to haunted houses – for most of his professional career. He has a Ph.D. from King's College, London, on modern witchcraft and magic, and is the author of *Witchcraft Out of the Shadows*, *Faustus: The Life and Times of a Renaissance Magician*, and *A Brief Guide to the Supernatural*, as well as being published in *Fortean Times*, *Paranormal* magazine and academic journals. His work has been mentioned in the media from the *Guardian* to Radio Jamaica, and his expertise has been sought by film companies and the likes of the International Society for Human Rights. He is an Associate of King's College and a member of Societas Magica, the European Society for the Study of Western Esotericism, the Society for Psychical Research, the Parapsychological Association, the Gesellschaft für Anomalistik and the Ghost Club. Visit him online at www.witchology.com and www.ruickbie.com.

Praise for *A Brief Guide to Ghost Hunting*:

'Dr Leo Ruickbie's latest book achieves a very rare feat indeed: it succeeds in being scholarly, informative, meticulously researched *and* very absorbing. If you have ever considered setting out to find a ghost you could do no better than take your information from the pages of this fascinating work, which is a textbook example of how it should be done.' Brian Allan, editor *Paranormal*, sub-editor *Phenomena* magazines

'Very useful and informative, extremely well researched and fluently written. Enjoyable and intriguing as well as exceptionally interesting.' Lionel and Patricia Fanthorpe, President and First Lady of the Association for the Scientific Study of Anomalous Phenomena (ASSAP)

'I have always admired Dr Leo Ruickbie's comprehensive expertise in the paranormal. *A Brief Guide Ghost Hunting* delivers more than most other ghost guides combined.' Rosemary Ellen Guiley, author of *The Encyclopedia of Ghosts and Spirits*

Recent titles in the series

A BRIEF GUIDE TO

GHOST HUNTING

DR LEO RUICKBIE

ROBINSON

RUNNING PRESS
PHILADELPHIA · LONDON

Constable & Robinson Ltd.
55–56 Russell Square
London WC1B 4HP
www.constablerobinson.com

First published in the UK by Robinson,
an imprint of Constable & Robinson Ltd., 2013

Copyright © Leo Ruickbie, 2013

The right of Leo Ruickbie to be identified as the author of this work has been
asserted by him in accordance with the Copyright, Designs & Patents Act
1988.

A copy of the British Library Cataloguing in Publication
Data is available from the British Library

UK ISBN: 978-1-78033-826-2 (paperback)
UK ISBN: 978-1-78033-827-9 (ebook)

1 3 5 7 9 10 8 6 4 2

First published in the United States in 2013 by
Running Press Book Publishers,
A Member of the Perseus Books Group

Books published by Running Press are available at special discounts for
bulk purchases in the United States by corporations, institutions, and other
organizations. For more information, please contact the Special Markets
Department at the Perseus Books Group, 2300 Chestnut Street, Suite 200,
Philadelphia, PA 19103, or call (800) 810-4145, ext. 5000,
or email special.markets@perseusbooks.com.

US ISBN: 978-0-7624-5077-0
US Library of Congress Control Number: 2013931824

9 8 7 6 5 4 3 2 1
Digit on the right indicates the number of this printing

Running Press Book Publishers
2300 Chestnut Street
Philadelphia, PA 19103-4371

Visit us on the web!
www.runningpress.com

Typeset by TW Typesetting, Plymouth, Devon

Printed and bound by
CPI Group (UK) Ltd, Croydon, CR0 4YY

To Bill and Bernice who made it all possible.
To Antje, Morgana and Melissa who make it all worthwhile.

FORMS or APPARITIONS. If seen, DO NOT MOVE AND ON NO ACCOUNT APPROACH THE FIGURE. Note exact method of appearance. Observe figure carefully, watch all movements, rate and manner of progression etc. Note duration of appearance, colour, form, size, how dressed, and whether solid or transparent. If carrying camera with film ready for exposing, quietly 'snap' the figure, but make no sound and do not move. If figure speaks, do not approach, but ascertain name, age, sex, origin, cause of visit, if in trouble, and possible alleviation. Inquire if it is a spirit. Ask figure to return, suggesting exact time and place. Do not move until figure disappears. Note exact method of vanishing. If through an open door, quietly follow. If through solid object (such as wall), ascertain if still visible on other side. Make the very fullest notes of the incident.

Extract from Harry Price, *The Alleged Haunting of B– Rectory: Instructions for Observers* (London: University of London Council for Psychic Investigation, 1937), p. 5.

CONTENTS

LIST OF TABLES

INFORMATION BOXES

ABBREVIATIONS

GCJ	*The Ghost Club Journal*
GCN	*The Ghost Club Newsletter*
GHS	Ghost Hunting Survey
JSPR	*Journal of the Society for Psychical Research*
PSH	Preliminary Survey of Hauntings
PSPR	*Proceedings of the Society for Psychical Research*
SPR	Society for Psychical Research
TAPS	The Atlanta Paranormal Society

ACKNOWLEDGEMENTS

It has been my great pleasure to meet many interesting living people through the course of this book and I would like to thank those who helped with my research, beginning, in alphabetical order, with Emil DeToffol, James Gilberd of Strange Occurrences, Ross Hemsworth, Vernon Holt, General Secretary of the Ghost Club, Michelle and Dave Juliano, Andy Matthews, Alan Murdie, President of the Ghost Club, Shawn Porter, James Tacchi, Technical Officer of the Ghost Club, Noah Voss, and Beth Watson, Director of Spookers. Thanks are also due to those who took part in the Ghost Hunting Survey; unfortunately time and space prevent me from listing everyone by name here, but my appreciation is heartfelt, nonetheless.

Of course, none of this would have been possible without my editor Duncan Proudfoot whose understanding of what it is like to work with two small children was particularly appreciated. My thanks also to Becca Allen and Charlotte Cole for their part in safely guiding this book through to its finished form, and to my agent Sonia Land for her perspicacity. Finally, no word of thanks can adequately express my gratitude for the support and encouragement of my wife Antje.

PREFACE

At midnight the lights went out. The house was plunged into darkness. Torches snapped on. The team were in place. Equipment tested. Sensors placed in the key locations. Outside doors locked and bolted. The ghost hunt had begun. What answers would the night bring? What terrors?

Everyone loves a good ghost story. That, in a nutshell, was how this book began. But it is a testament to current trends and the perspicacity of my editor that it became 'everyone loves a good ghost hunt'. When the first 'ghost hunters', such as Elliott O'Donnell, wrote about their exploits these were still good old ghost stories with the underlying assumption that ghosts were the spirits of the departed (or occasionally demons). Everyone knew what a ghost was and consequently few wanted actively to seek them out. But times have changed.

Do you believe in ghosts? It is a question that I often ask myself and I am sure that you have asked it of yourself, too. If you do not believe in ghosts yourself, then the chances are that the person sitting next to you on the bus, on the train, or at work, does. And if you have not seen a ghost yourself, then the chances are that you know someone who has. Not to speak of my own strange experiences, simply mentioning that I was writing this book elicited many personal accounts of the supernatural. To name just two, there was a haunted house in Aberdeenshire with moving furniture, footsteps and evil presences; and a woman in Germany who, after a teenage out-of-body experience, witnessed two crisis apparitions of the recently deceased, one a close childhood friend, the other a neighbour she barely knew.[1]

There has been a huge surge in books, television programmes, films and websites exploring the reality or otherwise of the spirit world. Not since the founding of the Ghost Club (1862) and the Society for Psychical Research (1882) has ghost hunting been this popular. Television and the internet, in particular, have fuelled this new level of interest, creating a modern media phenomenon that spans the globe. Clicks and viewing figures are in the millions. The demand for information is high. But good information is scarce.

Ghost hunting guides cover almost every corner of the world – well, mostly the UK and USA. There are shelf-fulls of ghost hunting titles from classics such as Andrew Green's seminal *Ghost Hunting: A Practical Guide* to the faintly ridiculous, although far be it from me to suggest that *The Girl's Ghost Hunting Guide* falls into this category. Even *Top Gear*'s James May covers ghost hunting in his book *Man Lab* alongside repairing dripping taps. Why does anyone need yet another one? As I said, good information is scarce.[2]

The book is structured in a way to take you through the process of ghost hunting, from initially weighing the first report, to choosing equipment, and investigating and identifying the phenomena, with an analysis of the best places to go looking, supposed methods of contacting the spirit world, how to explain paranormal activity and, crucially, how to survive the encounter.

However, this is not just a book about how to hunt ghosts. It is also about 'ghost hunting' itself. I have plumbed the cavernous archives of the Society for Psychical Research to draw on 130 years of research and reached back even further into history to find the earliest ghost stories. I have interviewed those calling themselves ghost hunters today to find out what their views, motivations and experiences are, for what I called the Ghost Hunting Survey (GHS).

There is much new and original research here into identifying and categorizing the paranormal phenomena of ghosts
and hauntings, especially using statistics to map and circum-
navigate this nebulous world. For the purposes of this book
I also conducted what I called the Preliminary Survey of
Hauntings (PSH). This was an analysis of 923 reported phenomena from 263 locations across the UK. I fear that I may
have gone beyond providing simply a 'brief guide', but this
work – any work on this subject – must fall short of being
encyclopedic.

A word should be said on the style of the book itself. I have
tried to present ghosts and ghost hunting in as objective a
manner as possible, but this is an emotive subject with ardent
supporters on both sides of the belief/disbelief divide. Sometimes I will present a story as it is, despite the obvious problems, but this should not be taken to mean that there are not
obvious problems. I frequently throw in words such as 'allegedly' and 'supposedly' to indicate that the phenomena under
investigation here are not proven, but where I may have omitted such words out of weariness at their over-use the reader
can easily insert them.

After studying all of the evidence it is almost impossible
for me to say, finally, what ghosts are and whether I 'believe'
in them, but after all that was not the purpose of the book.
Many of the explanations examined here seem to work at least
some of the time even when they are contradictory. It is no
wonder that mainstream science largely refuses to deal with
the subject: it is too complicated. As Daniel Defoe observed
many years ago, 'Of all the arcana of the invisible world I
know no one thing about which more has been said, and less
understood, than this of apparition.'[3] Without trying to convince you of any viewpoint, this book is intended to help you
understand *more*.

L.R.
Staudernheim
21 December 2012

'Mortui vivos docent'
('The dead teach the living')

I

PREPARE

It first began in a haunted house with groaning and rattling chains. It had to. All the stuff of the stereotypes was there from the start. The house was in Athens. The time: about two thousand years ago. The Roman writer Pliny the Younger (61 CE–c. 112 CE) described it as a capacious residence, but entirely undesirable:

> In the dead of the night a noise, resembling the clashing of iron, was frequently heard, which, if you listened more attentively, sounded like the rattling of chains, distant at first, but approaching nearer by degrees: immediately afterwards a spectre appeared in the form of an old man, of extremely emaciated and squalid appearance, with a long beard and dishevelled hair, rattling the chains on his feet and hands.[1]

The occupants of the house were terrified. Their nightly rest was instead a roller-coaster ride through Hell. Fear and exhaustion broke down their health. Illness and death followed. The house was abandoned. No one who knew of its reputation wanted it – and that was the whole of Athens – but a notice was pasted up informing all and sundry that the house was for rent or outright sale.

The philosopher Athenodorus (c. 74 BCE–7 CE) had then just arrived in the city and, taking a liking to what must have been a grand villa, inquired of the price. Suspicious of the low sum being asked, he nevertheless took the property. He would soon discover why it was so cheap.

Sitting up late one night, writing, Athenodorus heard the approaching rattle of iron. Looking up, he saw the wasted figure of the spectre. It seemed to see him, too, and beckoned for him to follow. Athenodorus had not quite finished his work and held up his hand to show that the spirit should wait. Athenodorus returned to his papers. Growing impatient, the ghost rattled his chains loudly over the philosopher's head. Again Athenodorus looked up. Again the ghost beckoned. This time Athenodorus took up the lamp and rose to follow it.

'The ghost,' wrote Pliny, 'slowly stalked along, as if encumbered with its chains.' It reached a certain point in the grounds and then vanished. Athenodorus had the forethought to mark the spot with a heap of grass and leaves so that he could find it in the morning. The next day he advised the magistrates of the situation, recommending that they should order the spot to be dug up. This they did, and under Athenodorus's marker the skeleton of a man bound in chains was unearthed. 'The body,' according to Pliny, 'having lain a considerable time in the ground, was putrefied and mouldered away from the fetters.'

The remains were gathered together and publicly reburied with 'the proper ceremonies'. The ghost was seen no more.

If it is not a personal experience, then it is the ghost story that brings most people to ghost hunting. Pliny himself was pondering the existence of ghosts after some unusual events had occurred in his household. Were ghosts real, or only 'the visionary impressions of a terrified imagination', he wondered. He was aware that he had to rely upon the testimony of others for the authenticity of this tale, but finished his letter with a more personal account. Two of his servants were molested in the night by a person or persons unknown, and, dreaming of having their hair cut, awoke to find the clippings lying around them and a new and unwanted tonsure. He interpreted this as a particular omen for himself and did not question who or what these night-time barbers may have been, but assumed that his servants had not been lying or given over to a 'terrified imagination'.

We find ghosts in every culture from the Australian outback to the Arctic Circle. The witnesses come from every level of society and every occupation civilization has devised. It comes as little surprise, then, to find that as many as one in two people in the UK or one in three people in the USA say that they believe in ghosts. Another one in three in both the UK and USA believe that one can communicate with the dead. Many people also claim to have seen a ghost: one in ten in the UK and one in seven 18–29-year-olds in the USA say that they have seen one.[2] The experience of 'ghosts', whatever they may be, is relatively common, ranging from 10 to 32 per cent across the Western world over the last hundred years or more, giving an average just shy of 21 per cent.

Perhaps this is unsurprising. If ghosts do exist, then there must be an awful lot of them out there and, regrettably, with more on the way. It was once calculated that Warwickshire had a ghost for every square mile, which, if it were a representative figure, would mean that the United Kingdom alone must be troubled by some 94,000 spirits of the dead.[3] In 1973 ghost hunter Andrew Green claimed that 150 hauntings were being reported each year and speculated that twice as many again were never publicized. Half of those appearing in the newspapers related to poltergeists, perhaps less than a quarter were long-established cases and the remainder new ones.[4] If a ghost really is the spirit of a dead person, then there must be

Apparitional experience in the general population

Study	Subject Group	Experience (%)
Sidgwick (1894)	17,000 British adults	10
Palmer (1979)	Charlottesville, USA, students and residents	17
Irwin (1985)	Australian university students	20
Haraldsson (1977)	Icelandic adults	31
Persinger (1974)	Canadian adults	32
Roper (1992)	American 18–29-year-olds	14.3
	Average	20.7

Note: E. Haraldsson, et al., 'National Survey of Psychical Experiences and Attitudes Toward the Paranormal in Iceland', in J. D. Morris, W. G. Roll and R. L. Morris (eds), *Research in Parapsychology 1976* (Metuchen, NJ: Scarecrow Press, 1977), pp. 182–6; H. J. Irwin, 'Parapsychological Phenomena and the Absorption Domain', *Journal of the American Society for Psychical Research*, 79 (1985), pp. 1–11; J. Palmer, 'A Community Mail Survey of Psychic Experience', *Journal of the American Society for Psychical Research*, 73 (1979), pp. 221–51; M. A. Persinger, *The Paranormal, Part 1: Patterns* (New York: MSS Information Corporation, 1974); Henry Sidgwick, et al., 'Report on the Census of Hallucinations', *PSPR*, 10 (1894).

trillions more. It was for this reason that the Greeks gave the name Pluto, meaning 'rich', to the God of the Underworld, for he was rich with the dead.

There are earlier accounts of spirits of the dead returning to confront the living. With the help of the sorceress Circe, Odysseus raised the spirit of Tiresias to learn his path homeward in Homer's *Odyssey*. The Old Testament has its tale of the Witch of Endor raising the spirit of Samuel. However, these are instances of what is properly necromancy – divination by the dead. Pliny gave what is recognizably the first ghost story.

He has also given us the opportunity to dissect his story. The ghost hunt begins with a rumour, story or report of a haunting. Pliny believed it. Should we believe it? And on what grounds? We have here a full apparition with auditory phenomena interacting with the living at close range. There were several witnesses to the ghost itself and others to the exhumation. The principal witness was a person of good standing. He had taught Octavian, who, as Caesar Augustus, would rule the Roman Empire, and after his death Athenodorus was commemorated with an annual festival and sacrifice at Tarsus. He also conducted himself in a manner that would not suggest that he was frightened or hysterical, or had his judgement impaired in any way.

However, the story is what is considered to be hearsay. It is not Athenodorus himself who tells the story – he may have in his now lost philosophical works – but Pliny. Pliny does not give his source, but could not have heard it directly from Athenodorus himself since the lifespans of the two did not cross. It is not a verifiable story. There are no other independent accounts of it. It cannot be further investigated since all of the principal witnesses are now dead. It is beginning to sound like an urban legend – it always happens to a friend of a friend.

The story also serves two purposes. Athenodorus was one of the Stoics and his teachings would have been concerned with the stoical principles of self-control and fortitude, excellent virtues for a ghost hunter. Firstly then, the story amplifies the stoicism of Athenodorus. Confronted by the ghost that has ruined the lives of others and brought them to their graves, he first bids it wait – showing self-control and bravery – then follows it to see what it wants – again showing self-control and bravery. His actions laudably demonstrate the Stoic virtue of mastering the emotions. Secondly, the ghost itself has a purpose. His *post mortem* mission on earth is to correct the omission of funerary rites, underlining their importance, more important than bringing his murderer to book, for example. Therefore the story serves to glorify Athenodorus and enforce social customs. This makes it doubly suspicious from a ghost hunting point of view.

Furthermore, the rattling chains were an unusual addition.

Iron and the noise it makes were generally held by the Greeks and Romans to scare away ghosts. Odysseus uses his sword to control the spirits of the dead during his necromantic invocation of Tiresias – not its keen edge, but its metal held terror for the dead. Lucian later wrote that if ghosts 'hear the clash of bronze or iron, they're off'.[5]

Pliny's story is generally seen as a variation of one told by both Plautus around 200 BCE (from an earlier Greek tale of the fourth to third century BCE) and Lucian in the second century CE, but the places, characters and action differ in each. Plautus uses haunting as a deceit practised by a servant against his master. Lucian sets his tale in Corinth where his protagonist actively investigates a haunted house and uses magical grimoires to exorcize it.[6]

A near exact replica of Pliny's story appeared in Spain in 1570. It concerned an unnamed law student rather than an esteemed philosopher, but the rattling chains, the insistent ghost, the marking of the spot, the finding of human remains and the decent burial are all there. Some have argued that this demonstrates that the story, whether told by Pliny or by someone 1,400 years later, is a type (in the sense of a literary or folkloric motif) and thus a falsehood. But we should be wary of dismissing anything merely because it is imitated, or, if not imitated, found again in the same form. Ronald C. Finucane, professor of history at Oakland University, thought it entirely unlikely that the same event could occur twice by chance alone, but because something is unlikely it is not therefore impossible. In the first place, any ghost would seem to be unlikely; that a ghost should behave in the same manner as another is actually more plausible than otherwise.[7] But we see how necessary it is to look forwards and back and around an account of a haunting to ascertain its context, its connections and its possible origins.

Pliny was no *venator phasmatis* ('ghost hunter'), as he might have called it, either. In the final analysis, Pliny's story is just a story. That is not to say that it is not a good one; it is, but it is not evidence. It is evidence that must be the first concern of the ghost hunter, but the question is still the same: are ghosts real or something else?

Early ghost hunters

'It is wonderful,' said Dr Samuel Johnson, sitting down to breakfast with his biographer James Boswell one day in March, 1778. 'It is wonderful' was his favourite way of launching one of his famously sardonic comments. 'That five thousand years have now elapsed since the creation of the world, and still it is undecided whether or not there has ever been an instance of the spirit of any person appearing after death.' Then he delivered his classic line: 'All argument is against it; but all belief is for it.' As we now know, a great many more years have elapsed since the creation of the world, but the situation as regards ghosts of the departed remains much the same.[8]

Supposed encounters with the dead are anything but new. But ghost *hunting*, as the organized search for evidence relating to reports of 'ghosts', is. Ghost hunting is a modern phenomenon. It only becomes necessary to look for ghosts when we, as a society, start questioning their existence, or stop believing in them entirely; when argument prevails over belief. Despite high numbers of people who do believe in ghosts, the theory that ghosts exist no longer forms part of the accepted, scientific worldview. In earlier times, the spirits of the dead were everywhere and, with the exception of Greek heroes, the occasional philosopher and a whole host of necromancers and black magicians, nobody wanted to meet them. Athenodorus, to take Pliny at his word, did not doubt that it was the spirit of a dead man who was rattling his chains at him and felt it unnecessary to conduct any experiments to prove the matter to his contemporaries. It is only now, when the existence of the spirit world is doubted, that we are forced to seek it out.

The 'ghost hunter' is a nineteenth-century invention. The *Oxford English Dictionary* traces the term 'ghost hunter' back to Andrew Lang's *Cock Lane and Common-Sense* of 1894, but the term is older than that. We find it in the 'Ingoldsby Legends' first published in *Bentley's Miscellany* and the *New Monthly Magazine* in 1837, but Michael Banim, under the pseudonym of the O'Hara Family, used it earlier in the title of his *The Ghost-Hunter and his Family* in 1833.[9]

Before the development of organizations specifically devoted to investigating alleged hauntings there were many sporadic attempts made by individuals to uncover the truth of the matter. Harry Price, himself a dedicated ghost hunter, credited Joseph Glanvill as 'the Father of Psychical Research' for his investigation of the Drummer of Tedworth case in the seventeenth century.[10] Glanvill's methodical approach was certainly enlightened for the period, but again we can find earlier examples of the systematic investigation of hauntings.

In 1323 Jean Goby conducted a very business-like investigation of a supposed haunting in the town of Alais (now called Alès) in the South of France. Prior of the Order of Preachers in Alais, he was commissioned by the townspeople to look into the disturbances at the house of Guy de Torno. Guy had died eight days before, but his voice was still to be heard and heard it was 'by many people of consequence'. With a 'team' of a over a hundred, including the Lord of Alais, he searched the house and neighbouring buildings as 'precautions against fraud'. He placed pickets at all the places most likely to admit a deception, even turfing people out of their houses for the purpose, and stationed an elderly matron in the bed of Guy's wife. Goby and three companions sat themselves upon Guy's bed, evidently a different one to his wife's, and, with lanterns in hand, waited. On the first night nothing was seen or heard, but later a glowing form appeared, announcing itself to be Guy trapped in Purgatory. Father Herbert Thurston noted that the Society for Psychic Research (SPR) could learn a few lessons from Goby's thoroughness, although one suspects that they would have difficulty expelling householders and camping out in people's bedrooms for the purposes of an investigation.[11]

In 1643 almost 30,000 men, Royalist and Roundhead, met
on the field of Edgehill, Warwickshire, and gave fierce battle.
Cries and clash of arms, crack of musket and roar of cannon
filled the air. All who saw and heard it were astonished: the
Battle of Edgehill had been fought the year before. The first
sightings of this wonder were attributed to shepherds, coun-
trymen and travellers, but the phantom battle was later certified by local worthies William Wood, Esq., and the minister
Samuel Marshall. Wood and others of faint heart quit the scene
as soon as they could, but Marshall stayed to watch it unfold.

Investigation report: Edgehill
At this Edge Hill, in the very place where the battell
was strucken, have since, and doth appeare, strange
and portentuous Apparitions of two jarring and
contrary Armies, as I shall in order deliver, it being
certified by men of most credit in those parts, as William Wood, Esquire, Samuel Marshall, Minister, and
others [. . .] Between twelve and one of the clock in
the morning, was heard by some sheepherds, and
other countrey-men, and travellers, first the sound
of drummes afar off, and the noyse of soulders, as it
were, giving out their last groanes; at which they were
much amazed, and amazed stood still, till it seemed,
by the neereness of the noyse, to approach them; at
which, too much affrighted, they sought to withdraw
as fast as possibly they could.
'A Great Wonder in Heaven, Shewing the Late Apparitions
and Prodigious Noyses of War and Battels Seen on Edge-
Hill' (London: Thomas Jackson, c. 1643)

Rumours of the event reached the king's ears at Oxford
and he dispatched Colonel Lewis Kirke, Captain Dudley,
Captain Wainman and three others to investigate. Kirke,

forty-four-year-old veteran of the Quebec campaign and soon to be knighted for his role in the Civil War, witnessed the whole spectacle, even to the point of recognizing Sir Edmund Verney who had been killed defending the Royalist colours. He reported back to Charles I and swore on oath to all that he had seen. There were still reports of this spectral re-enactment into the twentieth century.[12]

Joseph Glanvill was concerned to correct disbelief in the supernatural and wrote *Saducismus Triumphatus* to promulgate his views on witchcraft and apparitions. In doing so he gives a full account of the poltergeist activity that beset a certain John Mompesson, Justice of the Peace, and his family in Tedworth (today Tidworth), Wiltshire. The disturbances began after Mompesson had William Drury, a vagrant drummer, arrested for using a forged pass and confiscated his drum. Glanvill called the case the 'Daemon of Tedworth' and supposed that the whole affair had been caused by witchcraft, presumably on the part of the drummer. The initial investigation, if such it might be called, was conducted by Mompesson, following strange knocking sounds around his house armed with a brace of loaded pistols. The activity continued at irregular periods from 1661 into 1663.[13]

In late January or early February 1663, Glanvill himself arrived in Tedworth to examine matters. He listened to the reports of various witnesses and heard some of the strange noises for himself. He entertained several experiments in communicating with the supposed spirit, apparently successfully, and all the while kept a close eye on the children of the household to catch them at any trickery. After a thorough search he stated that, 'I was verily perswaded, and am so still, that the noise was made by some Daemon or Spirit.' Given Glanvill's bias, his testimony might be doubted, but he himself set about on a sceptical investigation, only considering the supernatural when he could find no natural explanation.[14]

In 1817 Edward Lewes Lenthal Swifte, Esq., Keeper of Her Majesty's Regalia at the Tower of London, reported his unusual encounter with the supernatural – bizarre even among annals of the unnatural – to the chaplain. An other-worldly tube of swirling fluid substance had appeared at the Keeper's dinner table to the horror of his family and molested his wife. The chaplain suggested that the Keeper's natural senses had been deceived as had those of the other witnesses, upon which Swifte noted the beginnings of a great theological error the clergyman was assaying: if he should deny one vision, especially a collective vision, as merely imagination, then why not all visions and therewithal would the edifice of religion crack and crumble. The chaplain retracted, but countered with the thought that someone had been playing some sort of prank upon the Keeper by means of projecting something through the window. Swifte stuck by his account. He knew what he had seen, even if it was impossible. Besides, on the night in question, 'heavy and dark cloth curtains were let down over the windows.' To resolve the matter the chaplain recommended that the case be investigated by a 'scientific friend' of his acquaintance. The scientific friend duly arrived and conducted a close examination of the Keeper's dining room. Although finding no satisfactory explanation for the event, he breezily offered to reproduce it if he were allowed to set up his equipment on the dining room table, or outside the walls with the curtains conveniently drawn aside. The mystery remains.[15]

Other notable nineteenth-century investigations include Major Edward Moor's assiduous documentation of the inexplicable bell ringing that plagued his home, Great Bealings House, Great Bealings, Suffolk, in 1834. 'Ghost-detector' Edward Drury started out ghost hunting at Willington Mill, Northumberland, in 1840. It was a choice location: Joseph Procter's household was in the midst of a range of phenomena, from poltergeist activity to full-blown apparitions. However, Drury's disastrous exploits resulted in his temporary loss of sanity and a complete end to his ghost detecting career, as will be revealed in Chapter 9. The copy of Moor's book

Early ghost hunters ·

Name	Known for	Date
Jean Goby	Guy de Torno case, Alès [Alais]	1323
William Wood et al.	Battle of Edgehill investigation	1642
Col. Lewis Kirke et al.	Battle of Edgehill investigation	1642
Joseph Glanvill	Drummer of Tedworth investigation	1681
Friedrich Nicolai	Investigation of his own ghost visions	Before 1799
unknown scientist	Tower of London investigation	1817
Major Edward Moor	Great Bealings House investigation	1834 (1841)
Edward Drury	Willington Mill investigation	1840
Brook Foss Westcott	Founded the Ghost Club	1851
Michael Faraday	Experiments with table-turning	1853
E. J. Simons	Meggernie Castle investigation	1862
London Dialectical Society	Report on Spiritualism	1869 (1871)
Sir William Crookes	D.D. Home investigation	1870–1
	Florence Cook investigation	1874
W. F. Barrett, E.D. Rogers et al.	Founded the Society for Psychical Research	1882
W. F. Barrett et al.	First Report of the Committee on Haunted Houses	1882
'Rose Morton' (pseud.)	The case of the 'black widow'	1882–9
H. Sidgwick et al.	Census of Hallucinations	1894
Ada Goodrich-Freer	Ballechin House investigation	1897

I happened to read through had the name 'Joseph Procter' inscribed on the title page.[16]

The publication of Catherine Crowe's *Night-Side of Nature* in 1848 kindled a popular interest in apparitions and related subjects that would embrace Spiritualism when it crossed the Atlantic from America to Britain in the 1850s. Sir David Brewster, the inventor of the kaleidoscope, noted with alarm that 'there are *thousands* of tables turning every night in London, so general is the excitement.' Even Queen Victoria sat down to a séance. In consequence of Spiritualism a great deal of ghost hunting at this time took place in the séance room. The claims and demonstrations advanced by Spiritualism were startling and profound. From the stage to the ordinary parlour, the dead returned to converse with and even appear to the living. If proof of the afterlife were needed, here it was in spades. Or was it?[17]

Michael Faraday's ingenious experiments with table-turning in the 1850s proved that it was the unconscious movements of the participants that were the real ghosts. Many more mediums were unmasked as frauds; some confessed to their duplicity. Both Maggie and Katie Fox, two of the sisters who spawned the Spiritualist movement, publicly revealed that the whole mystery of spirit communication was the secret snapping of toe joints, although several doctors and others had worked it out more than thirty years earlier. To the delight of her critics, Catherine Crowe went mad, running naked down an Edinburgh street after the 'spirits' told her she would be invisible. As her shocked neighbours confirmed, she was not.[18]

Despite such scandals and revelations many scientists were still convinced that real phenomena took place in the séance room. Founded in 1867 as a debating club, the London Dialectical Society appointed a committee to investigate Spiritualism in 1869, presenting its evidence before the Society in 1870 and publishing the year after. After numerous experiments they concluded that 'motion may be produced in solid bodies without material contact, by some hitherto unrecognized force', rather than pronouncing on the substance of Spiritualism: that there is an afterlife.[19]

At the same time, the respected scientist Sir William Crookes, FRS, was publishing in the *Quarterly Journal of Science* the results of what he called his 'experimental investigation of a new force'. To the outrage of many of his scientific colleagues this new force was a psychic one. His investigations of the mediumship of Daniel Dunglas Home appeared to demonstrate the non-physical application of a power sufficient to lift weights, apply force and play musical instruments. Crookes decided that there was no need for the action of miracles or spirits to account for these effects and looked to the theoretical work of Professor Thury of Geneva on nervo-magnetism, psychodes and ectenic forces. But he had also seen the appearance of phantom forms and faces.[20]

After the Foxes' downfall, the believers may have seemed entrenched in indefensible ground, but the findings of the Dialectical Society and Crookes greatly complicated matters. The Spiritualists simply marched on without the embarrassing Fox sisters. The Spiritualist Association of Great Britain was founded in London in 1872 and the National Spiritualist Association of Churches in Chicago in 1893 – both are still going today.

The involvement of the Dialectical Society was important, but its investigation had only been the work of one special committee. The first steps towards dedicated investigative groups began at the universities.

Ghost clubs

House haunted by ghosts – The Ghost Club, with a view to investigation, desire to obtain a house haunted by ghosts, in town or in country, for a limited period. Address, with all requisite particulars, to the Secretary of the Ghost Club, to the care of Joseph Clayton, advertising agent, 265, Strand, London.[21]

The French politician and *homme de lettres* Louis Blanc raised an eyebrow and remarked, 'There is not a syllable of the marvellous advertisement that is not worthy of attention.'[22] Blanc was then in exile in London and had innocently turned over the pages of the *Daily Telegraph* in the Autumn of 1863. In those days the 'Wanted' columns were usually full of invitations for applications from man-servants and maids-of-all-work, but here was something different, something marvellous.

A 'ghost club' holding 'weekly breakfast meetings' was mentioned as being in existence as early as 1802 by Revd J. J. Smith in his Cambridge miscellany. However, he chose only to remark upon 'what extent the spirit of clubbing may run' before reproducing a long poem 'The Cambridge Scholar and the Ghost of a Scrag of Mutton'. It raises a wry smile but aids us not one whit in understanding what this early club may have been.[23] It is in any case a curious fore-echo of the Ghost Club that caught Blanc's eye more than half a century later.

The mathematician Charles Babbage, inventor of the prototype computer, the Difference Engine, also laid claim to a 'ghost club'. Whilst an undergraduate at Trinity College, Cambridge, from 1810 to 1812 (from 1812 to 1814 he was at Peterhouse), he regularly met with ten or so friends to sit down to breakfast after Sunday chapel. 'We discussed all knowable and many unknowable things,' said Babbage, and 'at one time we resolved ourselves into a Ghost Club.' He described, briefly, their activities as collecting evidence, however that may have been done, and entering into 'a considerable correspondence upon the subject'. Although 'some of this was both interesting and instructive', he passed quickly on and spent more time describing the singularly undergraduate regulations of The Extractors, a far-fetched society consisting of members who had been judged both sane and insane, and not just once, but three times on each account. All this whilst assiduously playing chess, sixpenny whist and boating, to say nothing of actually studying.[24] The Venerable

Archdeacon Denison expressed his regret, as we all do, that
Babbage had not said more about 'the investigations of the
great mathematician into the theory of phantoms'.[25]

Under the heading of 'Modern Necromancy' in the *North
British Review* we discover that in 1851 a society was formed
at the University of Cambridge for the purposes of conducting, according to their literature, 'a serious and earnest inquiry
into the nature of phenomena which are vaguely termed
supernatural'. This, we are told, was popularly called the
'Ghost Club'.[26] Its members were clergymen and Fellows of
Trinity College. Even then, in its early days, it had reached the
conclusion that 'there is sufficient testimony for the appearance, about the time of death, or after it, of the apparitions of
deceased persons'. The *Review* scoffed at the notion.[27]

The printed circular of this society broke down its intended
subject matter into a series of classes: 'appearances of angels',
both good and evil; 'spectral appearances', including 'Fetch-
es' and second-sight; 'shapes' that were neither angels nor
'spectral appearances', according to their definition, including the Banshee and Mawth Dog; remarkable dreams; 'feelings', including 'future presentiment'; and 'physical effects',
such as sounds and the impression of touch. Interested persons were directed to contact Revd B.F. Westcott of Harrow,
Middlesex.[28]

It was remarked that this Ghost Club 'attracted a good
deal of attention outside its own circle', but information
concerning its members and activities remains surprisingly
scarce. The *North British Review* may have pulled a face, but
they were reputedly said to have amassed over 2,000 cases of
apparitions.[29]

Meanwhile, Blanc would have been amused to read in *The
Illustrated London News* about the fashion for 'table-turning,
spirit-rapping and mountebank-medium patronising' in addition to, of course, 'advertising for a "haunted house"'. The
author mused that he had heard of 'The Ugly Club' – and
indeed intended to apply – and 'The Unfortunate Club' for

the twice bankrupt with a near relative who had been hanged, but was simply taken aback by the appearance of the Ghost Club. 'Do they believe in ghosts,' he asked, 'or are they rather playful humourists?'[30] The Ghost Club was also mentioned briefly in a skit on haunted houses that appeared in the satirical magazine *Punch*.[31] They even got a mention in the prestigious medical journal *The Lancet*.[32]

It was to this group that George Cruikshank – Dickens's illustrator – dedicated his short book *A Discovery Concerning Ghosts*.[33] Either the dedication was in jest, or it demonstrated the sceptical turn of mind of the Club's members, for Cruikshank's slim volume sets out to debunk the whole idea of apparitions.

A veil of mystery is largely drawn over the next twenty years. It is believed that Charles Dickens was a member, which may account for Cruikshank's dedication as well as his interest in the subject. After the death of Dickens in 1870 the club seems to have gone into abeyance.[34]

A 'Phasmatological Society' appeared at Oxford University in 1879. Although relatively short-lived, the 'Phas', as it was familiarly called, conducted some interesting research. They collected and classified over a hundred first-hand accounts. Most they put down to natural causes, hallucination or coincidence, but there were still a few that defied tidy explanation. The military historian Sir Charles Oman, KBE, was a member and fondly recalled their activities in later years as an excellent training for a barrister or, indeed, a historian. Other members included the philosopher Ferdinand Canning Scott Schiller and the liturgical scholar Dr Frank Edward Brightman. It was rumoured that an early member had once put a bullet through a ghost, unsurprisingly, to little effect. The Phas also made a brief appearance in M. R. James's story 'The Mezzotint', and one editor, at least, has supposed that it was an invention aimed at slighting the Society for Psychical Research (SPR). In fact, many old Phas men, including Sir Charles, would go on to join the SPR.[35]

A further incarnation of the Ghost Club appeared on 1 November 1882. Re-founded by Alfred Alaric Watts and William Stainton Moses, it was a dining club for 'the confidential reporting and discussion of psychic phenomena'.[36] They met at the Hotel Previtali, 14–18 Arundel Street, a location popular with foreign travellers and noted for its Italian cuisine. Meetings generally comprised fewer than ten members and guests, some others usually absent on account of their living too far away. An eavesdropper would have heard accounts of premonitions, strange visions and experiments in table-rapping.[37]

Blanc saw the Ghost Club as only another 'page to be added to the history of human oddities and English eccentricities', but he was wrong.[38] It was the Ghost Club of the 1860s that attracted the attention of three young Fellows of Trinity College; Henry Sidgwick (1838–1900), Frederic W. H. Myers (1843–1901) and Edmund Gurney (1847–88). All had achieved some measure of excellence as prize winners, medallists and academics at Cambridge – Sidgwick would become professor of moral philosophy, Myers a lecturer in Classics – but it was their interest in ghosts that would win them a place in history.[39]

The Committee on Haunted Houses

The idea for a new society to study psychic phenomena was born of a meeting between William Fletcher Barrett (1844–1925), professor of physics at the new Royal College of Science for Ireland in Dublin, and the journalist Edmund Dawson Rogers (1823–1910), founder of the National Press Agency. A general call for interested persons went out and a meeting was held at the headquarters of the British National Association of Spiritualists at 38 Great Russell Street on 6 January 1882. At the meeting were two of that influential cabal of Trinity scholars, Myers and Gurney, together with the remarkable Frank Podmore (1856–1910), soon to be one of the founders of the Fabian Society (1884). At 23 St Swithin's Lane on 20

February the new Society for Psychical Research was formally constituted. Myers and Gurney co-opted Henry Sidgwick as the society's first president.

One of the first moves made by the newly founded SPR was the formation of a Committee on Haunted Houses, comprising Barrett, the wonderfully named Alfred Percival Perceval Keep, a former president of the Phasmatological Society, the Theosophist Charles Carleton Massey, also of the Ghost Club, and the etymologist Hensleigh Wedgwood with Frank Podmore and fellow socialist Edward Reynolds Pease as honourable secretaries. The object of the committee was 'to investigate the phenomena of alleged hauntings whenever a suitable opportunity and an adequate *prima facie* case for inquiry might be presented.' 'We have held ourselves in readiness,' they stated, 'to take any favourable opportunity for personally investigating the phenomena.' Unfortunately, no opportunities to investigate haunted houses presented themselves.[40]

Although they received a number of witness testimonies, they found that the owners of reputed haunted houses were reluctant to let the fact be known for fear of damaging the property's value and other witnesses were equally reluctant to give them the names of owners. When they asked owners about rumours of haunting they encountered 'a diplomatic reserve' or professed ignorance and found that they 'distinctly decline to offer any facilities for their investigation'. When the reputation for being haunted became too overwhelming to be ignored, people would prefer to tear down the house, or at least remodel it, rather than have it investigated. In the end this reduced them to interviewing witnesses, either in person or, less satisfactorily, by letter. They ended the report with an appeal to fellow members of the SPR to help them find a proper haunted house.

Podmore would join forces with fellow SPR members Myers and Gurney to work on what would be published as *Phantasms of the Living* in two volumes in 1886. This emphasis was perhaps inspired by Catherine Crowe who had already published a large number of such accounts. Working with over 700 reports, the authors presented convincingly the argument that ghosts were telepathic projections originating in the mind of a living person experiencing acute distress – the 'crisis apparition'. Two of their cases came from the earlier Phasmatological Society.

Unfortunately, the attack on *Phantasms* was swift and decisive. Shortly after publication it was argued that despite claiming to base itself on authenticated first-hand evidence, the book contained no corroborative documentation of this. Despite a vigorous defence, Gurney could only supply three letters supporting the cited reports.[41]

Work continued after Gurney's untimely death two years later, culminating in the monumental 'Census of Hallucinations' in 1894. In all, some 17,000 people had been surveyed on their experiences of hallucinations, including to a lesser extent 'phantasms of the dead'. With all this additional evidence behind them, Sidgwick and the others determined that crisis apparitions could not be explained away: 'Between deaths and apparitions of the dying-person a connexion exists which is not due to chance alone. This we hold as a proved fact.'[42]

Much else of the society's important work at this period falls more generally under the heading, quite properly, of psychical research and thus beyond the scope of ghost hunting. In addition to the Committee on Haunted Houses, there was a Committee on Thought-Reading, a Committee on Mesmerism, a Committee on Spontaneous Experiences, a Committee on Physical Phenomena, a Literary Committee, and a Reichenbach Committee to explore the wondrous research of Baron Karl von Reichenbach.[43]

Membership would approach a thousand in the Victorian period and include many of the great names of the day. Serving Prime Minister William Gladstone, Alfred, Lord Tennyson, John Ruskin, the future Prime Minister (1902–5) Arthur

Balfour, Lord Rayleigh and others, all lent their support; the Revd Charles Lutwidge Dodgson, better known by his pen-name Lewis Carroll, was a member, as were Robert Louis Stevenson and Sir Arthur Conan Doyle. Barrett travelled to the USA and in 1885 founded an American Society for Psychical Research. The astronomer Simon Newcomb was its first president and the famous psychologist William James was its most notable member.[44]

Popular ghost hunting

It was not just Trinity Fellows and Oxford undergraduates who were hunting ghosts. Rumours of ghosts have often drawn large crowds of prospective 'hunters'. In 1862 'a dense mass of people of all ages, sizes, sexes, and nationalities' turned out to catch a glimpse of New York's sensational Twenty-Seventh Street Ghost, with nearby off-licences supplying spirits enough of another vintage sufficient to draw out a large body of police to maintain order. P. T. Barnum noted that the fuss had a bizarre knock-on effect so that 'the whole country seemed to have gone ghost-mad'.[45] In 1884 the police were again called upon to control huge crowds of ghost hunters, this time in Vienna. The so-called Vienna Disturbances centred around the Fünfhaus, but when after two days no ghost appeared, the crowd dissipated, believing the whole affair to have been 'humbug'.[46] A ghost encounter in Tondu, Glamorganshire, in 1904, caused 'bands of stalwart men' to 'sally forth to lay the terror of Tondu'.[47] In the same year, a report of haunting in the schoolhouse of Blyth, Northumberland, caused a 'ghost scare' drawing large crowds intent on 'solving the mystery', according to the papers.[48] Towards the end of 1904 another posse was formed to apprehend 'a spectral figure clad, apparently, in a long grey sheet' that had taken to haunting the railway station at Kirkstall, Leeds.[49] In 1908 a group of men described in the press as 'ghost hunters' endeavoured to ambush a nine-foot-tall ghost at Glanville outside Galway. On levelling his pistol at the apparition, one of the ghost hunters was rendered powerless in his arm before he could discharge a shot.[50]

As can be seen, these ghost hunting mobs were generally unsuccessful in finding their quarry, with the notable exception of the Glanville gang. Such ad hoc ghost posses were never going to amount to more than a fun or frightening night out, but with the demise of the university clubs and the changing focus of the SPR – never quite going after ghosts – ghost hunting was still in the hands of the amateur.

The first ghost hunter

'This is a curious yarn that I am going to tell you,' said Carnacki, as after a quiet little dinner we made ourselves comfortable in his cozy dining room.

William Hope Hodgson entertained the reading public in 1910 with his stories of a paranormal investigator in *Carnacki the Ghost Finder*.[51] It is a book full of curious yarns, but none quite so curious as that of the first ghost hunter. The phrase had been bandied about before, in serious and less than serious books, and in the Press; however, the first person to use the term 'ghost hunter' of himself was the Irish writer Elliott O'Donnell (1872–1965) in the title of his 1916 book *Twenty Years' Experience as a Ghost Hunter*. In 1928 he published *Confessions of a Ghost Hunter*. Harry Price would later catch on to the term and publish his own *Confessions of a Ghost Hunter* in 1936.[52]

To say O'Donnell was a prolific writer is an understatement. He wrote more books on the subject than anyone could possibly want to read and it is this that throws one of the greatest doubts upon the veracity of his supposed nonfiction. Like Hodgson he began with occult fiction, writing *For Satan's Sake* in 1904, before he found his metier in the semi-autobiographical true-life tales that feature in *Bona-Fide Adventures with Ghosts* and *Some Haunted Houses of England and Wales*, both published in 1908. Like most of his works, *For Satan's Sake* was written in the first person; here it was the fictional 'Paul Penruddock'. O'Donnell simply exchanged 'Paul Penruddock' or perhaps 'Carnacki' for himself in most of his subsequent works.

Whatever the real truth of the matter, O'Donnell presented himself as a ghost hunter and his many cases as true. He eschewed the scientific approach, if not actually pouring scorn upon it, describing himself as 'formerly of the Psychical Research Society'. He claimed a degree of mediumship, although sceptical of professional mediums – 'unmitigated humbugs or hysterical dupes' he called them – and whatever this facility may be, it certainly allowed him to access a wider spectrum of experience. His fascination with the paranormal stemmed from this ability and he sought his subject more for enjoyment than in the interests of gathering evidence. He was not so much a ghost hunter as a ghost connoisseur.[53]

The contrast between O'Donnell's lurid tales of hauntings and the more sober and undramatic accounts given by subsequent ghost hunters like Andrew Green and Peter Underwood is striking. O'Donnell is nine-tenths novelist, which always makes him an entertaining read, but as a source he should be used with caution, if at all. A modern ghost hunter might spend years on the job and have only a few cases of creaky floorboards to show for it, but for O'Donnell the supernatural was around every corner in all its fantastic guises. Ghost hunter John Fraser also draws our attention to the fact that most of his locations remain anonymous, always a hindrance to further investigation and a red flag for mendacity.[54] O'Donnell remains of interest, however, not least because his stories are still doing the rounds and are often the first point of entry for many investigators. Some of the first ghost stories I read – the 'Death Bogle of the Crossroads' and 'Pearlin' Jean' – were O'Donnell masterpieces. In a way O'Donnell makes it all seem possible, if not actually real. Undaunted by the demands of science, O'Donnell invites one into the mystery.

Harry Price

O'Donnell inhabited another world, somewhere between dream and reality like a figure of Irish mythology himself. To deal with the paranormal is to run the gauntlet of fantasy and unreality, and some do not pass through unscathed. As Nietzsche so famously remarked, 'If you gaze for long into an abyss, the abyss gazes also into you.'[55] Like O'Donnell, Harry Price would also bear the stigma of fraud without ever being caught out in it.

Born only a few years after O'Donnell, Price took the different road, advocating science over psychic impressions. He began his career in psychical research with work on mediums, but it was his investigation of Borley Rectory that both set him apart and cemented his reputation, for good or for ill. Between the Ghost Club advertising for haunted houses, the Committee on Haunted Houses failing to find any, and O'Donnell finding too many, Price took the necessary step of actually leasing a 'genuine' reputedly haunted house.

Price's 'haunted house' had everything he could have wished for: footsteps in empty rooms, a human skull in the library, lights in unoccupied parts of the building, slamming shutters, locking and unlocking doors, vanishing keys and ringing bells, a voice crying out 'Don't, Carlos', not to mention the headless coachmen and phantom nun. When Revd Guy Eric Smith and his family arrived from India in 1928 to take up the living of Borley, they found more than they expected waiting for them in the rambling and decrepit twenty-three-room mansion that was the rectory. Smith wrote to the *Daily Mirror* requesting the name of a reputable organization involved in the investigation of psychical phenomena. The paper sent a reporter.[56]

That summer the *Daily Mirror* ran a number of stories from V. C. Wall in the haunted rectory. Shortly afterwards, Harry Price was on the scene, invited by the newspaper's editor, with his secretary and former model, Lucy Kaye, in tow.[57] Price was then running the National Laboratory for

Psychical Research (NLPR) – an organization founded in
1925 under the aegis of the London Spiritualist Association
– but in an effort to keep out the SPR, he told the Smiths that
he represented the American SPR.

After all the initial excitement of having a haunted house
in his hands, Price suddenly abandoned the rectory to pursue
a round of crazy adventures that found him analysing ectoplasm, casting spells on the Brocken mountain in Germany,
sleeping in a haunted bed, looking for a talking mongoose on
the Isle of Man and spending the night with Aleister Crowley.
At the same time he managed to sabotage all his attempts to
put the NLPR on a more secure footing.

At the instigation of the cousin of Lionel Foyster, the new
incumbent, he returned to Borley Rectory in 1931. This time
he put all of the phenomena down to the fraud, conscious or
unconscious, of the rector's wife Marianne.[58] With his NLPR
in packing crates and its offices closed, Price was back at the
rectory in 1937 with a team of investigators. Lacking the funds
or inclination to buy the house outright, Price rented it from
17 May 1937 to 19 May 1938. Strangely, none of the investigators came from the Ghost Club, which Price had joined in
1927 and revived in 1937. The rectory was sold in November
1938 and burnt down in February 1939. This did nothing to
prevent Price returning again in 1943 to dig up the cellars.
He found what he claimed to be human bone fragments, and
a service was held to re-inter them. The ruins were finally
demolished in 1944.[59]

Many of those involved would later suspect Price himself of engineering the poltergeist activity, including Revd
Smith's wife, Lord Charles Hope who bankrolled the NLPR
in the early days, and *Daily Mail* journalist Charles Sutton
who once found Price's coat-pockets incriminatingly full of
pebbles. One of Price's 1937 investigators caught him using a
concealed pencil to draw on the walls.[60] Price's background
as a magician and his earlier unmasking of fraudulent mediums certainly gave him the necessary knowledge to forge the

paranormal and his showmanship always made him seem suspect. However, it would be the SPR's investigation into his account of Borley that would leave his reputation in tatters. Published in 1956, Price was lucky enough not to have lived to read it. He died of a heart attack in 1948.[61]

Post-war ghost hunting

Whatever the truth, the legend of Borley lives on. Peter Underwood was there in 1947 and reported unaccountable footsteps in the dark. In time he would be regaled as 'the Sherlock Holmes of psychical research', 'Britain's ghost hunter supreme' and the 'undisputed king of ghost hunters'. As a mark of the great respect in which he is held he would be invited to become the patron of Paranormal Site Investigators, the Ghost Research Foundation and Ghost Investigation, as well as being granted life membership of the Vampire Research Society.[62] He was one of the last members to be invited to join the Ghost Club by Harry Price and would go on to become president of the club from 1960 to 1993. Underwood would write his own books about Borley, among many others, perhaps even more than Elliott O'Donnell, but of a different style and calibre altogether. After sixty years researching the haunting of Borley, he concluded that: 'I do think Borley Rectory justified the term "the most haunted house in England".'[63]

Opinion is still divided. According to Andrew Green, 'Borley isn't haunted!' Green, dubbed the 'spectre inspector' by the *Daily Telegraph*, was another industrious investigator who helped to define the character of post-war ghost hunting. It was he, after all, who wrote the first introduction to investigation, called *Ghost Hunting: A Practical Guide*, in 1973. It is still highly regarded.[64]

His interest in the paranormal seems to have been shaped by a number of experiences in childhood: two near-death experiences, a fight with an invisible force pulling the bedclothes and a brush with death at 16 Montpelier Road, Ealing. Soon after leaving the army, following obligatory National Service, he founded the Ealing Society for Psychic Phenomena in 1949 aged just twenty-one. He met his first ghost in 1951, but it would not be his only encounter. The strange thing is that these experiences combined with his years of research led him to believe that ghosts were not the spirits of the dead.[65]

Described as 'a "slumbering giant" of paranormal research' by John Fraser, the perceived situation in the SPR led a group of modernizers to break away and establish the Association for the Scientific Study of Anomalous Phenomena (ASSAP) in 1981. They wanted to set up an organization with a more inclusive policy on contributors, investigations and publications. The term 'anomalous' was carefully chosen over such things as 'parapsychology' and 'psychical research' as better encompassing the broader range of their inquiries into such subjects as UFOs, legends, earth mysteries and cryptozoology. Founding members included Hilary Evans, the author and co-founder in 1964 of the Mary Evans Picture Archive, ufologist Jenny Randles, *Fortean Times* founder and former editor Bob Rickard, Dr Vernon Harrison, a specialist in forgeries, and Dr Hugh Pincott, a former chemist for British Petroleum and SPR council member. Despite the broad remit, much of the society's research focuses on sites of alleged haunting, including pioneering work on orbs and their ultimate explanation as optical 'circles of confusion'. The organization was fully incorporated in 1986 and became a recognized charity in 1987. In 2011 it was recognized as a professional body (consultation stage) and can offer training as an accredited investigator. The current president is the remarkable Revd Lionel Fanthorpe, prolific author, former star of Channel 4's *Fortean TV* and much else besides.[66]

The ghost hunting reality show

Explain it? We cannot. Disprove it? We cannot. We are simply inviting audiences to explore the unknown.[67]

The paranormal has always been a fascinating subject, so it is unsurprising that television has sought to explore the subject. The first programme to broach the subject was the documentary series *Ripley's Believe It or Not!* hosted by the famous popularizer of the bizarre, Robert L. Ripley, in 1949. However, the focus was more on the weird and wonderful than the truly paranormal. From 1959 to 1961 the US network ABC broadcast *One Step Beyond* with John Newland. Charles Bronson, William Shatner and Christopher Lee ('The Sorcerer') made early career appearances in this anthology series of stories supposedly based on real events, such as President Lincoln's premonition of his death, and in one episode Newland ingested Mexican magic mushrooms (*Psilocybe mexicana*).

Although undoubtedly pioneers in this field, a more lasting impression would be made by science fiction writer Arthur C. Clarke and his *Mysterious World* in 1980, followed by *Arthur C. Clarke's World of Strange Powers* in 1985 and *Arthur C. Clarke's Mysterious Universe* in 1994, and actor Leonard Nimoy as the presenter of *In Search of . . .* which ran from 1976 to 1982. The shows' remits were broad, covering cryptozoology, ufology and the sort of popular thaumatology that is now called Fortean. It was the short lived *Haunted Lives*, again with Leonard Nimoy and later Stacy Keach from 1991 to 1992 and 1995 (renamed *Real Ghosts*), that focused more exclusively on the experience of ghosts, using actor re-enactments and interviews to tell supposedly true ghost stories. Whilst an important milestone, it was Ian Cashmore's *Ghosthunters* (1996–7) that brought audiences closer to the realities of actual ghost hunting.

In recent years the number of ghost hunting reality shows on television has mushroomed. As well as demonstrating the public's interest in the paranormal, these shows have also brought new audiences to the subject. However, it is advisable to take all of these programmes with a large pinch of salt. To work on television they have to be geared towards entertainment. Ghost hunting, as the diehards will tell you, is not entertaining. Many programmes tend towards the hysterical Scooby-Doo end of the spectrum. Turn out the lights and run around in the dark, scaring the pants off yourself and hopefully your audience, seems to be the general formula. The use of mediums is dubious at best, and accusations of outright fraud have been levelled at some of the participants.

From the defining format of *Most Haunted* the ghost hunting show has diversified into every conceivable TV friendly area. Children get their own shows, such as *Ghost Trackers* and *Psychic Kids: Children of the Paranormal*. Animals appear on *The Haunted*, and lower down the evolutionary scale celebrities flaunt their way through *Celebrity Ghost Stories*, *I'm Famous and Frightened* and *Celebrity Paranormal Project*. Hardboiled Chicago policemen go sleuthing after spirits in *Paranormal Cops*. The newbies try their luck in *Ghost Hunters Academy* and antiques get their own slot with Derek Acorah's *Antiques Ghost Show*. Seeing the potential comedy of the situation, *South Park* writers got in on the act with *Ghost Hunters*' Jason Hawes and Grant Wilson turning up in a 2009 episode called 'Dead Celebrities' with predictably puerile results.

Summing up the genre for *The New York Times*, Mike Hale noted how such shows have 'created a new career – the paranormal investigator – that requires neither good looks nor any discernible skills beyond the ability to walk through an old building waving a flashlight'.[68] Although one fails to see how good looks should come into it, excessive torch waving is an occupational hazard, quite necessary to avoid stumbling in the dark. However, as journalist Will Storr said about *Most Haunted*, 'I got the distinct impression that proper paranormal researchers consider it to be a bit silly.'[69]

Most of the people I interviewed were either negative towards ghost hunting TV (32 per cent), or held at best mixed views (32 per cent). A typical comment along these lines came from Ghost Club member Alan Hetherington: 'Some of these

programmes are very good while others are a load of rubbish.'
Only 16 per cent had a positive opinion. Despite that, many
of the people behind such shows are genuinely interested
in paranormal investigation. It is also the case that 'proper
paranormal researchers' were involved with *Most Haunted*,
at least, at various times, notably Jason Karl, Dr Matthew
Smith and Dr Ciarán O'Keeffe. It is also the case that, inevitably, ghost hunting TV has changed the way in which people
investigate the paranormal in the real world.

Chronology of ghost hunting on television

Name	Country	Main Presenter(s)	Original Run
Ghosthunters	UK	Ian Cashmore	1996–7
Scariest Places on Earth	USA	Linda Blair	2000–6
Ghost Watch Live	UK	Claudia Christain, Paul Darrow	2001
Scream Team	UK	Ben Devlin, Phil Whyman	2001
Creepy Canada	Canada	Terry Boyle, Brian O'Dea	2002–4, 2006
Most Haunted	UK	Yvette Fielding	2002–10
Most Haunted Live!	UK	Yvette Fielding	2002–10
Ghost Hunters	USA	Jason Hawes, Grant Wilson	2004–
Haunted Homes	UK	Mia Dolan, Chris French	2004–10
Dead Famous	UK	Chris Fleming, Gail Porter	2004–6
Ghost Hunt	New Zealand	Carolyn Taylor, Michael Hallows, Brad Hills	2005–6
Celebrity Paranormal Project	USA	various	2006–7
Paranormal State	USA	Ryan Buell	2007–11

Chronology of ghost hunting on television *continued*			
Name	Country	Main Presenter(s)	Original Run
Ghost Adventures	USA	Zak Bagans	2008–
Ghost Hunters International	USA	Andy Andrews, Barry Fitzgerald	2008–
Ghost Hunters Academy	USA	Steve Gonsalves, Dave Tango, Jason Hawes	2009–10
The Othersiders	USA	Derek Shetterly and others	2009
Northern Ireland's Greatest Haunts	UK	Andy Matthews, Marion Goodfellow	2009–10
Ghost Lab	USA	Brad and Barry Klinge	2009–11
Fact or Faked: Paranormal Files	USA	Ben Hansen, Jael de Pardo	2010–
The Dead Files	USA	Amy Allan, Steve DiSchiavi	2011–
Haunted Collector	USA	John Zaffis	2011–
Nachtwakers	Netherlands	Dennis de Boer	2011–

Today's ghost hunters

To find out who today's ghost hunters are, I did what any good sociologist should, a survey. As far as I know this is the first time that such an attempt has been made. I contacted established ghost hunting groups with a published record of investigations and the Ghost Club generously allowed me to send my questionnaire to their members. From the responses, which may or may not be representative, a picture emerged of a dedicated group of paranormal investigators. Looking at the demographics, most were men (60 per cent), but there was still a large female participation. The average age was 43 and the majority (98 per cent) were white (Caucasian).[70]

In total, our ghost hunters had spent 490 years investigating 4,861 cases. This gave an average of 9 years spent investigating 92 cases. One individual had spent 40 years in pursuit of ghosts; another had chalked up over a thousand investigations single-handedly. One or two others had lost count, there were so many.

Given such dedication, I was particularly interested to find out what had started people ghost hunting in the first place. In the largest number of cases (29 per cent) it had been some sort of childhood experience, such as seeing a ghost, that had sparked an interest in ghost hunting, just as it had for Andrew Green. For example, Christian Adams of www. ghostalone.co.uk said:

> I witnessed my Uncle John come into my room [. . .] when I was 13. He was not there. The next morning we received a call to say he had passed away the evening before.

Many others (19 per cent) simply described their interest as lifelong. The media, of course, played its part, with 13 per cent saying that film, TV or radio had started them on the path of ghost hunting. Colin Conkie, a founder member of Cambridgeshire Ghost Research, put it well when he said that 'certain TV shows made it seem possible to participate'.

Most (83 per cent) of the ghost hunters had experienced what they would call a 'ghost'. There were many more opinions on what a 'ghost' is than could be effectively reduced to statistics, but I noted that many held a dual-source theory involving recording-like 'ghosts' and spirits of the dead who might manifest in other ways. There was a tendency, too, to talk of energy rather than soul as something persisting beyond physical death.

Just under a third (30 per cent) considered themselves to be psychic, or 'sensitive'. Few (17 per cent) were outrightly negative as to the use of psychics on investigation, being generally more positive (44 per cent).

I also wanted to know how people thought their non-ghost hunting friends and family viewed their activities. This was generally a mix of acceptance, interest and horror. For example, Ghost Club member Nicola Taylor wrote:

> Some accept this is what I like to do and encourage it, some are fascinated but don't want to join me, my husband's grandparents for example think it is dangerous and some friends think I am stark raving mad!

When asked who they thought were the foremost ghost hunters, historically as well as currently, Harry Price's name topped the list at 16 per cent, although some made this with reservation given all the controversy. Hans Holzer (14 per cent) and Peter Underwood (12 per cent) came next, although a pioneer such as Andrew Green was only mentioned by one person. Inevitably, TV cast its shadow, with TAPS members from the shows *Ghost Hunters* and *Ghost Hunters International* accounting for 24 per cent in total. Jason Hawes and Grant Wilson were mentioned by an equal number of people (7 per cent). None of the Ghost Club members mentioned any of these characters. Interestingly, neither Yvette Fielding nor Derek Acorah from *Most Haunted* were spoken of, but Ciarán O'Keeffe was held in some regard (5 per cent). Two people, surprisingly, mentioned Sir Arthur Conan Doyle. The man who invented the ghost hunting genre, Elliot O'Donnell, got a single mention.

Asked why they went ghost hunting, the people I interviewed gave a number of different responses. Of course, many were seeking evidence of the afterlife, of 'the survival of consciousness', of 'survival after bodily death', of 'the existence of ghosts' and so on. But others were also interested in simply exploring the unknown, the mysterious and 'phenomena which seem to violate the laws of physics'. Helping people, even helping spirits, was also mentioned. It was also interesting that some people saw the 'thrill' of this as its main attraction, as well as the social aspects – 'meeting interesting people' – or simply doing 'something different'. On this subject, however, the last word belongs to Ghost Club member Monica Tandy, who said:

> [I] can't understand why everyone isn't out there trying to answer the most fundamental of questions about life and death.

2

EQUIP

It was 4 p.m. on an autumn day in 1936 and Captain Hubert Provand had his head under a black cloth. The idea was to keep light from entering the back of the camera. The gloomy, dark oak staircase of Raynham Hall stretched up before him as he adjusted the focus. His colleague, a Scotsman going under the *nom de plume* of 'Indre Shira', stood idly by, toying with the flashgun in his hand. Suddenly he called out 'Quick! Quick! There's something! Are you ready?' Provand replied with a muffled, 'Yes.' Shira fired the flashgun and Provand opened the shutter.

About six seconds later Provand extricated himself from the cloth. 'What's all the excitement about?' he demanded.

Shira breathlessly explained. He had, he said, 'detected an ethereal, veiled form coming slowly down the stairs.'

Provand complained that he had not seen anything. He promptly bet Shira five pounds that when they developed the photographic plate there would nothing unusual there either.

Shira readily accepted.[1] Events would tell who would be the winner.

Basics

The old-school ghost hunter went in with little more than his wits about him. Elliott O'Donnell might have occasionally taken a candle with him, but that he often blew out. On another occasion he tells us how he 'felt in my pocket for pencil, notebook and revolver' and was known to rely on a hip flask to 'keep the cold out'.[2] Andrew Green listed the essentials as 'a shorthand notebook, a ball-point pen and a measuring tape'.[3] Tom Perrott, former chairman of the Ghost Club, disappointed an enthusiastic media producer by saying that all he needed for ghost hunting were 'a pencil and paper and a sympathetic ear'.[4] The Ghost Club's current chairman, Alan Murdie, is equally spartan: 'At its simplest, my ghost-hunting equipment would consist of a notebook, a pencil and a sympathetic ear.'[5]

Although Green's classic *Ghost Hunting: A Practical Guide* is a short book, he did expand on the list, but the range of equipment and materials had little changed since Harry Price's day in the 1920s and 30s. With a nod towards Sherlock Holmes, Green threw in a magnifying glass, and other items included chalk, flour, graphite powder and sewing thread. It all sounds like the average contents of a Boy Scout's pockets, but since then the range of equipment has grown considerably in type, complexity and expense.

I looked at twenty-eight different 'ghost hunting kits' currently on the market.[6] They ranged in price from an affordable $34.95 to a staggering $810.00. Most (85.7 per cent) of them contained some sort of electromagnetic field (EMF) meter or EMF-related device, an infrared (IR) thermometer (50.0 per cent), an audio recorder or electronic voice phenomena (EVP) device (39.3 per cent) and a motion sensor (35.7 per cent), all bundled up in a suitable case (64.3 per cent). Less than a quarter (21.4 per cent) included some sort of book or booklet to explain how to use the equipment. However, the kit is not an entirely accurate reflection of what serious ghost hunters consider to be the most necessary tools of the trade.

I also talked to Noah Voss, paranormal investigator and owner of www.getghostgear.com, about ghost hunting equipment. According to Voss, the big change in demand occurred after *Ghost Hunters* hit US TV screens. 'Within a year,' he said, 'there was a dramatic shift industry wide. People wanted what they saw on that TV show and other programming that followed.' People wanted 'unintimidating tools' that were easy to use 'allowing for no to little learning curve and no specific skill set to operate'. To begin with this was the EMF meter, but later people started adding digital audio recorders to the list before 'more metaphysical devices', such as the Ovilus, became popular.[7]

Shawn Porter runs GhostStop, a website and bricks-and-mortar shop in Orlando, Florida. Inside, the colour scheme is red and black. Muted lighting picks out the quirky items in display cases and wall boxes. Short of being a haunted house, this is a ghost hunters' paradise. Porter also believes that the TV shows are driving what sells. 'The most popular items,' he said, 'are those used on paranormal related television shows.'[8]

Asked what three essential items they would bring to an investigation, today's ghost hunters are more likely to favour a camera of some description, an audio recorder and a camcorder, with other essentials being an EMF meter and a torch. In total, I received thirty-seven different types of answer, including 'myself'. One person sensibly mentioned a first aid kit and others added food and warm clothing. Going against the grain, one ghost hunter packed a spellbook, candles and Ouija board, but this was very much the exception in today's technologically driven investigation. Where Perrott and Murdie focused their attention on interviewing witnesses, we see a trend towards monitoring the environment. Fortunately, no one followed O'Donnell's example and included firearms.

Popular investigative equipment

Rank	Item	GHS Respondents (%)
1	Audio recorder	60.38
2	Camera	49.06
3	Camcorder	33.96
4	Torch	30.19
5	EMF meter	20.75
6	Notepad	18.87

Note: the respondents column does not sum to 100% because each respondent was asked to provide three answers.

In general, the choice of equipment follows the process of investigating an allegedly haunted site: define the locus of the investigation; secure the area; field monitoring devices; and analyse the data. As we can see, certain types of instrumentation or methodologies will be deployed with different aims in mind and only a portion will be concerned with detecting physical sources of the alleged haunting.

Map
The ghost hunter needs to know the lie of the land. For the UK, Ordnance Survey provide detailed and up-to-date maps, but the Land Registry will provide the best overview of the property, its boundaries and its neighbours. The local library should be able to provide historical maps of the area and these might prove useful in cases where the property has undergone additional building work over the years.

A geological map can also be useful. Clay, chalk, sand and gravel can all cause movement in a property, particularly when a heavy downpour follows a period of drought. The resultant extreme shrinkage and expansion of soil strata will affect building structures. Andrew Green tells the story of the phantom flames of Charmouth that burnt along the clifftop in 1908. Known as the Lyme Volcano, the rumour was that a witch had been burnt here in the seventeenth century and had supernaturally returned to burn again. However, the spontaneous fire was in fact a freak of nature caused by the friction of iron pyrites in a combustible substratum of slate. There was also evidence of paraffin having been used to keep alight what had by then become a popular tourist attraction.[9]

The best map, however, is going to be the one you draw yourself. Walk round the property and note the geography. Look for natural features that may account for supposed paranormal activity. Water, present in wells, drains, rivers and underground streams, poses risks for buildings potentially leading to a range of structural problems through subsidence and damp. These can be the cause of much mysterious moaning and groaning.

The ghost hunter also needs to map the interior of the building. Here the measuring tape and graph paper will come into their own, although today laser and ultrasound measuring devices make the task easier. In an old property one should especially look for fault lines in the structure that may be evidence of subsidence and the origin of a range of 'paranormal' sound effects. It is also important to note the location of electrical supply and installed appliances.

Secure

To rule out the involvement of human agents, ghost hunters strategically create barriers across thresholds or the believed path of an apparition. This is where Green's flour comes in useful. Peter Underwood used chalk powder in Langenhoe Church to the same end. Investigating the haunting of her own home in the late nineteenth century, Rose Morton used the simple expedient of tying threads across the route of the 'black widow'. The apparition was seen to pass through the threads without breaking or displacing them.[10]

Modern investigators can resort to more technologically sophisticated means, employing beam barrier alarms. The set-up uses a transmitter and receiver unit to create an invisible infrared beam barrier, triggering an alarm or other action when broken. A motion detector provides greater coverage using a passive infrared field to detect movement within a given area, typically a 60° to 110° arc, again activating an alarm or other function.

As well as being used to exclude human interference, area security methods can also document the unexplained. When Sir Max Pemberton and news editor Ralph Blumenfeld investigated a haunted Georgian house in Lincoln's Inn, London, in 1901, their attempts to catch anybody up to mischief caught something else entirely. Not having night-vision goggles, they simply left the electric lights on – quite a novelty at that time – and sprinkled chalk dust on the floor of the rooms. After going to investigate the mysterious movements of doors, they discovered large, turkey-sized bird footprints in the middle of each room. Apart from the investigators, the building was empty at the time. The story was covered by the *Daily Mail*, but being Sir Max's newspaper, it spared us any jokes about 'fowl play'.[11]

When The Atlanta Paranormal Society (TAPS) investigated St Augustine Lighthouse, Florida, in 2006, Jason Hawes and Grant Wilson saw someone lean over the railings and look at them. Curiously, the motion sensor controlling the lights failed to go off. When Hawes pursued the figure up the tower he found no one there. It was a case of the dog that did not bark in the night and Hawes drew the obvious conclusion that what he had seen and pursued was not of this world.[12]

Detect

The search for some indicator or source of paranormal phenomena is all about energy. Many ghost hunters talk about 'energy' in an undefined way as somehow powering 'ghosts'. For example, both Jason Hawes and Grant Wilson of TAPS make statements to this effect: 'supernatural entities need energy to manifest themselves', according to Hawes; and 'ghosts draw on energy in order to manifest', according to Wilson. They do not explain what that energy is and assume that it can be taken from sources such as the manmade batteries used in their equipment without describing the process at work.[13]

Energy can be defined as 'the ability to make a force act through a distance'.[14] Energy can take several different forms, including thermal, chemical, electric, magnetic, electromagnetic, nuclear, sound and mechanical, and can be transformed from one form to another. As we know from school, the Law of the Conservation of Energy states that energy can neither be created nor destroyed. Energy is everywhere all of the time and it does not go away, but it does move. In order to understand common monitoring equipment and its uses in ghost hunting we should think in terms of energy first and bits of kit, like cameras and EMF meters, second.

The electromagnetic spectrum is the infinite and continuous range of electromagnetic radiation (EMR), or radiant energy. It is measured in terms of frequency in hertz (Hz), wavelength in metres (m) and energy in electron volts (eV), currently from Extremely Low Frequency (ELF) with wavelengths the size of mountains to high frequency gamma rays with wavelengths the size of atomic nuclei. Frequency is the number of waves that pass a point in a given period of time, which is in an inverse relationship to wavelength, the distance between two successive equivalent points at the same phase (crest, trough, or zero crossing) in the wave. This range is often differentiated in terms of effect as non-ionizing and ionizing radiation. Non-ionizing radiation comprises that part of the spectrum from ELF to UV. Ionizing radiation is defined from X-rays and above, although as UV radiation approaches the X-ray part of the spectrum it begins to exhibit ionizing behaviour (photoionization). Ionizing radiation also includes alpha and beta particle radiation generated by radioactive decay or fission/fusion reactions (nuclear energy). When passing through a substance, ionizing radiation causes it to lose one or more electrons from one or more atoms or molecules (combinations of two or more atoms). Ionizing radiation is particularly noted for its damaging effect on biological tissue.

The highly radioactive alpha particle emitter polonium-210 was used to assassinate Alexander Litvinenko in 2006, for example. So when ghost hunters talk about 'energy' what do they mean and how do they measure or record it?

Visible light

Shira won his bet. He and Provand were in their dark room, and together they saw a mysterious figure materialize in the centre of the plate. Shira ran downstairs and dragged chemist Benjamin Jones out of his shop to come and witness the extraordinary development. Jones later signed a declaration, stating 'I am satisfied that the ethereal figure on the staircase was there when the film was being fixed.'[15]

Harry Price looked into the matter. Although he suggested that the same result could be produced fraudulently, he admitted that 'I could not shake their story, and I had no right to disbelieve them [. . .] The negative is entirely innocent of any faking.'[16] Several other experts have all declared the photograph genuine, all except C. V. C. Herbert, investigations officer for the Society for Psychical Research.[17]

A camera has become a standard piece of kit for the ghost hunter. The idea is, reasonably enough, that if an apparition can be photographed then it can be presented as strong proof of the existence of ghosts. Since the invention of the photographic process, almost no convincing photographs of apparitions have been made despite the fact that an untold mass of such photographs has accumulated. No well-known photograph that I can think of has been taken whilst the photographer was also observing the phenomenon. The supposed proof is usually only discovered after the fact. Even the most famous photograph, that of the Brown Lady of Raynham Hall, was only and allegedly seen by the photographer's assistant prior to shooting and not by the photographer himself. With his head under the camera hood and the shutter open for the exposure, Provand would have been entirely in the dark.

It is taken for granted that 'the camera cannot lie', but it does and often. Early 'spirit photographs' caused considerable controversy in their time; understandably, as here, suddenly, was apparently the proof everyone had been searching for. During New York's great Twenty-Seventh Street Ghost sensation of late 1862, P. T. Barnum recalled that the ghost had 'his daguerreotype taken on prepared metal plates set upright in the haunted room', whilst someone else claimed to have captured an 'exact photographic likeness' and 'made immense sales'.[18]

The pioneer in this field was American William H. Mumler. He first came to note in 1862 in Boston before moving to New York where his success in spirit photography eventually had him up in court. The trial in 1869, fittingly at Tombs Police Court, was front-page news. *Harper's Weekly* was amazed that spirits of the deceased could be raised 'from the vasty deep' for $10 a head. P. T. Barnum testified against Mumler, as did many others, but Mumler called photographers to his defence who stated under oath that they had been unable to detect any charlatanry in his technique. The judge was forced to concede 'not guilty' from lack of evidence.[19]

By 1875 William Stainton Moses had already examined some 600 supposed spirit photographs. His judgement was harsh. 'Some people would recognise anything,' he wrote. 'A broom and a sheet are quite enough for some wild enthusiasts.'[20]

Illusionist and psychic investigator William Marriott gave a presentation to the Ghost Club on spirit photography in 1939. He showed the audience a spirit photograph which 'had been recognized at séances as a new-born baby, a mother, grandmother, and great-grandmother.' He concluded that it was 'not what the sitter saw so much as what the sitter imagined was seen which counted at a séance.' Marriott declared that 'every spirit photograph he had seen was a fake, including those he had taken himself.'[21]

Strangely, Stainton Moses still endorsed the results produced by Frenchman Edouard Isidore Buguet. A month after

Stainton Moses's article was published, Buguet was arrested and charged with fraudulently manufacturing his spirit photographs. At his trial Buguet made a full confession. All of the 'spirits' had been produced by double exposure. In the early days of his career he had used confederates to pose as ghosts. Later, fearing exposure himself, he used a doll and a large stock of interchangeable heads (photographs mounted on cardboard). Even someone as sceptical as Stainton Moses, at least in this regard, was still likely to be duped.[22]

Despite all these court cases and carefully scrutinized photographs, the lesson was not learned. In the first two decades of the twentieth century, William Hope claimed to have taken over 2,500 photographs of what he called 'extras', or spirits.[23] In 1919 a Society for the Study of Supranormal Photographs (SSSP), with Sir Arthur Conan Doyle as Vice-President, was formed to organize and analyse this 'new' evidence.[24] To rebut Harry Price's conclusion that Hope was faking it, Conan Doyle would publish *The Case for Spirit Photography* a few years later in 1923. Although Fred Barlow, another member of the SSSP, changed his mind about the genuineness of Hope, the big names in psychical research – Sir William Crookes, Sir William Barrett and Sir Oliver Lodge – all supported him.[25]

All sorts of strange fogs and mists – sometimes erroneously termed ectoplasm – are routinely shown as evidence of the paranormal, often with claims as to discernible forms and faces in the nebulous swirls. Uncap a camera still warm from the car, camera bag or pocket in cold conditions and condensation will fog the lens, no doubt producing some of these aberrations. The converse is also true: a cold lens in warm, humid conditions will also fog. The photographer's breath condensing in the air on a cold night, and even cigarette smoke, also produce 'mysterious' mists that are apparently unseen at the time the photograph is taken. Vapour or smoke near the lens is illuminated by the camera's flash, thus making the form seem to appear only on the image. Aware of these explanations, investigator Jason Karl has nonetheless been perplexed to 'have caught this kind of picture when no-one has been smoking in the vicinity and the weather has been mild.'[26]

Flash photography is known to produce aberrations in the film. These are caused by particles, such as dust, snow, raindrops or insects, close to the lens reflecting flash light. Because the camera is focused on a more distant object these particles appear as soft spheres of luminescence that can overlap the background image. To solve this problem manufacturers, such as Fujifilm, recommend shooting in better lighting conditions or using a separate flash unit. Ghost hunters are unlikely to want to flood a supposedly haunted house with studio-level lighting, so using a separate flash unit placed at a distance and different angle to the lens is likely to be the best option. This will require a higher-end camera with flash sync capability. Mediums, however, usually insist on darkness or near darkness for the manifestation of supposed spirit phenomena, claiming that strong light inhibits communication and can be harmful to the medium.

Without flash, longer shutter speeds will be required to capture any available light. Holding the camera in the hand for longer exposures will typically result in blurring due to hand shake. Although vibration reduction technology onboard many cameras can reduce this, better results will be produced by using a tripod. With long shutter speeds normal objects moving through the camera's field of vision will produce blurred and distorted forms that could be mistaken for paranormal activity. Supposing that apparitions can be photographed and are visible to the naked eye, their movements would likewise cause blurring, making them potentially unrecognizable and evidentially useless.

A wide-angle lens is needed to photograph interiors. Many modern digital compacts feature impressive zoom ranges from wide angle to telephoto, although a digital SLR or mirrorless system camera will allow you to change lenses and

Photographic evidence of alleged ghosts

Subject	Location	Photographers	Date
Lord Combermere	Combermere Abbey, Cheshire	Sybil Corbet	1891
Jonathan Owen	Risea, Monmouthshire	unknown	1916
Freddy Jackson	Cranwell, Lincolnshire	unknown	1919
The 'Brown Lady'	Raynham Hall, Norfolk	Capt. Hubert Provand and Indre Shira	1936
'The Back Seat Ghost'	unknown	Mabel Chinnery	1959
Hooded figure	Newby Church, Yorkshire	Revd Kenneth Lord	1963
Kneeling figure	Church of St Mary the Virgin, Woodford, Northamptonshire	Gordon Carroll	1964
Figure ascending staircase	The Queen's House, Greenwich	Revd R.W. Hardy	1966
Figure in balcony	St Botolph's Church, London	Chris Brackley	1982
'The Madonna of Bachelor's Grove'	Bachelor's Grove Cemetery, Illinois	Mari Huff	1991
Figure of girl	Town Hall, Wem, Shropshire	Tony O'Rahily	1995
Figure closing doors, aka 'Skeletor'	Hampton Court Palace	CCTV footage	2003
'Victorian' ghost	Tiger Bay, Cardiff	Google Street View	2008

achieve the best from a dedicated wide-angle lens. Prosumer compacts are an affordable alternative. By resisting the craze for more and more megapixels, these cameras are able to deliver better low-light photography, and with a restricted zoom range employ better optics. In most multifunction or cheaper lenses, distortion will be a visible problem: barrel at the wide angle; pincushion at the telephoto. Whilst this can usually be corrected by photo manipulation software either onboard the camera or on a computer, the less you have to manipulate the photo the better for obvious evidential reasons. The moment you say Photoshop you can kiss your perfectly exposed, pin-sharp ghostly nun goodbye.

The heart of a digital camera is its sensor. In low- to mid-range cameras this is typically a Charge Coupled Device (CCD). In top-range and professional cameras this is a Complementary Metal Oxide Semiconductor (CMOS), also called an Active Pixel Sensor (APS). The essential difference between them is size and hence the number of megapixels that can be comfortably accommodated, which means better results when it comes to blowing up an image to scrutinize that potential anomaly.

Another factor to contend with is compression. Lower-range cameras will record compressed JPEGs, often in a variety of quality settings, whereas higher-end cameras will allow RAW format capture. RAW is more like a digital version of the old film negative compared to the finished JPEG. The JPEG format uses lossy compression, which means that it discards some of the information to produce a smaller file. The effects of low to moderate compression are not usually noticeable to the naked eye when the image is viewed at its intended size, but enlargement will magnify the problem. In contrast the RAW format retains almost all of the detail, creating a larger file that requires more disk space to store. The RAW image still requires processing before it can be printed, or viewed in some graphics programs, due to the large number of different standards in use. Some models get around this problem by allowing simultaneous RAW and JPEG photography.

Of course, quality will be tempered by practicality. Price, portability and ease of use will be important limits to any camera choice. A top-of-the-range DSLR might shoot the best images, but it comes with a price tag to match and will require greater technical skill to capture those images, not to mention the muscles (and masochistic streak) to lug all the gear around.

Even if one manages to photograph something, then what? The most famous photograph of all – the Brown Lady of Raynham Hall – has been reprinted far and wide as proof of the paranormal, but is it? Even the best photograph we have is not without its criticisms.

After the *Country Life* article was published publicizing the photograph, Shira had a blown-up copy of the photograph outside the premises of Indre Shira Ltd, 'court photographers', and was selling 8×10 prints at a guinea a time. Nandor Fodor, research officer for the International Institute for Psychical Research (IIPR), wrote to Lady Townshend, owner of Raynham Hall, giving his opinion that 'Indre Shira is out to make capital out of your ghost'.[27]

Provand and Shira were not there on a photo shoot for *Country Life*, as is so often asserted. Shira had written to Lady Townshend asking for permission for himself, his wife and Provand to come and photograph the ghost, particularly wanting to stay up during the night to try and do so. Lady Townshend was having nothing of any ghost hunting, but did allow them to visit when she had a large group from the Archaeological Society of Norfolk there. She later noted that Mrs Shira 'behaved as a psychic' and 'described to me exquisite influences all over the house'. The presence of his wife is largely unknown yet she clearly had a strong interest in the ghost. Added to the fact that 'Indre Shira' was the pseudonym of an as yet unidentified Scotsman and it is beginning to sound like the Twenty-Seventh Street Ghost all over again.[28]

However, financial gain was not the chief allegation against the authenticity of the photograph. Everyone who met Shira and Provand thought them honest and unlikely to defraud – traits also found in the best con men. But even in 1936, it was remarked that the camera was 'old'. Provand himself was worried that the camera's faulty bellows might admit unwanted light. The SPR's Herbert interviewed both photographers and examined the negatives for himself:

> The second film (both were in one dark slide) i.e. the one with the 'ghost' is obviously shaken in a vertical plane, causing doubling of all horizontal lines (or else is two exposures?) Provand said he had not noticed this, which surprised me, as it is very obvious even in the process block. Provand says camera was on a marble table or pillar and was not very rigid. He uncapped in a hurry.[29]

If the photograph was not a fake, was it simply a bad photograph badly taken? If so, then what had Shira seen on the staircase as Provand opened the shutter? His wife? A stray archaeologist?

Infrared

'Ghosts for some reason,' explained Dale Kaczmarek, president of the Ghost Research Society (GRS), 'always seem to be on the IR spectrum. We've gotten a lot of interesting photos of spirits using IR film.'[30]

All objects above absolute zero (−273.15°C) emit infrared radiation. This means that infrared devices can be used as a means of seeing in the dark, but are to be distinguished from 'night-vision' devices that operate by amplifying available light rather than using infrared. They also 'see' more than would be apparent to the human eye in daylight, such as drag marks on carpets and explosives residue at crime scenes, and can be used to determine the precise time of death of corpses less than fifteen hours old, for example.[31]

Infrared photography has been used to great effect by Sir Simon Marsden in his many atmospheric and haunting photographs, but the technique is not easy to emulate. Filters can achieve something of this look – a red filter will turn your sky a suitably apocalyptic black – but the point here is to try and record what cannot be seen by the naked eye. Old film SLRs can take expensive infrared film stock, but both the sources of film and the places to develop it are becoming rarer, which may require setting up a home darkroom, supposing one can still buy the film. Dedicated digital infrared cameras are available, but they are specialist pieces of kit with a price tag to match. Modern digital cameras can be converted to infrared by a little home surgery to remove the device that normally blocks the infrared end of the spectrum from being recorded. This is not a complicated operation, but neither is it something to try out on your new top-of-the-range digital SLR.

Most séances are conducted in darkness or semi-darkness. When light is used it is usually a muted red-light of the magnitude of a photographic darkroom, or a little brighter. In his séance experiments Dr W. J. Crawford, lecturer in mechanical engineering at the Queen's University and Technical College, used a gas light shining through ruby-coloured glass, for example. At this time, it is not clear why the red end of the spectrum should be non-destructive as opposed to the violet end. As early as 1919, W. Whately-Smith hoped that Crawford would experiment with the light used to discover 'the particular wave-lengths which prevent phenomena developing'.[32]

Temperature
Temperature fluctuations are one of the most commonly reported signs of supposed paranormal activity. These have been recorded at least since 1936 when Harry Price investigated Dean Manor, Kent, for the BBC.[33] From my preliminary survey of hauntings I found that 3.93 per cent of all non-visual phenomena were described in relation to cold, but given the partial reporting in the sources consulted this may not reflect the true picture. Interestingly, in Gauld and Cornell's analysis of poltergeist/haunting cases they found that 4 per cent involved 'cold breeze, air movement etc.' – they did not

have a 'cold spot' category.[34] In addition, Hilary Evans found the sensation of cold to be sometimes reported at séances.[35]

Harry Price even had expensive Negretti and Zambra thermometers in every room of the offices of the NLPR, as well as a specially designed 'transmitting thermograph' in the séance room and maximum and minimum thermometers outside the windows.[36] Today, many ghost hunters, such as Joshua P. Warren, use non-contact IR thermometers to find cold spots in a reputedly haunted location. Again these devices were not designed for finding 'cold spots' and frequent errors arise from their mishandling. Jason Hawes once described how TAPS team member Paula managed to 'detect some cold spots with her EMF detector'.[37] This, of course, is impossible. As the Ghost Club's Technical Officer, James Tacchi, explains:

> To me, the biggest error most investigators make is not knowing how their kit works, e.g., chasing cold spots around a room with a laser thermometer, unaware that the unit is effectively a camera, in that it detects IR radiation (instead of light for a camera) via a lens from a solid surface and interprets it as a temperature – it cannot detect temp. in mid-air, and the laser dot is just a guide, so even though the spot is on a wall, depending on the accuracy of the unit, you could actually be measuring an area many feet in diameter.

Another problem arises out of the fact that most thermometers are only accurate to within two degrees at best. This means that apparently differing readings can actually be the same absolute temperature. As a way round this Tacchi suggests that investigators should calibrate their instruments at the beginning of the investigation and choose one device to be the 'master' against which all other readings can be compared for accuracy. He also recommends setting up temperature dataloggers that can be started via a laptop and left alone in their recording positions. By using both thermistor-based loggers for recording long-term measurements together with thermocouple devices that are sensitive enough to register small and rapid changes, a more complete picture of onsite temperature can be recorded for later analysis.[38]

Temperature is also relevant to electromagnetics. A relationship exists between the temperature of bodies emitting EMR and the frequency/wavelength of the EMR. We should be aware that temperature and thermal energy are different things. Heat is caused by molecular motion (kinetic energy) within a substance, which can be measured as a total (thermal energy), or an average (temperature).[39]

Humidity
People frequently mention a certain 'atmosphere' in conjunction with supposed haunted locations. But these are not always, if ever, paranormal in origin. Using humidity dataloggers, Tacchi found that the recurrent 'heavy atmosphere' reported at an allegedly haunted site corresponded with an over-active air-conditioning unit.[40]

Joshua P. Warren has taken a different approach. He argues that a dry environment is conducive to paranormal phenomena, connecting this somehow to air ionization. Interestingly, he found that running strategically placed humidifiers at the scene of a particularly disturbing haunting caused the 'malevolent activity' to cease within forty-eight hours.[41] Confusingly, Maurice Townsend, writing for ASSAP, found that high humidity is usually associated with haunted locations, among other factors.[42]

Electromagnetism
Spontaneous fires, bursting water pipes, exploding light bulbs, loosening bolts, dead family pets – the bungalow in Minsterworth near Gloucester seemed to be the epicentre of something wicked, but when exorcism failed to put an end to the phenomena, psychical researcher Tony Cornell got involved. The site was surrounded by government communications bases, some

of them highly secret, such as the GCHQ (Government Communications Head Quarters) facility at Cheltenham, the Cinderford Radio Station and the radar research establishment at Malvern, which gave rise to the theory that secret government research might be the cause of the phenomena.

According to former NASA scientist, Dr David Baker, the sort of electromagnetic radiation involved in experimental radar research 'can melt plugs. It can disassemble wire. It can create harmonic vibrations that will unscrew pipes. It can create all the wealth of things we are seeing reported by various people in various places.'[43]

The idea that electromagnetism might be involved in paranormal phenomena can be traced back to the 1870s and the researches of Dr Francis Gerry Fairfield:

> The writer has personally witnessed, under conditions of test provided by himself, in his own room, in full daylight, with the medium seated upon a sofa from six to eight feet from the table hovering upon which the apparition (the hand) appeared. The application of the poles of a horse-shoe magnet to the hand caused it to waver perceptibly, and threw the medium into violent convulsions.[44]

Fairfield concluded that the apparition was generated by the medium's nervous system. This is by no means established, but, if his experiment was as reliable as he claimed and events took place as stated, then he did demonstrate that apparitional phenomena could be influenced by magnetic fields. The problem for ghost hunting today is whether they are generated by (electro)magnetic fields or produce them: is electromagnetism causal or incidental?

A scientific team from Malvern was brought in by the local Environmental Health Officer to test the Minsterworth bungalow. It was, curiously enough, Friday 13 March 1987 when they set up their equipment to conduct what they called an electromagnetic compatibility (EMC) evaluation. Using a

Hewlett Packard RE spectrum analyser they tested the property for radiation in the range 100 Hz to 22 GHz. They found nothing unusual.[45]

The Malvern scientists may have been looking in the wrong wavelength. Cornell noted that readings in the range 4–20 Hz have been taken in areas where paranormal activity is believed to have produced physical effects.[46] The Canadian scientist Michael A. Persinger began working on the biological effects of electromagnetism at Laurentian University in the early 1970s, but there is no evidence that ghost hunters were aware of this research at the time.[47] In 1973 Green only mentioned a voltmeter to check for electrical faults that might be responsible for the strange behaviour of lights.[48]

In 1976 Peter Underwood was invited to take part in an experiment at Borley Church with John Taylor, professor of mathematics at London University, for the BBC.[49] Taylor set up a range of equipment, including magnetometers and 'electric field measuring devices'. The equipment failed to register anything out of the ordinary, but when Underwood came to write his own guide to ghost hunting in 1986 he added them to the list.[50]

Electromagnetic Field (EMF) meters are now widely available. Commercial meters are calibrated to the frequency of mains electricity in the range 50 Hz (Europe) or 60 Hz (North America). This is fine for finding cables buried in walls and floors, but is still too high for the sort of ranges said to be involved in paranormal cases. More sensitive devices are available, but these come at a greater cost.

The most popular device is the KII (or K2) Meter. Almost half (45 per cent) of the GHS respondents who mentioned an EMF meter specified this product by name. It is a basic single axis meter with five lights indicating the strength of field detected from 0 to 20+ mG. It is calibrated at 60 Hz, but has a frequency range of 30 to 20,000 Hz.[51]

While brandishing an EMF meter, Phil Whyman, investigating Edinburgh's Niddry Street Vaults with *Most Haunted*, stated that 'anything between two and eight, they reckon, could be significant of paranormal activity'.[52] According to New Zealand show *Ghost Hunt*, 'a reading of 7 mG may indicate spiritual activity'.[53] Troy Taylor used to believe that a reading somewhere between 2 and 8 mG qualified as 'ghostly'. However, he confessed that he had no idea why this was so and found that his own research contradicted this assumption.[54]

When actually used in a scientific manner, different results have been obtained. During their investigation of a reputedly haunted farm in Cheshire, Para.Science found that more than 80 per cent of reported paranormal activity occurred in areas where EMF levels were consistently above 10 mG, in some cases above 25 mG. In one case, Michael Persinger recorded levels of 157 mG.[55] So, who is right and why? This is something we will have to return to in Chapter 8, 'Explain'.

Air ionization

A self-descriptive piece of kit, the Air Ion Counter detects natural and artificial ion levels, either scaled to show negative ions (Negative Ion Detector, or NID) or both negative and positive ions. Ions have a considerable impact on our day-to-day mood. Too many positive ions, as is typical in airless buildings running a lot of electrical equipment, such as the modern office, produce negative mental effects: headaches, tiredness and so on. Negative ions, in contrast, produce positive mental states. A good example is the light, refreshing feeling one experiences after a rain shower. Ions can produce the sensation of coldness or even touch on the human skin, so an Air Ion Counter can be used to determine whether such experiences – typical in a haunting – are due to atmospherics or the paranormal. Although not routinely in use, the Burnley Paranormal Research Association was using air ion counters in the early 1990s.[56]

Ionizing radiation

A Geiger counter measures ionizing radiation consisting of alpha and beta particles, and gamma rays and X-rays. The scale for alpha and beta particles is in counts per minute (CPM) or counts per second (CPS). Gamma rays and X-rays are measured in microSieverts (µSv) per hour, milliSieverts (mSv) per hour or milliRoentgens (mR) per hour. Accuracy is typically ±15 per cent relative to Cesium 137.[57] Some units will also measure in electron volts (eV), kilo electron volts (keV) and mega electron volts (meV). For industrial models, prices range from $350 for analog models up to $556 for digital devices, and all the way up to $1,799.99 for state-of-the-art Model 1703MO Personal Radiation Detector and Dosimeter for emergency services and military use.[58] Cheaper gadgets are available, such as the $175 NukAlert nuclear radiation detector key chain or the tiny K8 Nuke Safeguard Radiation Detector Geiger Counter for $189.99.[59] According to the EMF safety and health website, EM Watch, there was a huge rush on Geiger counters after the Fukushima nuclear disaster in 2011.[60]

Oliver J. Lodge first proposed the use of X-rays in psychical research in 1919, but as a means of determining whether they had an influence on séance phenomena as light in general is believed to have.[61] The Ghost Research Society was using a Geiger counter at least as early as 2000 during their investigation of Danaka Fey's home in the Chicago area.[62] TAPS first used a Geiger counter during their investigation of St Augustine Lighthouse, Florida, in 2006, claiming that 'the theory is that supernatural entities emit a radioactive frequency'.[63]

Sound waves
Sound is another energy also measured in terms of frequency and wavelength. Sound is defined as a mechanical or material wave of pressure that requires a medium to travel through. This differentiates it from electromagnetic waves which can travel without a medium. Thus electromagnetic radiation can travel through a vacuum whilst sound cannot.[64] We hear only a limited range of pressure waves as sound, typically between 16 and 16,000 Hz.[65] Infrasound (lower frequencies, longer wavelengths) is anything below this and ultrasound (higher

frequencies, shorter wavelengths) anything above. Common uses of ultrasound are medical imaging and sonar, but it can also be used to pasteurize milk and clean teeth, as well as to electronically eavesdrop without the use of microphones.

What we hear is the result of pressure waves vibrating a thin membrane in the human ear which sends signals to the brain that we interpret as sounds. We can feel these same pressure waves vibrating the whole body, such as at a rock concert or at the scene of a bomb blast. The technology has advanced from using soot-covered barrels to wax cylinders to discs to magnetic tape to digital to record sound waves and, from the later part of the nineteenth century, to enable their play back.

As early as 1889 Arthur Palliser, Jr, suggested the use of a phonograph, as well as a 'detective camera', to verify apparitional experiences.[66] The phenomenon of 'speaking in tongues' – defined at the time as 'a case of psychic automatism' – was recorded by William James in the USA in the 1890s and the SPR in London was able to hear 'specimens of the unknown tongues recorded by the phonograph' at their general meeting.[67]

One of the first attempts to record paranormal sound effects was made in 1915. Dr W. J. Crawford was investigating séances held by the medium, teenager Kathleen Goligher, in Belfast and using a phonograph to record the sounds produced, supposedly by paranormal means. He recorded a range of noises from 'scarcely audible taps to real "sledge hammer" blows', as well as sounds made by a trumpet and a bell. On hearing the recordings for himself, the editor of the spiritualist magazine, *Light*, noted that they ruled out the possibility that such sounds were simply 'the collective hallucination' of those present during the séances.[68]

Electronic Voice Phenomena (EVP)
When the Swedish artist and film-maker Friedrich Jurgenson (1903–87) heard the voice of his deceased mother calling him by her pet name for him, he was convinced that he

had established 'a radio-link with the dead'. In the summer of
1959 he had been recording bird song, but when he played the
tapes back he was surprised to hear faint voices. Intrigued,
he conducted further experiments into what he called 'voices
from space' and eventually heard his mother.

The Latvian scientist Dr Konstantin Raudive (1906–74),
then lecturing at the University of Uppsala, heard about Jurgenson's work and after making over 100,000 recordings of
his own published his findings as *Breakthrough: An Amazing Experiment in Electronic Communication with the Dead*
(1971). This led to the phenomena being called Raudive Voices
for a time.

During their investigations TAPS have recorded a number
of EVP: 'Fine, take it' coinciding with the appearance of six
pennies apparently apported during an investigation in Massachusetts in 1996; 'Water' and 'get out' during the investigation of a private home in southern Connecticut; a male voice
saying something like, 'Now, now, now, dirty folk . . . mean'
in a house built on sacred native American land in western
Rhode Island; 'Get out now' and others in a private home in
Connecticut; 'Leave . . . leave, gather' at a warehouse in New
Jersey; 'I miss Adam' and another message in Polish whilst
investigating Adam Zubrowski's home in Connecticut; 'have
them go' at the DiRaimos's family home, Cranston, Rhode
Island; 'the ship' or 'long ship' on board the USS *North
Carolina*.[69]

Generally, the recordings sound like a word or small group
of short words of few syllables, what Dr Carlo Tajna called
the 'psychophonic style'. Other researchers, such as David
Ellis and Professor James Alcock, have suggested that such
'voices' could be misinterpreted terrestrial radio signals,
static interference effects, or auditory apophenia (also parei-
dolia) – where the brain finds meaningful patterns in random
stimuli. Professor Hans Bender in Germany thought that the
effect might be a demonstration of psychokinesis, rather than
a spiritual phenomenon.[70]

After the early audio experiments, German pensioner Klaus Schreiber became famous for receiving images of his dead relatives on a television set in the 1980s. Using a variation of Schreiber's technique, Martin Wenzel even claimed to have received a picture of Jurgenson. The range of phenomena reported has grown to include telephone, video, television and computers – leading to the new term 'instrumental transcommunication' (ITC).[71]

Carbon monoxide (CO) detector

This is not used to hunt ghosts, but rather to rule out carbon monoxide poisoning as a possible source of alleged haunting phenomena. Carbon monoxide is produced by the incomplete combustion of materials containing organic compounds due to inadequate oxygen supply. Around the home or office these are typically fuel-burning devices that are not working correctly. Because carbon monoxide is invisible and difficult for people to detect it has become known as the 'silent killer'. Depending on concentration and length of exposure, carbon monoxide can cause headaches, dizziness, convulsions and death. It can also cause delirium and hallucinations. In a case investigated by William Wilmer, which we will discuss in detail later, it was found that the supposed haunting experience by one of his patients was a result of carbon monoxide poisoning.[72] Appliances for detecting CO in the home are relatively inexpensive and easily available; handheld units for professional use are considerably dearer. TAPS deployed one during their April 2005 investigation of a private home in Springfield, Massachusetts.[73]

Composite and custom devices

'Every ghost hunter worthy of the name,' according to Underwood, 'will invent simple gadgets for himself.' Some of these gadgets, however, have been far from simple. Foremost amongst them is the legendary SPIDER, nicknamed the 'spectre detector' by Underwood.[74]

Developed by Tony Cornell and Howard Wilkinson, the Spontaneous Psychophysical Incident Data Electronic Recorder (SPIDER) was a large box on a trolley with a web of cabling connecting it to various cameras, lamps and a monitor. Inside the box was an array of recorders and sensors in a rich complexity of spaghetti wiring. The set-up included two floodlights (75/150 watt tungsten and near infrared), a 35 mm camera, a stereoscopic camera, one camcorder or more, an infrared video camera with monitor, a tape recorder and four thermocouples. The devices were wired to be triggered by onboard sensors monitoring the infrared spectrum, normal sound and ultrasound, and temperature variation, with everything recorded on a print-out. It also had sensors to monitor electrical activity.[75]

Ghost Adventures lead investigator Zak Bagans' favourite piece of kit is the Mel Meter designed by Gary Galka. Featuring an EMF detector and emitter operating in the range 30–300 Hz, with ambient thermometer and red-light torch, Bagans described it as 'the Swiss Army knife of paranormal meters'.[76]

A retired engineer, Galka has produced over thirty different products for ghost hunting with prices ranging from $79 to $349.90 for the top-of-the-range Mel-8704-SB7-EMF meter.[77] His latest device also incorporates what he calls a 'spirit box' to record EVP. He later appeared on Bagans's TV programme *Ghost Adventures* to demonstrate it. Operating the device in the Trans-Allegheny Lunatic Asylum on 30 October 2009, he apparently received the message 'Hi Daddy, I love you'.[78]

Other composite custom devices are altogether more suspect. The Ghost Meter Pro has a transparent case with a bulbous, red-nosed end, a small dial and 'Ghost Meter Pro' stamped on it. It is a basic EMF meter, just like its cousin the Ghost Meter, but with a number of additional modes. According to the product description mode 1 covers 'Recent Ghosts [that] appear every 3 to 5 minutes', mode 2 'Ancient Ghosts [that] appear every 7 to 15 minutes', mode 3 is an 'EMF Gauss

Meter mode' and mode 4 is 'Dialog Mode'. In dialog mode the product claims that: 'the ghost can answer 4 to 9 questions in a yes or no format, for example Are you a good ghost? Move the needle once for yes and twice for no, or Are you a happy ghost? Sound once for yes and twice for no.' A number of customers have noted that in dialog mode the device appears to give 'answers' in a pre-programmed manner. The company, for its part, insists that 'it is reacting to all the paranormal activity in its presence'.[79]

Other extraordinary devices include the pocket-sized GhostRadar marketed by Japanese company SolidAlliance. As to how it works, the company's Vice President Yuichiro Saito said, 'This detects invisible phenomena and so the system is confidential.'[80] For about $20, Strapya World sells the Baketan Ghost Radar – a small red chunk of plastic on a chain that flashes and buzzes when ghosts are about, or so it is claimed.[81] There is now a range of iPhone apps for ghost hunters: the Ghost Radar from Spud Pickles; the retro-look Ghost-O-Meter; and the Spectre Detector – 'the one trusted by professionals'.[82] A range of more useful apps has been developed by Richard Holland, former editor of *Paranormal* magazine.

Trigger objects

Many investigators use ordinary objects to stimulate paranormal activity. The object is placed on site and its position recorded and later monitored for signs of having been moved. Typically, a coin is placed on a sheet of paper and a line is drawn round it.

A new variation attributed to Leinster Paranormal is the 'Irish wind chime'. This is a wind chime suspended within a glass receptacle, usually a jar. The idea is that, being shielded from breezes, any movement of the chime has a paranormal cause. Groups such as Champaign County Paranormal and Southwestern Ohio Night Stalkers have experimented with the chimes.[83] Champaign County Paranormal use the chimes as a response mechanism to questions asked, as well as a passive object placed under camera observation. The Ghost Investigation Team and R.I.P. South Wales set up a wind chime during their investigation of Mulberry House in 2010. As team member Gareth Mates joked that 'we're sat here watching this and meanwhile a full apparition will walk behind us', the camera operator gasped as what she took to be a paranormal light drifted past Mates's back.[84] Other devices using things like crystals suspended within an airtight transparent vessel work on the same principle and are sometimes referred to as 'spirit bottles'. It should be noted that sound vibrations, including those that are inaudible, will also cause the wind chime to move.

The ghost-sniffer

When journalist Will Storr was staying in 'the haunted room', everything seemed fine until the family pets, a cat and dog, stopped enjoying his strokes and tickles under the ear to stare at the stone wall. He followed their gaze, but there was nothing there. That did not stop the animals from turning-tail and exiting post haste. Most people have seen a cat or dog stare at something that we cannot see and react to it by barking, growling, hissing or high-tailing it out of the room. This has led some researchers, such as Green, to suggest their use in ghost hunting.[85]

There are many accounts in the annals of ghost hunting concerning the strange behaviour of dogs. The earliest would appear to be the Wesleys' mastiff barking, whining and fleeing whenever 'Old Jeffrey', the infamous poltergeist of Epworth in the eighteenth century, was about to put in an appearance.[86] The reaction of dogs to alleged paranormal phenomena was also documented by the SPR as early as 1889 in the much discussed (at the time) case of General Barter's sighting of an apparition and his dogs' independent reaction to the same.[87] Modern examples include Willington Manor near Bedford and the old vicarage at Elm near Wisbech in Cambridgeshire.[88]

The otherwise inexplicable behaviour of the dog has become a stock feature of the ghost story. I have seen our black Labrador Pixie behaving strangely, suddenly growling at the empty air, but then, she is a strange dog. Given the animal's greater sensory range it should come as no surprise for it to react to things that we cannot sense ourselves. Animals can hear well beyond the human range: dogs to 40,000 Hz, cats to 60,000 Hz and rodents to 100,000 Hz.

The first deliberate use of a dog in paranormal investigation was in 1969 when the BBC's *Twenty-Four Hours* programme brought one in to investigate Southport's Palace Hotel.[89] Since then no one seems to have explored the possibility further until in 2011 TAPS added Maddie – a German Shepherd/Australian cattle dog crossbreed – to the *Ghost Hunters* team. Grant Wilson described the dog's talents:

> She's basically an untainted investigator. She's not bringing in any predispositions, she hasn't made any judgments ahead of time, whether this place is haunted or not. You can't get more honest than a dog.[90]

Despite TAPS deploying Maddie the 'investigative canine' on cases, in general, it is not advisable to take the family pet along when ghost hunting. For starters, poor Rover has no idea that his master is going to try and scare the bejesus out of him. Then, when the ectoplasm hits the fan, the last thing anyone wants is a terrified and out-of-control animal trying to escape the carefully controlled investigation site.

The five-field complex processing unit
The most important piece of equipment is the ghost hunter himself. One's five senses form the basis of all investigations. An EMF meter spike without someone seeing something is just an EMF meter spike. An apparition without someone seeing it might just as well have not happened at all.

Then there is that extra something, that sixth sense that

sets alarm bells ringing inside. TAPS can back me up on
this. 'Very often,' wrote Jason Hawes, 'our best tools are our
human instincts.' But, as Hawes also noted, instinct alone is
not enough to substantiate a haunting.[91]

As every court and police officer will tell you, a single
witness is unreliable. The SPR's Committee on Haunted
Houses made the observation policy: 'the unsupported evidence of a single witness does not constitute sufficient ground
for accepting an apparition as having a *prima facie* claim to
objective reality.'[92] Peter Underwood recommended at least
three witnesses to any phenomena to rule out 'imagination or
a trick of the light'.[93]

Early ghost hunters usually did not mention much else
beyond the contents of their pockets, but there are many
more easily overlooked essentials other than technological
gadgets. During the operation you will need to sustain body
and soul, so pack something to eat and drink. This should ideally be something other than the hip flask routinely carried
by Elliott O'Donnell. Green also suggested 'camping gear'
and Underwood added Primas stove, kettle and 'unbreakable
mugs'.[94]

As much of the hunt may be conducted in low light in
unfamiliar terrain, a first aid kit should also be included.
O'Donnell would have been grateful for this after tripping
over a tramp in the dark interior of a supposedly haunted
house. Many locations might be outside, ruinous, or not otherwise supplied with facilities required to answer the call of
nature. The wise ghost hunter packs a roll of toilet paper.

Peripherals

Finally, as Green and others since have suggested, make up
a 'kit bag' so that all of the ghost hunting essentials will be
on constant standby[95] – the ghost hunter's equivalent of the
survivalist's 'bug-out bag'. Underwood had his gear in a 'type
of leather carpet bag',[96] but someone like Joe Nickell carries
a modified pilot's case to contain the expanded set of tools.

Some companies now sell durable aluminium cases with custom partitions to accommodate basic, intermediate and advanced equipment sets.

The bag should also contain some essential peripherals such as spare batteries for all of the different equipment types being used, spare bulbs for lighting equipment and cleaning materials such as lens cloths and brushes. Chemical-based light sources called glow sticks are a fast and reliable alternative to candle and matches. Extensive camera equipment will be better stored in a separate case. Tripods come in a variety of models, some extremely portable, but again these will probably require a separate bag.[97]

In the days when a gentleman's word was enough, old-school ghost hunters like Andrew Green and Peter Underwood never thought to mention carrying some form of identification. Times are different and ID is essential, but many ghost hunters still neglect to mention this. Fielding and O'Keeffe were probably the first to list it and Paul Keene and fellow writers put ID in their top ten tips for ghost hunting.[98]

In addition, TAPS have been known to include fart machines and tiaras among their ghost hunting equipment, and recommend bringing an extra pair of shorts (underpants, presumably) – evidence of the same humour that led two plumbers to call themselves TAPS in the first place.[99]

Communications

An investigation involving several researchers, especially when positioned at or patrolling separate locations, undoubtedly benefits from the use of walkie-talkies – handheld radio transmitter/receiver units. Relatively inexpensive models are easily purchased these days, but better-quality ones will have the power to send signals over greater distances and across more complex terrain, such as building interiors where most ghost hunting takes place. One should be aware that their use of radio waves may interfere with other detecting equipment, or even become detecting instruments themselves. Joshua

P. Warren noted that 'ghosts may even communicate via the radios!'[100]

Mobile (cell) phones are also useful in case of emergency. It should go without saying that a strict 'phones off' protocol should be rigorously adhered to during the investigation.[101]

Weapons

Elliott O'Donnell was not the only one to investigate the paranormal armed and dangerous. James Turner, who stayed in Borley Priory near the remains of the infamous and ruined rectory, came home late one evening to find a group of 'ghost hunters' in his garden, one of them sporting a 12-gauge, ready to blast the phantom nun, presumably just to make sure she was dead.[102] Loaded pistols may have been counted among the 'appurtenances most approved, when people have the prospect before them of a long night to be spent in ghost-hunting' in the once well-known *Ingoldsby Legends*, but current firearms regulations no longer countenance such bravado.[103]

Ghost hunting may require one to travel to isolated places, investigate unstable structures and keep unsociable hours; however, common sense, a mobile phone and several companions are all that are required to stay safe on the job. While the media and certain celebrity hunters play up the dangers of poltergeists and even demons, the common-or-garden ghost is unable to do you any harm. Even if it were, shooting one is unlikely to prove much of a defence. O'Donnell reported that a woman living at the edge of the Sussex Downs had discharged a firearm at a phantom 'but the bullets had had no effect whatever'.[104] Most ghost hunters are agreed that ghosts present no physical danger.[105]

There may well be mental danger – you are, after all, trying to come face to face with the presumed spirit of a dead person. Consider Andrew Green. It was, as we shall see, a disembodied voice telling him to jump off a high tower that got him into ghost hunting in the first place.

The gadget trap

Everyone wants to snap another Brown Lady just like the one famously photographed in Raynham Hall. But even that photograph fails to be final proof of the existence of ghosts. Ultimately, it is just another negative with an indeterminate misty something obscuring part of the frame. Equipment alone is no guarantee of finding anything, especially anything *convincing*. This problem was noted as early as 1894 when only photography and phonography (as it then was) were available to the ghost hunter, since the recording alone cannot rule out non-paranormal explanations, notably that of fraud.[106]

Despite using an array of recording and measuring devices in some of the most haunted locations over a fourteen-year period from 1982 to 1996, Tony Cornell obtained no evidence of the paranormal. He estimated that his equipment was up and running for something in the region of 1,200 hours in total. Long enough, he thought, to capture anything out of the ordinary. Cornell also noted that despite the widespread use of CCTV for security purposes nothing paranormal, so far as he was aware, had ever been captured on film. One case he investigated was at the Police Staff College at Bramshill, Hampshire. The Jacobean mansion had plenty of witnesses to several ghosts throughout the building, but surveillance cameras covering the property, including most of the allegedly haunted sites, failed to provide objective verification.[107] Since then there have been a number of claims of ghosts being caught on CCTV. The most famous was captured at Hampton Court Palace in 2003.[108]

Peter Underwood listed an impressive inventory of ironmongery for the ghost hunter, but noted that one acquaintance who routinely fielded over five tons of equipment was unable to procure results of greater scientific interest than the most basically outfitted amateur.[109] The TAPS team have their own 'mobile command center' packed with 'monitors and hard drives' to save themselves 'a good half hour of setup time'.[110]

To an extent, equipment creep is inevitable. None of the gadgets being fielded is specifically designed to detect ghosts – despite the claims – because we do not know what ghosts are or what causes them. For example, EMFs may be involved, but at the moment that is simply one hypothesis amongst many.

It can also become a case of self-validation through technology: the more gadgets I have, the better I must be. According to one ghost hunter, having an EMF meter 'give[s] the researcher credibility'.[111] Even though it might look and sound impressive, having something that beeps does not make a scientific investigation.

With so much equipment available, James Tacchi recommends choosing a particular area to focus on, such as audiovisual, or temperature and humidity. In this way one can build up expertise instead of being overwhelmed by excessive gadgetry and the extensive data it churns out.[112]

The lesson has to be: choose your equipment with care; concentrate on the essentials; and be thoroughly familiar with the workings of any sophisticated measuring/recording devices being used. But beyond what and how, know *why* any piece of equipment is being used. As Ghost Club chairman Alan Murdie stressed, 'there is no such thing as a ghost-detecting device.'[113]

3

INVESTIGATE

Haunted House. – Responsible persons of leisure and intelligence, intrepid, critical, and unbiased, are invited to join rota of observers in a year's night and day investigation of alleged haunted house in Home Counties. Printed instructions supplied. Scientific training or ability to operate simple instruments an advantage. House situated in lonely hamlet, so own car is essential.

Ghost hunters wanted: 200 people applied when this notice appeared in *The Times* on 25 May 1937. After careful screening, Harry Price chose forty-eight to help him investigate the infamous Borley Rectory. Each of his 'Official Observers', as he called them, was required to sign the ' "Haunted House" – Declaration Form', preventing any of them from acting, especially publishing, independently. It was a smart move for Price. Borley made him famous.

The personal characteristics that Price looked for – intelligence, bravery, critical thinking and lack of bias – are still needed today. When asked what makes a good ghost hunter, open-mindedness, patience and scepticism were the most frequent answers given by the ghost hunters in my survey. Other terms often used included rational, logical, analytical, scientific and objective. Some also saw the need for humour and the ability to actually enjoy ghost hunting as important. Others noted that a degree of nerve was also necessary. One said that his background as an intelligence officer was advantageous when ghost hunting. Given that many haunted places are still in lonely or inaccessible locations, 'own car' is probably also a good investment.

Viewpoint: the good ghost hunter
Someone who is patient – be prepared for the fact that you might have a whole evening of nothing if you're honest about it. Also someone who doesn't see the majority of the dead either as horrible (after all most living aren't so why should they be) or as beings to be bossed about and commanded in a very strict voice. I think it's good to be polite to someone whether they're down here with us or not. Also someone who is open-minded: if someone says something odd has happened, be prepared to look into it; if someone says there's a perfectly rational explanation for something, be prepared to look into that, too.

Jonty Stern, Ghost Club (GHS, 2012)

Price supplied instructions to his observers in the form of an eight-page booklet called 'The Alleged Haunting at B— Rectory – Instructions for Observers'. The colour of its cover lent it the more informal title of the 'Blue Book'. This covered such things as how to write up reports and what to do when dealing with unexplained phenomena.

Before his big Borley investigation, Price had already been

involved with the first live broadcast from a haunted house. On 10 March 1936 the BBC rigged up four microphones to try and record the 'muffled footsteps and tappings, a cellar door which opens suddenly, and cold, uncanny winds' that were said to haunt Dean Manor near Rochester in Kent. As listeners learned, Price sprinkled powdered starch on the floor to detect footprints, used powdered graphite to dust for fingerprints and set up thermometers to record temperature drops.[1]

Investigative structure

Structure	Task	Purpose
Phase 1: 'Before'		
	Clarification	Ascertain the merits of the case: should it be investigated?
	Interviewing	Obtain a precise record of experiences reported by witnesses (if any) and establish their credibility.
	Site Investigation (Recce)	Map the physical location, noting areas of reported activity and any relevant structural or physical aspects.
	Background Research	Part history, part geological survey to determine the context and environment of the case.
Phase 2: 'During'		
	On-Site Observation (Vigil)	Document evidence of anomalous phenomena.
Phase 3: 'After'		
	Data Analysis	Review equipment recordings for evidence pertaining to anomalous phenomena.
	Conclusion	What does the evidence or lack of it prove?

Unless, like Athenodorus, the ghost hunter happens to live in a haunted house, or like Price is lucky enough to be invited to investigate one by a newspaper, it will be necessary to plan the ghost hunt. Most investigations comprise several distinct phases from preliminary research into the evidentiality of the case through to forming a conclusion based on observation and analysis.

Historical research can be conducted before or after the vigil. It is inevitable that the investigator will be influenced beforehand by interviewing the witnesses, but without ascertaining the nature of the alleged haunting it will be next to impossible to decide whether to pursue the matter further and then, having done so, how to go about it. Green advises that the ghost hunter should make it clear at the outset that repeat visits may be necessary.[2]

Viewpoint: the investigation

1. Initial interview with at least two witnesses. (If only one witness, and no corroboration, I feel that does not support conducting an investigation.)
2. Group discussion on best way to conduct initial observations.
3. Physical investigation/inspection of the premises.
4. Conduct observations, trying to duplicate the original conditions at the time the events were witnessed (same time of day, same lighting conditions, etc.).
5. Group discussion on what was observed.
6. Development of hypotheses and 'tests' to rule out natural explanations for what was observed.
7. Report to 'client' outlining observations, but no conclusions unless absolutely certain.

Mark E. Reed, lead investigator, Litchgate Research Group
(GHS, 2012)

Open a case file and document everything relating to the investigation. You will need to consider apparently unrelated factors such as weather conditions, geology, lunar cycle, and even things like one's own mood at the time. We can only find patterns in the unknown by considering all of the things that *can* be known.

Investigative 'good practice'
When investigating a haunted building it is good practice to attempt to exclude as many possible normal causes for the 'haunting' as possible. The ways in which normal earthly events might conspire to convey an impression that a house is haunted are numerous. Thus, all of the following may well be the more mundane cause of an ostensible haunt: water hammer in pipes and radiators (noises), electrical faults (fires, phone calls, video problems), structural faults (draughts, cold spots, damp spots, noises), seismic activity (object movement/destruction, noises), electromagnetic anomalies (hallucinations), and exotic organic phenomena (rats scratching, beetles ticking). The exclusion of these counter-explanations, when potentially relevant, must be the first priority of the spontaneous cases investigator.

Vic Tandy and Tony R. Lawrence, 'The Ghost in the Machine', *JSPR*, vol. 62, 851 (April 1998), p. 360.

Asked what a typical investigation usually involved, Ghost Club member Andrea Harvey said:

Lots of sitting around in the cold, damp and dark. Lots of recording of any events as they happen. Lots of time to set up and dismantle any equipment. More often than not it is an uneventful night. I believe it's all about being in the right place at the right time!

This was a common description and it is surely no coincidence that patience was widely thought to be a necessary attribute to good ghost hunting. Attending a ghost hunt organized by a third party will usually involve an initial walk-round before participants are divided into groups to conduct vigils in various parts of the chosen location. There will usually be some rotation of the groups and at the end a debriefing will be held with all participants to share and discuss experiences.[3]

The team

Back in the day before the idea of 'teams' was even vouched, Peter Underwood suggested that 'it is advisable to be accompanied by several reliable and sensible friends'.[4] Starting from scratch, the American Association of Paranormal Investigators recommends that an investigative team should have five clearly-defined roles:[5]

1. Lead, or Lead Investigator. This is the person in overall charge of the investigation. Responsibilities normally also cover filing reports and other paperwork.
2. The Researcher, or Research Officer, is detailed with sourcing background information on the case. Ideally, this should cover geological reports as well as location history.
3. The Science Officer, or Technical Officer, is responsible for the equipment used during the investigation, including its distribution among other team members.
4. Security is the health and safety officer of the team.
5. Medium.

Many groups eschew any sort of hierarchy, but at the very least, a group should have a designated leader and someone with knowledge of first aid, as most of the other roles can be subsumed. As for the use of mediums, this is a controversial topic. Looking at a programme such as *Most Haunted*, we see that mediums tend to take over an investigation by flooding

'Haunted house' – declaration form

I, the Undersigned, in consideration of having had my services accepted as an Official Observer, make the following Declarations:

1. I will fulfill all conditions and instructions, verbal and written, which are given to me.
2. I will pay my own expenses connected with the investigation.
3. I am not connected with the Press in any way.
4. I will not convey to any person the name or location of the alleged Haunted House.
5. I will not write, or cause to be written, any account of my visit/s to the Haunted House, and not lecture on my experiences there.
6. I will not photograph or sketch any part of the Haunted House or grounds without written permission.
7. I will not allow any person to accompany me on my investigation, who has not signed the Declaration Form.
8. I will fulfill my obligations as regards Observational Periods, at the times and on the dates as arranged.
9. I will furnish a report after each Observational Period.
10. I will not use the Telephone installed in the House except for the purposes of reporting phenomena to the person or persons whose names have been given me, or for requesting assistance from those persons.
11. I will lock all doors and fasten all windows on my leaving the House, and will deposit key/s to person as directed.

Harry Price, in Sidney H. Glanville, *The Haunting of Borley Rectory. Private and Confidential Report* (London, 1937–8) it with subjectively experienced information. This can seem exciting at the time, but the amount of unverifiable information produced by unverified means is usually unhelpful, even if the medium is sincere.

A larger organization, such as the Ghost Club, will have a number of other roles concerned with the running of the group itself. The Ghost Club has two administrative posts of general secretary and membership secretary, an events organizer and an investigations organizer, a journal editor and web administrator, a press officer for media relations, both a science officer and a technical officer, and a chairman.[6] Due to its wider remit, the Society for Psychical Research found it necessary to organize a variety of committees responsible for investigating different areas of the paranormal.

As we saw, Harry Price had his ghost hunting recruits sign a restrictive Declaration Form before he let them loose on Borley Rectory, and Hawes and Wilson had Brian Harnois sign a statement of conduct, but such forms are rare. Larger organizations, such as the SPR, will expect members to abide by a fairly broad set of rules generally to protect the society's reputation.

Haunting is only an hypothesis

Many investigations throw a multitude of different tools and techniques at the problem without specifying what it is that is being investigated. This may appear obvious: a haunting is being investigated. But scientifically speaking, a 'haunting' is only an hypothesis to be tested through experiment. The formal model of testing, universal in science, is that of falsification. One does not set out to prove what one believes or hypothesizes to be the case, because this sets loose a number of unconscious psychological biases that distort the experiment and the findings. Instead the experimenter seeks to find a way of showing that the hypothesis can be explained by other causes, that is, shown not to be true. This means that to conduct an investigation on scientific principles one must seek to falsify the hypothesis. This is not 'debunking' – 'debunking' is simply looking to explain away phenomena because they do not meet the debunker's mindset. Instead falsification aims to make the experimenter apply the toughest test of the hypothesis because only then can it be considered reliable.

A 'haunting', or 'this house is haunted', is not a sufficient hypothesis in itself because it does not stipulate what the said 'haunting' is supposed to be. Thus, 'this house is being visited by spirits of the dead', or 'unusual phenomena experienced in this house are being caused by abnormal electromagnetic fields' are better hypotheses because they are more specific. If possible, the hypothesis should be more than a bald statement and propose an explanation of the observed or reported phenomena, or formulate a correlation between two or more factors.

The double-blind experiment is the gold standard of science because it sets up a model in which experimenter effect and expectation of human subjects (if involved) are nullified. In a double-blind experiment the subjects to be tested are divided into two groups: the experimental group and the control group. The experimental group is administered the variable under investigation. The control group is not; typically in human studies it is administered a placebo. The test is carried out by researchers who do not know which is the experimental and which the control group.

Unfortunately, the double-blind experiment is not always applicable. For example, archaeology or astronomy could not use such a method. In sociological research it is often the case that the researcher stipulates his or her personal beliefs and biases so that these can become apparent if they influence the result. Where the double-blind is most useful is in medical and psychological research. It would be difficult to apply this approach to ghost hunting.

Ghost hunting usually proceeds along two routes: (a) the investigators are contacted by a person or persons claiming that a haunting is taking place; or (b) the investigators seek out places reputed to be haunted. In the first case, a consultative client relationship is established in which the client (as the one forwarding evidential claims) must also become part of the study, although this is rarely seen in practice. It is particularly important to clarify at this stage whether the investigator is working for a client or conducting a scientific investigation because the ethics and requirements of the two are not the same. A client relationship must be confidential; a scientific experiment must be fully disclosed so that it can be tested by others. The second case is more straightforward, but the investigators must subject the reputation to testing and in the first instance this will be a historical procedure to determine on what factual basis that reputation rests.

In the 1950s several prominent members of the SPR led by Professor Hornell Hart developed a protocol for rating reports of apparitions. Their basic criterion was that 'the

Authenticating historical sources

Level	Function	Key Question
External Criticism		
Higher Criticism (Origination)		
	Date	When was the source material produced?
	Localization	Where was the source material produced?
	Authorship	By whom was the source material produced?
	Analysis	From what pre-existing sources was it produced?
Lower Criticism (Textual Criticism)		
	Integrity	In what form was it originally produced?
Internal Criticism		
	Credibility	What is the source material's evidential value?

Based on Gilbert J. Garraghan, *A Guide to Historical Method* (New York: Fordham University Press, 1946).

individual who had the psychic experience reported its details before receiving evidence of their verdicality'. From a literature search of what they called 'ESP projection' they found that only 99 out of 288 (34 per cent) published cases met this stipulation. They rated the remaining cases based on five factors:[7]

1. What written or oral testimony was given as to evidential details before confirmation had been secured?
2. What confirmation was secured later as to the correctness of these evidential details?
3. What investigation of the case was made by a competent and independent researcher?
4. How full a documented record was made of the case?
5. What time interval elapsed between the evidential events and the making of the report?

Most investigations, however, field a number of pieces of equipment under various controls in the hope of documenting evidence of the paranormal. Where a case has been reported by a living witness, it is better to focus initial efforts on interviewing the witness and establishing the credibility or otherwise of both the witness and the claims being made. The investigators need to ask 'why has this person reported this event?'

The interview
'Nothing can affect the human mind with greater terror,' observed the Northamptonshire clergyman Revd E. Gillespy in 1793, 'than the dread of an interview with the souls of deceased persons.'[8] It is fortunate then, that, except in rare cases, the prospective ghost hunter will be interviewing living witnesses. However, they too bring their own problems.

Interview kit
Voice recorder with spare batteries and memory.
Witness statement form(s).
Charts/maps for plotting witness locations.
Compass to align maps and record positions.
Writing materials: paper, pen, etc., or laptop.
List of pre-prepared questions.

The credibility of witnesses is an important part of judicial proceedings and often insisted upon in paranormal investigation. To be credible, a witness needs to be trustworthy and believable.[9] These terms are open to interpretation, but the key issues to consider are:

1. Whether the witness is capable of knowing the thing thoroughly about which he testifies.
2. Whether the witness was actually present at the transaction.
3. Whether the witness paid sufficient attention to qualify himself to be a reporter of it.
4. Whether the witness honestly relates the affair fully as he knows it, without any purpose or desire to deceive, or suppress or add to the truth.[10]

It is usual to subdivide the question into the competency of the witness and the credibility of the statement. This is an important distinction since a competent witness can still give an incredible statement, or an incompetent one a credible account.[11] By definition, the witness of the paranormal is giving an incredible statement and therein lies much of the problem.

Unsupported assumptions are often made about the types of people who become witnesses. Back in the first century CE, Plutarch thought that philosophers made more reliable witnesses because, apparently, they were 'not to be easily deluded by fancy or discomposed by any sudden apprehension', which brings us back to Athenodorus again and his impressive stoicism.[12] Today, workmen are often considered 'practical and hard-headed',[13] but in the absence of evidence to this effect, such as psychological testing, this is simply opinion and does not make them any more credible. Sworn statements from witnesses would be legally more convincing and are sometimes recommended – as by Andrew Green, for example – but they are difficult to arrange and still unlikely to convince a sceptic.[14]

Even if competent, witnesses are notoriously unreliable. During jury service in London I had first-hand experience of this when no two people could accurately describe the street in which a robbery had occurred. Despite compelling evidence to his guilt, the accused was nearly acquitted due to a disagreement over the number of parked cars.

Andrew Green tells the story of a group of senior policemen being examined for promotion. As they left one lecture room to go to another, a man wearing a trilby, a grey suit and black shoes with an umbrella in one hand and a large fluffy toy panda in the other passed them. When they got to the next room they were asked what they had seen on the way. Almost all of them mentioned the man, some describing him quite exactly, but out of sixteen only one recalled the fluffy toy and he said it had been a 'teddy bear'. Most of those highly trained police minds had done a quick calculation: soberly dressed man plus totally incongruous item equals soberly dressed man. The huge fluffy black-and-white animal was out of the window. Derren Brown has done a similar trick with a man in a gorilla suit in front of live audiences. Despite the get-up, nobody ever spots him walk on stage and steal a banana. The lesson is, even if someone does not see something, it does not mean that it was not there.[15]

The responsible ghost hunter needs to take every interview seriously. Seriousness opens up witnesses who might otherwise be afraid of being laughed at. Seriousness keeps the

interview on track. Even if the witness starts laughing as he
tells the story – a stress reaction – the interviewer must not
join in. Andrew Green warns that doing so encourages the
witness to embellish the story.[16]

Ask the interviewee to identify him or herself for the
benefit of the recording, as well as identify yourself as the
interviewer. Also give the date and time of the interview, its
location and the subject of the interview. One should, however, avoid making it sound like a police interrogation. In the
event that the recording becomes separated from its accompanying documentation the ghost hunter will thus still be
able to identify the precious witness interview. In the days
of tape, interview cassettes could be labelled appropriately,
but with digital media this is less convenient. After recording it may be useful to back up the digital content on another
device or medium to guard against data loss and for archival
purposes.

Privacy and data protection
It is advisable not to publish anything in any form, including those which are yet to be invented, unless the interviewee
gives consent. According to Green, most people do give consent, but never assume it.[17] Get them to sign a form so that
you have proof. This can be part of the questionnaire to make
it less intimidating. And approach the subject with the assur-
ance that you will not publish anything without their explicit
consent.

Data protection also covers what sort of information you
store about people and what you do with it. The ghost hunter
should reassure people that their data will be protected, but be
aware that raising this issue can make people nervous about
the very things they are being assured will be protected. For
research construed as journalistic or historical, data protection will not normally be an issue, but ghost hunters need
to be clear about what they are going to do with data collected before it becomes problematic. For example, creating

an online database of witness testimony with names and addresses, etc., is likely to fall under the terms of the UK's Data Protection Act, or the European Union's Data Protection Directive – the USA has no comparable single law.

Questions
Ask, but do not lead. 'Have you seen a ghost?' is a leading question. It firstly assumes (a) that there are such things as ghosts, and (b) that it is possible to see them, but also leads the subject by stating (c) that the experience that the subject has had was of 'seeing a ghost'. A less leading question would be: can you describe to me the experience you have had? This also has the advantage of being an open as opposed to a closed question. A closed question can be answered with a simple yes or no; an open question invites more.

Leading questions, as Tony Cornell admitted, had led him and his group to construct the personality of 'Juliet' during Ouija board sessions in the reputedly haunted Ferry Boat Inn, Holywell, in the 1950s. The story consequently snowballed out of control and is now an established 'fact' repeated in numerous guides to haunted locations in the UK.[18]

It is also helpful to use standardized questions. With a standardized questionnaire, information can then be entered in a database or computational program to draw up statistics. This allows you to compare the information and discover patterns, if there are any, in it.

Questions will naturally cover two main areas: (a) the nature of the event being alleged; and (b) the nature of the witness. It is important not to overlook what may seem obvious at the time. The interviewer should record name, address, age, sex, nationality, education and occupation at the least. Ethnicity may be important so far as it is related to cultural beliefs. Elliott O'Donnell, for example, always attributed his particular success as a ghost hunter to his Celtic background. Religious beliefs are also important to determine; however, this is a notoriously difficult area to probe. For example, many people will describe themselves as nominally religious (or spiritual), but seldom take part in any organized religious events, or attend religious events but have no or little religious beliefs. Therefore, one must also determine the extent to which that religion is adhered to. This leads naturally to a discussion on belief in the afterlife, which may, all things considered, be the better starting point.

The Tatler's *guide to ghost hunting*
There are certain points worthy of notice in all cases relative to spectural illusion. The principal party concerned is sure to be in one of five predicaments. Either he is of a morbid temperament, or superstition was inflicted upon his childhood (which is sure to be the case where clever men are concerned); or he is a rogue and a sharper; or he is grossly ignorant; or he is a liar. The habit of lying is often mixed up with narratives of people otherwise honest, but who are unable to resist the excitement afforded by it to their own fancies, and the temptation to aggrandize their importance with others. The first thing to be ascertained is the existence of the party which is said to have seen the ghost, and the next that the report is the same as he gives it: you then inquire into his character, which is sure to square with one of the above descriptions. Finally, it is to be observed, that you never catch a ghost, in broad daylight, in the midst of a great metropolis. He must have darkness, or loneliness, or ignorance, or superstition, to help him. You will never find him on the pavement in Whitehall, or in the court-circle at St James's. Or at a meeting of the Royal Society.

'Ghosts and Visions', *The Tatler*, 45
(26 October 1830), pp. 177–8.

In cases where the witness is alleging to have seen or heard something, the interviewer must establish the acuity of the witness's eyesight and hearing. Do they wear glasses or contact lenses? Or have they had corrective surgery? When did they last have their eyes checked? Are they colour-blind? Do they have any issues with their eyesight? One ghost hunter suffered from a complete lack of night vision, for example.[19] Most people only have their hearing checked in infancy and old age, so it may be better to ascertain any occupational or recreational noise hazards.

The interviewer will also need to establish the general health of the subject. In the case of the witness's mental health this will be difficult. Direct questions on this subject may meet with resistance and produce defensive answers.

Assessing witnesses
The US Air Force advises its Safety Investigation Board investigators to assess the quality, reliability and credibility of witnesses, although in practice these separate considerations tend to blend. Each variable can be influenced by a number of factors from such things as the physical fitness of the witness to his or her attitude towards the interviewer.[20]

Factors affecting the quality of witness testimony typically concern environmental conditions, such as time of day, quality of light and the weather, the witness's understanding of the event and the stress or even trauma that it may have produced. The more personally significant the event is, the better it will be recalled. The length of time the event is observed for will also aid recall, but the length of time that has elapsed since it occurred will be detrimental. Unsurprisingly, a negative attitude towards the investigator will affect the information being given, but so too will an overly positive attitude, with the witness embellishing the account in an attempt to be more helpful. A shadow seen at the corner of the eye might become a nun gliding by, for example.

The informant's ability to recall and organize thoughts will determine the level of detail and its presentation in a logical and coherent manner. The informant's emotions will play their role, too the more emotionally involved the informant is, then the more emotionally coloured is the information given, which may be prejudicial. It is also a peculiar thing that the more often a story is repeated, the more likely it is to become distorted and embellished. Some details may become transposed, that is, accurately described but in the wrong sequence, omitted altogether if the witness is not aware that they may be important, or repressed if they are linked to a frightening experience.

The USAF further noted that, when questioned, witnesses become aware of gaps in their knowledge and consequently attempt to fill these in, generalize or apply logic to the event remembered. Overly specific information is generally to be viewed with caution as in most cases it is difficult to accurately estimate most factors. Statements such as, the temperature dropped by ten degrees, or, as in the case of reporter Kim Lenaghan at Ballygally Castle, rose by ten degrees, are unlikely to be accurate unless the witness observed the indications on a thermometer at the time.

The USAF found that gender did not seem to be an influencing factor, but age could be. Old age can affect a number of senses as well as the ability to recall events. Very young age, too, causes witnesses to be more influenced by their preconceptions. However, nobody will remember everything all of the time, which makes the number of overall witnesses an extremely important consideration. Yet this too brings additional problems. To reconcile and corroborate testimony from several sources, the USAF suggests using a 'matrix' with the witnesses on one axis and the information given on another.

Technique

'Did any of you men have an erection at the time?' Eric Dingwall had a reputation for being straightforward. When he was investigating Tony Cornell's paranormal 'smell' he did not

beat around the bush, but as Cornell noted, 'his very outspo-
ken if not outrageous comments were a little disconcerting to
our group.' It is not too obvious to point out, then, that tact
should generally be observed.[21]

That goes for the use of equipment as well. As Green said,
'never push the microphone under the speaker's nose'.[22]
Put recording equipment in a discreet place. A small sound
recorder is better on the table between you than being waved
around or thrust menacingly under facial protuberances. It
is unlikely that filming an interview will produce better data
and may meet with more resistance, but it will give you a more
complete historical record and in a form that is better digest-
ed by others. Filming an interview will require attention to
lighting and it may be necessary to use additional light sources or reflectors. You will need to minimize outside interference, whether it is background noise or other members of the
interviewee's family being overcome with curiosity.

If more than a simple Dictaphone is being used, ask to set
up the equipment beforehand. This allows the interviewer to
check sound and light levels, if necessary, and make sure that
everything is working correctly.

The interview should take place with the person who has
allegedly experienced the event and that person alone. In cases
where the witness is underage, the interviewer should always
have the witness's responsible adult present. Where the event
has been witnessed by more than one person at the same location, for example by husband and wife, then the interviewer
should still interview the witnesses separately. Loyd Auerbach recommends interviewing witnesses both separately and
together. However, only interviewing them separately will help
to avoid any undue influence during the interview and produce
returns that can be compared for accuracy and consistency.[23]

The recce
A first search of the area should be conducted in daylight
or good lighting. It is at this stage that the investigator will

sketch his own ground plan of the site, noting anything that may have a bearing on later data gathering. This can be anything from noting possible health and safety concerns to establishing the presence of nearby water or power lines, for example. The internal power supply – cables, outlets, fuse-boxes, etc. – should be marked, and here is where the EMF meter will probably be most useful. The area should also be photographed and/or filmed prior to the vigil. Sketch the scene and record the positions of witnesses and other people in the vicinity relative to the anomaly.

Peter Underwood also recommended noting other factors such as the presence of pets and where they usually sleep and the number of occupants in the building (if any). It may be useful to compile a quick character summary covering things such as occupation and hobbies, as well as their attitudes towards the alleged phenomena, even if they are not witnesses.[24]

The recce can be combined with a re-creation of the experience with the witness. This may be helpful in jogging the memory of the witness and will certainly provide the investigator with a better opportunity to explore the nature of the experience. Both Troy Taylor and Loyd Auerbach, for example, use this strategy.[25]

Ghost hunting and the law
You should read the local laws and regulations of the land, country, state, county, city, etc., and be up to date on legal requirements for your hobby. You can be sued for damage to property or perceived damage to persons (physical and mental) if you do not follow lawful procedures. AAPI has a standard set of forms which we require to be signed by the interviewees and the property owners in order to protect both parties; this includes confidentiality clauses for both parties.
Sharon Raines-Weidner, lead investigator, American Association of Paranormal Investigators (GHS, 2012)

The vigil

The building is in darkness. The alert faces of ghost hunters are illuminated in the pale green glow of night-vision sensors. It is the familiar scene from any ghost hunting TV show. Indeed, it is a truism that ghost hunting must take place at night and in darkness. The setting undoubtedly creates the right atmosphere for susceptibility to experiencing what is taken for the supernatural. However, the reasons for this self-imposed blindness or near-blindness are not clear.

Mediums frequently assert that the spirits require darkness or low lighting to be able to manifest, but this has so often been associated with fraud on the part of the mediums that it cannot be accepted at face value.[26] On the contrary, many reports of ghost sightings have taken place during daylight hours or otherwise under good lighting. As early as the fourteenth century note was made of ghosts seen by day.[27] The brother of Rose Morton, identified as W. H. C. Morton, reported having seen the apparition at the centre of the Morton case in what he called 'full light'.[28] Again an encounter with the ghost of former master Dr Henry Butts at Corpus Christi College, Cambridge, occurred at three in the afternoon.[29] It should not be forgotten that it was 4 p.m. in the afternoon when the famous 'Brown Lady' of Raynham Hall was caught on film.

It should be established where and *when* the haunting has been experienced. In many cases hauntings are repetitive, sometimes re-occurring at the same time as well as place. Attention to this important detail could save the ghost hunter a sleepless (and fruitless) night. The vigil can be thought of as the experimental phase of the investigation and in some situations it may be desirable to try and replicate the exact conditions of the original experience as near as possible.

Psychologically, it may not be beneficial to stake out a location from dusk to dawn. Sleep deprivation is known to

Investigating a séance

The séance was fixed for December 15, 1937. After I had had supper with the family I began my search of the house, a large detached building. I examined every room. I sealed all external doors and windows. I removed most of the furniture from the séance-room (the drawing room), examined the bare boards of the floor, sounded the distempered walls and ceiling, blocked up the chimney with newspapers, and finally sprinkled starch powder in front of the fireplace and locked door in order to register any possible foot or hand marks. Then I sealed the door and windows with adhesive tape and screw-eyes and drew the heavy curtains across the windows. A mouse could not have entered that room undetected. We were ready for the séance.

Harry Price, 'I Really Saw a Ghost', *The Herald*
[Australia] (3 April 1948)

precipitate hallucinations, as my investigation of the Angel of Mons story from the First World War demonstrated.[30] Factor in darkness, unfamiliar surroundings with all their unfamiliar noises, and the expectation that the location is haunted, and the scene is set to hallucinate the very phenomenon the ghost hunter is trying to scientifically record. It might make good television, or an adventurous night out, but the data will be suspect.

The full moon has been flagged as a prime time for investigation, but more often it is a particular hour of the night that gets all of the attention.[31] Midnight, 'the witching hour', has always had a certain reputation. It was at midnight, for example, that 'Leathery Colt', a phantom coach and headless horses driven by a headless coachman, would haunt the Westgate, Elland, near Halifax.[32]

From his own experience Joshua P. Warren argued that paranormal phenomena were more frequent from midnight to 4 a.m.[33] Another number to come up is 3 a.m. Ryan Buell, director of the Paranormal Research Society and star of TV show *Paranormal State*, calls it 'Dead Time', but explains that due to editorial error this was mislabelled '3 a.m.' throughout season one of the show. Buell defined 'Dead Time' as essentially the same as Zak Bagans's 'Lock Down', or any other term such as 'stake out' or vigil used to refer to the on-site observation period of the investigation when lights and power sources are typically shut down to provide a dark, quiet environment. Peter Underwood was using periods of 'silence and darkness' in his investigations long before the advent of the TV ghost hunters.[34] Buell noted that although many of these observations were conducted at 3 a.m., they could just as easily take place in the middle of the afternoon.[35]

Advice for the vigil
Keep calm and your eyes and ears open!
> Max, Ghost Club (GHS, 2012)

Listen to your instincts and always mind your step in dark places.
> Samuel, Ghost Club (GHS, 2012)

Wear something warm and take a flask of something hot, and be ready for a long wait with nothing at the end of it.
> Cara, Ghost Club (GHS, 2012)

However, there is a perception amongst some that 3 a.m. is paranormally significant because it stands opposite on the clock to the time of 3 p.m., which is traditionally given as the time of Jesus' death on the cross.[36] The time 3 a.m. was popularized by the 2005 film *The Exorcism of Emily Rose* – one of the 100 scariest films ever made, according to the Chicago

Film Critics Association.[37] The time is referred to frequently in the film at the commencement of paranormal activity,
and one of the characters, the priest Father Richard Moore,
explains that 3 a.m. is 'the Devil's hour' used by demons to
mock the death of Jesus.[38]

According to Jason Hawes, 3.30 a.m. is 'the time, worldwide, when the most paranormal activity is reported'.[39] This
idea has been around for a while. There was even a 1969 horror
film called *3:30 a.m.* (dir. Mick Davis). But there are a number
of instances when 3.30 was noted as the start of an anomaly.
In Cambridgeshire in the 1950s Tony Cornell was awoken at
3.30 a.m. by a smell that seemed to have strange independent
properties and had decided to settle on his face.[40] In Massachusetts in 1996 TAPS investigators Jason Hawes and Grant
Wilson saw faint blue lights appear and move around the room
they were in 'at around 3.30 a.m.'. Then again at The Stanley
Hotel, Colorado, in 2006, 'it was about 3.30 a.m.' when TAPS
saw a table levitate.[41]

The problem is that Hawes and Wilson had already generalized the reporting of their experience – using words like
'around' and 'about' – to approximate with the desired time
of 3.30 a.m. Whilst staying at The Stanley, Hawes noted a
number of incidents that occurred at around 1.00 and after
5.00 a.m. In fact, more events (two in total) were logged
between 5.00 and 5.59 than for any other hour, making it statistically more significant. Thus the importance of 3.30 seems
to be determined more by expectation than by fact.[42]

Others have made much out of 3.33 a.m. Chase Daniels,
co-founder of the South Georgia Paranormal Research Society, states that this is 'widely belived [sic] to be the "Witching Hour"'. There is even an organization from Woodbridge,
Virginia, calling itself '3:33 a.m. Paranormal Research'.[43]
Some sources joke that 3.33 is significant because there is no
6.66 a.m. (technically, there is: 07.06); state that the number
implies a threefold mockery of the Christian Holy Trinity; or
quote biblical verses with apparent meaning, such as Jeremiah

The structure of a vigil

Activity	Underwood (1986)	Taylor (2001)	Southall (2003)	Fraser (2010)
Assign time per room			x	
Pre-vigil tour by psychic(s)	x			x
Group familiarization				x
Familiarization with premises	x		x	x
Set up base room	x	x	implied	
Set up equipment	x	x	x	x
Split investigators into teams	x	x		x
Part-night vigil		x	x	x
Whole-night vigil	x			x
Investigator rotation	x			x
Room-by-room investigation			x	
Periodic black-outs	x	implied		
Periodic equipment checks	x			
Refreshment breaks	x	implied		x
Experiments (e.g., séances)			x	x
Pack up and tidy location	x			
Debriefing		x	x	x

33:3: 'Call unto me, and I will answer thee, and show thee great and mighty things, which thou knowest not'.[44] The time 3.33 is the ultimate 'mystical' number in this regard, multiplying the supposed significance of the number three in a manner we see replicated in the fuss over dates such as 6/6/6, 11/11/11 or 12/12/12 (21/12/12), with a suitable range of appropriate meanings. All of these sequences are psychologically suggestive, thus liable to create false experiential artefacts.

One case that appeared to demonstrate a connection between darkness and paranormal activity was that of Dr

Michael Clift. In 1983 he had been staying at Bearwood College, Sindlesham – a Victorian Gothic building dating from the 1870s. He was sleeping in the top-floor dormitory, but was woken by the sound of what he took to be furniture being moved about. He was disturbed several times and his investigations showed that it was not cleaners on the floor below, nor a friend moving about his room, nor a lorry off-loading planks outside, as he thought each time. It was on the last occasion that he realized that 'the noise came on when the light was out and faded away when I switched it on'. Clift reasoned that there 'was a clear relation between the two'. He spent the rest of the night in his car.[45]

At best all we can say is that anecdotal evidence from ghost hunters suggests that the period after midnight and before dawn is likely to be the most productive for ghost hunting. From other accounts of hauntings and apparitions reported by non-ghost hunters, an experience may occur at any time of the day or night, but that light may be involved as either facilitating (light of the full moon) or inhibiting (electric light) a haunting. Given the nature of ghost hunting and the paranormal itself, many people seem prone to romanticize certain numbers that appear significant for nonrational or unverifiable reasons often based on chance or coincidental occurrences, or even certain unofficial religious ideas.

Finally, for an effective investigation the location needs to be controlled as strictly as possible during the vigil. For example, all team members must be accounted for and their positions known at all times to eliminate accidental 'ghosts'. The entrances and exits must be locked or otherwise secured to prevent unwanted interference. In Lagenhoe Church Peter Underwood not only secured the points of ingress and egress, but strung thread across the interior as well. During his famous investigation of the Rosalie séance when Harry Price satisfied himself that 'a mouse could not have entered that room undetected', he was left with little other alternative than that the form he saw and felt must, therefore, have been

Hunting the Langenhoe ghost
I spent the night of September 24th, 1949 in Langenhoe Church [...] I had a number of instruments which I set up and I also scattered some 'controls' throughout the church and churchyard. I sealed the doors and windows, ringed a number of objects and even left paper and pencils here and there in case an entity should feel inclined to leave a message! Objects that had moved or had been disturbed were under particular observation throughout the night; powdered chalk was spread where the apparition had walked and where footsteps had been heard; threads were strung across the church at strategic points.

Peter Underwood, *The A–Z of British Ghosts*, p. 115.

the spirit of the dead child Rosalie. Despite all his precautions it later emerged that the ghost had been impersonated by a very much living girl.[46]

Professional conduct

'You ran like a sissy,' said Jason Hawes. Brian Harnois was out of breath. He looked like he had seen a ghost. It was possible that he had. Eastern State Penitentiary in Philadelphia, Pennsylvania, was supposed to be haunted, after all. In Cellblock 4 he said he had seen a 'black shape'. 'It went right across my face,' he said. 'I saw shoulders and a head.' But he had run from it. And that, in Hawes's eyes, was unprofessional. (Hawes himself has confessed that he has yelled out in panic, although what frightened him were bats rather than ghosts.) There is also a health and safety issue. As Troy Taylor points out, 'you are more likely to be hurt running away in terror from ghostly activity than you are by the activity itself.'[47] So the message is, try not to run like a sissy, but just make sure you packed that spare pair of underpants because at some point fear is going to make you do something against your best intentions.[48]

Investigation dos and don'ts
Please wear flat sensible footwear.
Ensure you wear warm clothing when required.
Always carry a torch.
Carry a camera and spare batteries.
Do not wander off alone.
Do not Ghost Bait.
Do not take or use recreational drugs or alcohol before or during an investigation.

Sentinel Paranormal Investigators[49]

Analyse

Once upon a time, analysing vigil data meant sitting for hours watching video tapes of nothing much happening. There were also indecipherable investigator notes to cross check.[50]

It is self-evident that the investigator needs to examine the data collected during the investigation. This can be a long and arduous process, and the more equipment used, the more data will be produced and need to be analysed. Hawes and Wilson were lucky enough to leave the mind-numbing footage reviewing to other members of their team, but even then noted that people missed things and often had to double-check. As Maurice Townsend notes, much of the work can now be done by computers, but not all of it, and even where it is he warns of over-processing or otherwise distorting the raw data. Video tape may have seen its last, but DVDs and other digital recording media are now capable of storing much more data.[51]

The analysis itself can also require repeat visits to the location to test any recorded anomalies. For example, Hawes and Wilson did not see the lamp move behind them at The

Myrtles Plantation until they reviewed their camera footage and returned to the site to ascertain whether this could have occurred naturally or not.

Viewpoint: using equipment
We use the equipment we have collected to help us describe the investigation environment, in a normal sense, so that we can identify factors that might cause people to believe they are experiencing the paranormal.

James Gilberd, leader, Strange Occurrences (personal communication, 9 September 2012)

As we saw, the method of modern science is to falsify hypotheses. A scientist comes up with a plausible explanation for a phenomenon and then seeks to prove himself wrong. If he fails, then he must conclude that he has proven himself right. This method has filtered down into some quarters of ghost hunting. As Jason Hawes writes, 'we examine that evidence five ways to Sunday, looking for a way to disprove it – to show that it's attributable to a breeze, or a reflection, or some other normal, everyday phenomenon.'[52]

Conclude

In the world of television the ghost hunters sit the 'client' down at a table, show him some suggestive clips, mention a few subjective experiences and then, drum roll, pronounce on whether the location is haunted or not. They call it 'the reveal' – a term from the stage magic business.

Most ghost hunts find nothing in the way of evidence of the paranormal. According to TAPS, 'eight out of ten times we have to tell our clients their place probably isn't haunted'. Twenty per cent is still a good hit rate. Many more seasoned investigators report much lower numbers. However, from a single investigation it is unlikely that anything as concrete as a 'yes' or 'no' answer will be forthcoming.

Modern ghost hunting has tended to revolve around the vigil, but as far back as 1882 when the SPR's Committee on Haunted Houses made its first report it was noted that 'it is very improbable that any result will be obtained by a single night's experiment'.[53] A TV show will typically make the rash judgement on whether a house is haunted or not based on a few hours roaming about the property in the dark, whereas a dedicated researcher, such as Steve Parsons, will spend a considerable amount of time at a given location: more than 900 hours over the course of three years at the Cammell Laird shipyard, for example.[54]

Real ghosts, if there truly are any, seem to be shy creatures. At the dawn of scientific research into apparitions, Barrett observed that 'ghosts, like aerolites, seem to be no respecters of persons; and no amount of scientific watchfulness will make them come to order.'[55] As Andrew Green observed, 'there are not many ghost-hunters, if any, who have seen ghosts when purposely looking for them.' Bill Bellars, former secretary of the Ghost Club, had also discovered that 'when a ghost hunter enters through the front door, the ghosts hurriedly leave through a back window'.[56] Often it is the people who do not believe in ghosts who see them and sometimes afterwards still insist on not believing in them.[57]

Over a hundred years after the Society for Psychical Research began its researches, groups like TAPS are still experiencing the same problem. As Jason Hawes said, 'ghost hunting is a difficult business. You can work at it for years and not record any documentation of your experiences'.[58] Despite the fact that ghosts are so widely and so commonly reported, they remain tantalizingly elusive.

After almost half a millennium in total investigative working on almost 5,000 cases, not one of the ghost hunters I interviewed has been able to scientifically prove or disprove the existence of 'ghosts'. But then that is the challenge that keeps dedicated researchers in the field.

Viewpoint: paranormal investigation
Paranormal investigation is a passion, but it's also very draining. I quit probably about six times a year in my mind. I get tired of the endless emails, critics and drama, but something always pulls me back. If you aren't passionate about helping people through the right techniques in investigating then you aren't here for the right reasons.
  Jessna A. Woods, lead investigator, Paraex (GHS, 2012)

4

IDENTIFY

> It is extremely difficult to give a very accurate description
> of it, because, like the generality of occult phenomena I have
> experienced in haunted houses, it was a baffling mixture of the
> distinct and yet vague, entirely without substance, and appar-
> ently wholly constituted of vibrating light that varied each
> second in tone and intensity.[1]

Elliott O'Donnell, if we are to believe him, must have seen
more ghosts than almost every other ghost hunter put together. Even so, he found the phenomenon of the ghost frequently
baffled his senses. Most books on ghosts, O'Donnell's included, are simply a jumble of supernatural stories. There is nothing intrinsically wrong with that because they do not attempt
to classify and scientifically describe the phenomena, merely
tell some good, spine-chilling yarns. The ghost hunter, however, needs to be able to sort the data.

The easiest and most common way to identify hauntings

is according to their visual representation, but of course there is a range of phenomena considered to be supernatural that are experienced in other ways. I have categorized according to form, beginning with the visual – animate: human, non-human, animal and vegetable; the inanimate, such as furniture and vehicles – and encompassing the non-visual – emotional, olfactory, auditory and tactile. This enables us to sort phenomena according to the sense through which they are primarily or exclusively experienced, including those 'feelings' often reported of something being amiss. Of course, a haunting may take more than one form. For example, for Athenodorus rattling chains (Non-Visual: Auditory) were heard before the apparition was seen (Visual: Animate, Human). This structured approach to the reporting of phenomena is particularly useful in compiling a database of cases, allowing the ghost hunter to quickly and easily calculate statistics on the hauntings studied or investigated.

Visibility

Consistency

Whatever form the anomaly takes, there are several factors to consider on how it takes that form. Ghosts are described in a number of conflicting ways as misty/shadowy and insubstantial, life-like and solidly three-dimensional, and life-like but two-dimensional. Sometimes they are seen to form and disintegrate, at other times they abruptly appear and disappear. Consistency is an important point to record or ascertain in any ghost sighting.

INSUBSTANTIAL

The insubstantiality of ghosts has been noted for some considerable time. According to Homer's *Odyssey* from about the eighth century BCE, the 'dead just flit about as shadows'. Likewise the Greek philosopher Socrates some centuries later talked of 'shadowy manifestations'.[2] Skip forward the millennia and Sir Walter Bromley Davenport saw what he described as 'a line of shadowy, spectre-like figures descending the steps into the family vault' at Capesthorne Hall, Cheshire.[3] A feature often reported is being able to see through an apparition. In other cases light is seen to pass through the apparition. Danny Bradshaw, nightwatchman on the WWII battleship USS *North Carolina*, described seeing a translucent human apparition, but it is not recorded whether he could also see through it.[4]

SUBSTANTIAL, TWO-DIMENSIONAL

Chris Halliday described his encounter with a phantom cat in 1999 as seeing something 'similar to what would be achieved if you cut a picture of a cat out and stuck it over a picture of our hall [where the encounter took place], taking no regard of lighting and shadows'. This was confirmed by Trevor Ouellette who described his apparition, also of a cat, as 'distinctly two-dimensional and sharply triangular'. There have also been similar sightings of human apparitions. Chris Shilling described seeing a 'person-shaped hole' with clearly defined edges but no content. Andy Hinkinson-Hodnett and a friend both saw what he described as 'a cardboard cutout, flat and one-dimensional [sic]'.[5]

SUBSTANTIAL, THREE-DIMENSIONAL

Sometimes ghosts are experienced as if they had solid bodies, either monstrous ones like the 'Terror of Tondu' reported in 1903, or human, and to all appearances fleshly, bodies in the form possessed whilst living. Athenodorus's visitor looked like a real person – a starved, grubby old one – who was substantial enough to rattle his chains. At other times spirits can touch, attack or make love to humans as if they had physical bodies, paradoxically, often at the same time as they demonstrate incorporeality. The ghost of a woman raised by a witch in a Roman novel of the second century CE, physically touches someone like a living person, but then vanishes like a ghost from a locked room.[6]

Another aspect of these apparitions is that in some cases they seem to be able to optically influence their surroundings, as well as blocking the witness's line of sight through them. Sir Edward Wills, staying in what was then his brother's house, Littlecote Manor, Wiltshire, in 1927, saw an apparition carrying a light that threw shadows on the ceiling as she passed.[7]

INCORPOREALITY

Whatever the reported consistency, the apparition is usually incorporeal; that is, it has no physical substance. Bayonets have been thrust through ghosts, as by at least two sentries on guard duty at the Tower of London. Pokers have been thrown at ghosts, as by a Mr G. Varley who ineffectually hurled an iron poker at the ghost of Meopham Manor House, Kent. Cars have been driven through them, as by two sailors motoring over The Strood, Mersea Island, in 1970. Captain Marryat put a bullet though the Brown Lady of Raynham Hall. But the ghosts never seem to notice, or simply disappear.[8]

Attempts to merely touch apparitions, rather than assault them, likewise usually meet with no success. Rose Morton, who described the haunting of her home to the SPR's Frederick Myers, several times tried to touch the mysterious 'black widow'. She found that the apparition always seemed to be just out of reach.[9]

This characteristic of incorporeality accords with another: famously, ghosts are reputed to be able to walk through walls and other solid objects. To pluck just one of many examples, a woman sitting in a flat in Glasgow in the 1990s watched a tall transparent figure swathed in a shroud that 'came from one end of the wall and walked through into another wall.'[10]

However, not every reported apparition has been incorporeal. G. N. M. Tyrrell described laying his hands on 'something soft, like flimsy drapery, but whatever it was seemed dragged

from me by some invisible power.'[11] The widow Mother Leakey
of Minehead, Somerset, returned after her death in the seventeenth century to become the notorious 'Whistling Ghost',
responsible for calling up storms and wrecking ships, as well
as strangling to death her five-year-old granddaughter.[12] The
revenant Kasparek was even held responsible for fathering children on his wife and maidservants after his death. Several more
sorts of 'tactile' aspects to hauntings are frequently reported
and are dealt with under 'Form'.[13]

Other characteristics

Consistency seems to be related to other aspects of a haunting. It is usually the unseen 'ghost' that has the power to move
objects or physically engage with percipients. The visible
apparition, by contrast, moves through people and things as
if they were not there. Kenneth Mason of the *Daily Graphic*
had first-hand experience of this when no less than six ghostly monks walked through him during a vigil in St Dunstan's
Church, London.[14]

Strangely, ghostly footsteps are seldom heard in conjunction with an apparition,[15] although footsteps themselves are
frequently reported. At Langenhoe Church, Essex, Revd
E.A. Merryweather heard a variety of unexplained noises,
but when he saw the ghost of a young woman she made no
sound as she crossed the flagstones. The visible apparition
tends to be silent, although there are some exceptions. In
some instances the rustling of clothing is heard. A certain
Colonel A. Kearsey, visiting an undisclosed address in Berkeley Square, saw and heard a sobbing woman. Rose Morton
reported that if light footsteps were heard, it was a prelude
to the appearance of the apparition. When the apparition did
appear the only sound noted was that of a soft rustling as of
clothes, not footsteps.[16]

In addition, the facial characteristics of an otherwise life-
like apparition can be indistinct.[17] The Black Lady of Broomhill was sometimes described as having no face at all.[18]

The ghost that confronted Athenodorus was unusual, in that it was both seen and heard, and appeared to interact with the witness. Where apparitions are concerned they most frequently appear to act in a manner that is uninvolved with the world of the witness, in distinct contrast to poltergeist-type phenomena.

Presentation
Apparitions manifest in a number of ways. Sometimes it is the manner of appearance or disappearance that is the first clue to paranormality.

INSTANTANEOUS
These apparitions seem to be suddenly switched on and off, abruptly appearing and/or disappearing in an instant. Ruby Bower, staying with her aunt and uncle who owned The Black Horse Inn, Cirencester, was awoken by the apparition of an evil old woman creeping towards her. When she cried out 'No! No! Don't! Don't!' it vanished.[19]

GRADUATED
Certain ghosts are described as fading in and/or out of perception. Tony Kelly, who saw the ghost of Oscar Wilde whilst staying in his old room at Magdalen College, Oxford, described the ghost as having 'just faded out of sight'.[20] The Revd Merryweather experienced an interesting variation. As he read out 'my eyes gush out with water because men keep not my law' (Psalm CXIX: 129–36) from his pulpit, he became aware that someone was watching him. He turned round to find a young, sorrowful-looking woman in a cream dress staring at him. She abruptly vanished, but her dress apparently remained visible for some moments longer.[21]

RESOLVING
The former BBC newsreader James Alexander Gordon described an interesting presentation. He had retired to Room 333 in the Langham Hilton across the road from Broadcasting

House after reading the midnight news. He was awoken at
3 a.m. to see a 'ball of light' slowly resolve itself into a human
form. The night porter and fellow newscaster Ray Moore also
witnessed the phenomenon.[22] At her home in Springfield,
Massachusetts, Denise Tanguay saw swirling red lights coa-
lesce into a face.[23]

Locomotion

A common attribute of the apparition, usually human, is
movement that defies the laws of gravity. Sir Charles Taylor,
MP, described seeing the ghost of a 'lady in grey' float across
the floor, for example.[24] Notably, unusual apparitional loco-
motion tends to be described as the appearance of floating
above the ground, occasionally below it, but, as far as I can
tell, not up a wall or along a ceiling.

Coloration

Humanoid apparitions are frequently designated by colour.
Female ghosts are often named White Lady, Green Lady, etc.
Figures wrapped in black popularly become 'nuns'; those in
brown, 'monks'. This is frequently despite any direct evidence
that they are nuns or monks, although circumstantial details are
often later adduced, such as the site of a former monastery and
so on. Often there are not even enough details to confidently
describe the sex of the ghost. For example, an apparition without a face, hands or feet, that haunts Alwinton in Northumberland, is called a 'cowled monk-like figure'.[25] To complicate
matters, monks historically comprised different orders designated by a special colour of habit: Benedictines black, Francis-
cans brown or grey, Carthusians white, Dominicans black and
white, Cistercians white with a black scapula, and so on.

In my preliminary survey of 923 haunting phenomena
(PSH) most of the apparitions identified by colour were ach-
romatic. Out of 71 identified cases, 21 (28 per cent) were white,
16 (22.5 per cent) were grey, and a further 16 (22.5 per cent)
were classified as black, dark or shadows, giving a total of 73

The spectral spectrum

	Colour	Apparitions (%)*
Achromatic		
	White	28.17
	Grey	22.54
	Black	22.54
Monochromatic		
	Red	5.63
	Brown	5.63
	Pink	2.82
	Orange	–
	Yellow	1.41
	Green	2.82
	Blue	8.45
	Violet	–

* % of cases where colour is reported.

per cent. In contrast there were no orange or violet ghosts, and only a rare yellow one. Life-like apparitions where no overall colour is reported can be assumed to be polychromatic, i.e., displaying the appropriate range of colours from clothing to flesh tones.

Colour is usually a common designator of humanoid apparitions. Other animates, such as cats and dogs, are often described as being of a certain colour, but inanimates are typically not. Whilst there are phantom trains, for example, there are no 'white trains', 'blue trains', and so on. A reported case of a silver train owed its coloration to verisimilitude with its previous physical existence.[26]

A number of unusual lighting effects can also accompany an apparition. In the 1760s an apparition of a woman – the 'luminous lady' – was seen in Cock Lane, London, 'surrounded, as it were by a blazing light'.[27] Two recorded sightings of the legendary *Flying Dutchman* in 1881 and 1925 also noted that the phantom ship was luminous.[28] Glamis Castle has a female apparition surrounded by a red glow, said to be a former Lady Glamis charged with witchcraft and burnt to death on Castle Hill, Edinburgh. The dark shape encountered by two sailors as they drove across Mersea Island in 1970 was described as being surrounded by a white mist. In some cases the haunting seems to provide its own illumination. The Elizabethan procession witnessed by a captain of the guard at the Tower of London was unaccountably self-illuminated in a dark chapel at night. In other cases the luminescence is the haunting. For example, a red glow is reported to appear over the Pass of Killiecrankie on the anniversary of the famous battle fought there.[29]

Recognizing the 'normal type of phantom'
The normal type of phantom may be recognized by the absence, as well as the presence, of certain characteristics. To begin with, sensational features are extremely rare. Then again, these appearances scarcely bear any relation to a special time of the day or the year. [. . .] Another characteristic common in the 19 selected cases is the apparently casual and objectless nature of the apparition. A figure is seen which has no appearance of life, and which resembles closely the image thrown by a magic lantern. Sometimes the appearance is described as life-like; sometimes it is recognized at once as a phantom. Sometimes it is shadowy, but more often the dress is seen distinctly, and is described as that worn by living persons in recent times.

'The Second Report of the Committee on Haunted Houses', *JSPR* (April 1884), p. 36.

If apparitions are objective phenomena, i.e., exist outside of the percipient's mind, then the question is: how are they seen? Do they absorb light, reflect light or emit light? There are colours of light and colours of pigment, additive colours and subtractive ones. As we know, white light is the presence of all the colours (additive model), yet from playschool we also know that when you mix all the paints together you get black (subtractive model). Additive colour is the effect of transmitted light; subtractive colour the effect of pigment or reflected light.[30]

Visual form

Animate: human

Now the good old orthodox idea of a ghost is, of a very long, cadaverous, ghastly personage, of either sex, appearing in white draperies, with uplifted finger, and attended or preceded by sepulchral sounds – whist! hush! and sometimes the rattling of casements and the jingling of chains. A bluish glare and a strong smell of brimstone seldom failed to enhance the horror of the scene.[31]

This is, of course, the most obvious form of the ghost, here most eloquently described by the inestimable P. T. Barnum. Athenodorus's nocturnal visitor may have heralded his arrival with the rattling of chains, but it was his appearance over the philosopher's shoulder that caught Pliny's attention. The Society for Psychical Research found that 'visual hallucinations' of a recognized human face or form were experienced by one in every 247 adults (0.4 per cent).[32] In my analysis of hauntings (PSH), I found that a third (33.15 per cent) of all phenomena were reported as human apparitions. There are, however, many different aspects to the humanoid ghost to consider.

A human apparition may also involve other elements, such as animal, as in the case of phantom riders, or inanimate, as in the case of phantom motorists, and, of course, not forgetting the tricky question of ghostly clothes. Felix Darley was most perplexed on this point, wondering how it could be that there was 'the ghost of the clothes also – the ghost of the coat and unmentionables – the ghost of the cocked hat and wig'.[33] P. T. Barnum put it more directly: 'Can human credulity go further than to suppose that the departed still appear in the old clo' of their earthly wardrobe?'[34] He was discussing the case of spirit photography and noted how one man recognized his brother by the pattern of his cravat. However, the question has not gone unanswered and by no less an authority than one of the departed themselves.

There was once a boy who had frequent conversations with his grandfather (deceased). One day he asked him 'why he wasn't naked, or why spirits aren't naked'. His grandfather replied, 'Do you think of yourself as going about naked?' 'No,' said the boy. 'Well, neither do we,' said his grandfather. 'We look as we think of ourselves,' he explained, 'That is why people over here wear such a lot of different sorts of clothes, and why even I wear clothes that aren't the fashion any more with you in your world.'[35]

It is a neat explanation, but it assumes, of course, that ghosts are real. The SPR's Edmund Gurney was more inclined to attribute the 'ghosts of old clothes' to the memory of the witness rather than an independent thing.[36] But in some cases ghosts known to the witness whilst alive have appeared in clothes of which the witness had no memory.

Then there is the even more vexed question of naked ghosts. It is sometimes said that there are no naked ghosts and that this fact proves that they cannot then be spirits of the dead, since the clothes themselves were never alive and may indeed still be in existence. However, though rare, there are reports of naked ghosts: at Knebworth, Langenhoe Manor House, ruined Woodhouse Lee near Edinburgh, Hylton Castle, Durham, and further afield at Frankenstein Castle near Darmstadt in Germany, for example.[37]

Just as most ghosts appear clothed in the style of their time, most also appear to still have their flesh on their bones despite 'the worm that gnaws'. However, there was an old oak tree close to Broadwater in Sussex that had the reputation of being haunted by not one, but several human skeletons. They were wont, hand-in-hand, to dance round the tree every Midsummer's Eve.[38]

Many human ghosts are attributed to actual deceased persons or, in the absence of any other information, given quaint names of their own. Thus we find a 'Percy' and an 'Old Jimmy Garlick', a 'Spinning Jenny' and, best of all, a 'Scratching Fanny' who haunted Cock Lane.[39] The scene of a haunting when well-established in folklore is also likely to acquire a name, such as 'The Room with the Severed Arm' (Capesthorne Hall) or 'The House of the Screaming Skull' (Bettiscombe House).

There are also cases of haunting that involve more than one apparition. Battle scenes and phantom regiments marching to war are the most well known. We have already examined the whole fabulous replay of the Battle of Edgehill. Also worth mentioning is the attested sighting by two witnesses of a phantom army complete with camp followers on the march near Glen Array.[40] Church processions are also reported. The Chapel of St Peter-ad-Vincula in the precincts of the Tower of London has one. According to the story, a captain of the guard peered through a window to see a procession of men and women wearing Elizabethan costume walking slowly down the aisle. At their head was Anne Boleyn.[41] Group apparitions accounted for 6.21 per cent of all apparitions.

Since the laying of Athenodorus's ghost the oldest ghosts principally date from the Roman period. From the period of the Roman occupation of Britain (first to fifth centuries CE) we have modern sightings of single Roman soldiers, larger bodies of troops and even Boudica, Queen of the Iceni (died c. 60 CE). There are relatively few genuine reports of ghosts in the Middle Ages, even though belief in them was widespread; most are religious *exempla* intended to teach or reinforce moral and religious views. This state of affairs is largely on account of who was writing such stories: the clergy with a necessary and vested interest in the promulgation of the faith. By contrast, there are many more reports of ghosts reputedly *from* the Middle Ages and the Renaissance. The many accounts of ghostly monks and nuns, if they are such, can generally be dated to sometime before the Dissolution of the Monasteries (1536–41). Battlefield ghosts conveniently come with their own *terminus*, while for others we must rely on vague accounts of old-fashioned clothing. For example, the phantom ambush party of unknown vintage, but described wielding archaic weapons – spears, axes and clubs – seen setting upon a group of ragged refugees by the mountaineer Frank S. Smythe in Glen Glomach, Highlands, in 1941, is suggestive of some remote date of the event being replayed, but is lacking in sufficient detail to discover when it supposedly took place. The very oldest must be the primeval forest witnessed by a Welsh miner deep underground, according to Elliott O'Donnell.[42]

HUMAN BODY PARTS

Not all humanoid apparitions involve the whole body. They can involve almost any part of the body from otherwise complete but headless bodies, to mere heads, skull, hands and arms. Headless coachmen, such as those at Borley,[43] and headless horsemen are the mainstay of many a ghost story, but we also find a headless monk who strolls past the Georgian pub in Meopham, Kent.[44]

In one interesting case from 1862 the upper body and lower torso of reputedly the same apparition were described as behaving independently by haunting two different locations at Meggernie Castle, Perthshire.[45] More common, however, are human heads and skulls. Most well known are the various 'screaming skulls', physical skulls that seem to produce phenomena when moved from a certain location, usually a building. The most widely reported are the skulls of Wardley Hall, Burton Agnes and Turnstead Farm, but it is Bettiscombe House, a Queen Anne mansion standing in Marshwood Vale, Dorset, that has become 'The House of the Screaming Skull'.[46]

Of the same order as the skull is the head enfleshed, as it were, in the same manner as it was in life. A house in Mary King's Close, Edinburgh, was haunted in the seventeenth century by the apparition of an old man's head complete with a grey beard, but minus body.[47]

Spectral arms and hands are also sometimes reported. Again from Mary King's Close, came the report of a naked arm appearing in mid-air, 'the hand streatched [sic] out as when one man is about to salute another'.[48] Twenty-three-year-old William Bromley-Davenport was awoken one night in 1958 by the sound of the window rattling in his bedroom in Capesthorne Hall, Cheshire. In the dim light he saw an arm, and only an arm, extending towards the window. Since then the bedroom has acquired the name of 'The Room with the Severed Arm'.[49]

As well as having two screaming skulls, Warbleton Priory is also visited by 'a pair of ghostly white hands' that flutter outside a small window under the roof. A hand and wrist were reported by two observers during the poltergeist out-break at 'Old Gast's House', Little Burton, Somerset, in 1677. A pair of hairy hands terrorized a lonely stretch of Devon road in the 1920s.[50]

At other times it might only be the impression of a hand that is seen. Such an example was reported by Revd Merry-weather during the Langenhoe Church haunting episode. In another case the landlord of the White Hart Inn, Caldmore Green, Staffordshire, found the handprint of a child's hand on a dust-covered table in the empty attic where a mummified baby's arm had been earlier discovered.[51]

So-called pseudopods have reportedly been created during spiritualist séances. These are animate human-like or less fre-quently tenticular forms supposedly created out of ectoplasm extruded from a medium's body during trance. Eusapia Palla-dino is credited with producing the first pseudopod – a third arm and hand – during a séance in 1894. The medium 'Eva C.' (real name Martha Beraud) was alleged to have produced ectoplasmic tentacles from her mouth, eyes, ears and nose that could take the shape of human faces. Irish medium Kathleen Goligher used 'psychic rods' to lift tables. 'Margery' (Mina Stinson Crandon) claimed to be able to materialize pseudo-pod hands that could ring bells and move objects. Most of these instances have been convincingly demonstrated to be fraudulently produced by the medium.[52]

HUMAN BODILY SUBSTANCES

Not to be ignored are human bodily substances. Mysterious bloodstains are a widely reported feature, usually attributed to some terrible murder on that spot. The usual motif is that, even after scrubbing, such stains stubbornly re-appear, thus attesting to their supernatural origin. I have seen the dark patch on the floor in Holyrood Palace, Edinburgh, where David Rizzio was stabbed to death. Warbleton Priory, famous for its skulls, also has a bloodstain. The 'screaming skull' of Bettiscombe House is said to have exuded blood in 1914, which was taken as an omen of the Great War. Less common, thankfully, is urine. Roz Wolseley-Charles reported that in her old house in Malvern, Worcestershire, urine would mysteriously appear in frying pans, covered pots and casserole dishes, as well as occasionally flooding the cooker, but never on the floor. She nicknamed it the 'phantom piddler'.[53]

Animate: non-human

'Demonic' form that may or may not be humanoid in shape, usually distinguished by provoking a great sense of dread in the percipient. The range of descriptions is most varied, but such types very often have some power of independent action.

A humanoid apparition might take the phantastic forms of the so-called 'Terror of Tondu' in Glamorganshire. It was described as 'an exceptionally tall, cadaverous figure . . . shrouded in white' with a head 'like a death's-head covered with wrinkled parchment' and 'the eyes were hollow sockets, in which was a cavernous glow'. It exhibited supernatural strength in attacking a respectable local resident – 'he felt himself held as though in the folds of a python' – but had no corresponding physical substance – 'nothing more tangible than air'.[54]

O'Donnell called spirits that had never inhabited a physical human body 'neutrarians' and described them as 'grotesque and awe-inspiring', classifying them as 'spirits of the most dangerous type'. He even explained cancer or otherwise undiagnosable and usually fatal illnesses by their unwelcome ministrations. O'Donnell is not alone in this unusual diagnosis, as the section on human illness, below, demonstrates. O'Donnell's 'neutrarians' are functionally similar to the more familiar 'elementals', although he disparaged this word as one of the occultists' 'high-falutin terms'. He did, however, use it himself often enough.[55]

Black smoke or smoke-like forms have been reported on occasion. Dennis Wheatley recalled a story told to him by Harry Price concerning a haunted bedroom in an old house in Sussex. Occupants trying to get a good night's sleep there were frequently awoken by the sensation of being strangled. Food left in a semi-basement room became rotten within the space of some hours. An exorcism was performed in the bedroom shortly before dawn. A black ball of smoky substance appeared and rolled out of the room, down the stairs, out of the window in the semi-basement, and across the lawn into a nearby pond. When the pond was dredged, three human skeletons were discovered lying at the bottom.[56] A high-ranking officer at the Tower of London saw a whiff of smoke exit one of the disused cannons, drift across the ground and then appear to perch on top of a wall.[57]

Wheatley was also on familiar terms with Montague Summers – an author still widely read for his lurid accounts of witchcraft and vampirism. Summers claimed to have performed an exorcism himself and told Wheatley the gory details. It took place on a farm in rural Ireland. A farmer's wife was said to be possessed by an evil spirit. Summers arrived in the evening to find a cold leg of mutton laid out for supper and the wife going into violent fits at the sight of him. As she was held down, Summers sprinkled her with holy water and commanded the evil spirit to depart. A cloud of black smoke issued from her lips and entered the leg of mutton. Within minutes the meat was crawling with maggots.[58]

A particularly interesting case of a non-human haunting was related by Edward Lenthal Swifte, Keeper of the Crown Jewels at the Tower of London. It was a Saturday evening in October 1817, and Swifte was dining with his wife, sister-in-law and young son in their apartment in the Jewel House, which was then in the Martin Tower. His wife lifted her cup to her mouth, but paused midway. 'Good God! What *is* that?' she cried. Swifte followed her gaze and saw 'a cylindrical figure, like a glass tube' of an arm's thickness, hovering in the air. It appeared to be filled with something like a continually swirling white and blue liquid. It remained stationary for approximately two minutes before moving towards Swifte's sister-in-law. Its route took it in front of Swifte and his son, and behind his wife where it paused by her right shoulder. She watched it in the mirror. Suddenly, she threw herself forward on the table, her hands protecting her head. 'Oh Christ! It has seized me!' she screamed. Swifte leapt to his feet and swung the chair at *the thing*. It immediately disappeared. Afterwards, Swifte found out that although he and his wife had seen the object distinctly, neither his son nor sister-in-law saw anything at all.[59]

A non-human encounter that may be related occurred a few days later. A sentry standing guard at the Jewel House saw a large shaggy form, which he described as being like a bear, emerge from under the door of the Jewel Room. The soldier lunged at the intruder with his bayonet, but the bayonet passed through it and lodged in the door. The sentry collapsed. He was carried in a dead faint to the guardroom and, according to the story, died a few days later.

Lastly, an apparently human apparition can be a fictional creation, not a fraud, but a character and hence, categorically, non-human. The New York illusionist and author Walter Gibson, best known as the creator of *The Shadow* under the pen name of Maxwell Grant, seems to have also created The Shadow's ghost. An unusually intense man with astonishing powers of concentration, Gibson wrote 283 books about his crime-fighting hero, sometimes churning out a novel in less than a week. During one excessively creative period of his career, he sequestered himself in Greenwich Village and wrote with demonic intensity. It is said that for years afterwards his characters could be seen 'haunting' the place where they had been born.[60]

Animate: animal
Domestic pets, livestock and exotic species have all been reported to have returned from the dead. According to some research, as many as 20 per cent of experienced apparitions may be of animals, especially pets, although from the PSH I found that only 4.01 per cent of all phenomena, or 9.23 per cent of apparitions, fitted this category.[61]

DOMESTIC PETS
Dogs have a long association with the Devil and devil-dogs are as old as the hills.[62] These creatures, known by various folk names, such as Black Shuck or the Manx *Moody dhoe*,[63] seem more to inhabit the world of Fairy than that of the spirit, assuming there is a difference. There have been numerous sightings down the years usually involving a black dog of enormous proportions and burning red eyes. Recent eyewitnesses, such as Victoria Rice-Heaps, report 'a huge black dog [. . .] like something from hell!', and G. E. Thompson noted the 'glowing red eyes' during an encounter in 1996.[64]

Black Shuck usually seems to take an all too active interest in those who witness him, but there are more traditional 'replay' phantom dogs, such as the one at Hampton Court, said to reside in Cardinal Wolsey's former closet. A strange black dog haunted a bedroom in a house in Woodseats,

Sheffield, in the 1930s, terrifying at least one young girl who slept there.[65] A whole pack of phantom hounds is said to still enjoy the chase in the vicinity of an old Roman wall outside Haltwhistle in Northumberland.[66] Edward Lloyd claimed to have photographed the apparition of Gellert, the faithful hound of Llewellyn, whilst photographing the grave in Beddgelert, Wales.[67]

Graeme Cammack of Edinburgh reported what he believed was the crisis apparition of his own pet dog. During a period of hospitalization, an elderly patient in the bed next to him was under the distinct impression that there was a dog at the foot of his bed and tried to get the nurses to give it some of his breakfast milk. When Cammack's wife arrived during visiting hours, he learnt that his one-year-old dog had had an epileptic fit that morning and had been found in a death-like condition.[68]

Veteran psychical researcher Tony Cornell told the story of how his own dog, Boozer, appeared to his mother shortly after it was put down at the local veterinary surgery. His mother described how the dog had come in through the open kitchen door, looked at its rear leg, then back at her, repeating this several times before running out of the door again. What she did not know at the time was that Boozer had received a lethal injection in its rear left leg.[69]

A family renovating an old farmhouse in England found a number of strange things under the floorboards, in wall cavities and, in the attic, a small desiccated cat. It appeared to have crawled into the attic, died and naturally mummified in the warm, dry air. Not sure what to do with it, they popped it into a box and put it into a room they were using for storage. When the woman's mother came to visit she remarked, 'Oh, you never said you'd got a cat.' The family did not have a cat, or at least not a live one, but the woman's mother insisted she had heard one purring in the storage room. Philip Evans was surprised when his cat – distinctively coloured and with one eye – returned from the vets where he had been put down after a long illness. A retired police officer called Ian was relieved when, finally, someone else saw what he had been seeing all along: his old cat, Wellington, dead for the past six years.[70]

Phantom creatures were reported to haunt a house in Mary King's Close, Edinburgh, in the seventeenth century. They included a dog and a cat, as well as others of unknown form.[71] A location near Fulletby, Lincolnshire, was once said to be haunted by the ghost of a girl in the shape of a white rabbit. According to the story, she had fallen from her horse in 1766 and been killed outright.[72]

AVIAN

The White Bird of Arundel Castle, Sussex, is said to be an omen of death for members of the Howard family, the heredi- tary Dukes of Norfolk. In a reputedly haunted house in Lin- coln's Inn, London, the footprints of a large, turkey-sized bird were clearly marked in the powdered chalk in the middle of two separate rooms. St Martin's church in West Drayton, Greater London, was plagued by a large black bird that used to peck at the coffins in the vaults. Locals believed that it was the spirit of a murderer who had taken his own life.[73]

LIVESTOCK

Horses[74] are familiar as part of the horseman/rider type of haunting. Appropriately, Ascot, in Berkshire, has a phantom rider seen at night in the vicinity of a roundabout constructed in 1967. The 'wicked' Catherine Ferrers – lady of Markyate Cell in Hertfordshire by day, highwayman by night – is said to still ride her pitch-black horse through the countryside that she terrorized during the seventeenth century. Interest- ingly, she has also been seen without her horse in the house and grounds.[75] The question naturally arises: are her phan- toms one ghost or two?

Other strange things to happen to horses include the appearance of having been ridden during the night and their manes being braided, again mysteriously, overnight. An interesting account comes from Furnace Mill, Lamberhurst,

Kent, in 1906. Horses were found reversed in their stalls, tails
in their mangers, without apparently having the necessary
space to perform this manoeuvre themselves. Another horse
was found in the nearby hay room despite the fact that the
door was barely large enough to admit a man.[76]

The most ferocious livestock ghost must be that of the
legendary Roaring Bull of Bagbury. An evil character living
at Bagbury Farm sometime in the age of fairytales, expired
having done only two good deeds in his life. His spirit was
nowise less unkind and would impose itself upon his neighbours in the form of a bull whose roaring would quite shake
the building to pieces. It took twelve parsons to lay the ghost,
casting it into the Red Sea for a thousand years.[77]

A 'fyerin' – a fairy or apparition – haunted an old house in
Stanicliffe, near Middleton, during the years of the English
Civil War, and was said to manifest in the form of a calf, as
well as that of a dog and a human.[78] A ghostly calf at Weobley,
Herefordshire, was said to be the ghost of a farmer who had
taken his own life.[79] Another phantom calf haunted a field by
Ham Court, Bampton, Oxfordshire.[80] A whole drove of black
cattle sometimes seen roaming Highstane Common, Bewcas-
tle, was said to be the ghosts of murder victims. They also
turn up as a coach and pair, and a herd of wild horses. Anyone
unlucky enough to see them 'knew that his end was near'.[81]

As well as ghostly calves, phantom sheep were reported
to wander Cowleys Corner, Oxfordshire, at the spot where
suicides were once buried.[82] Other flocks of phantom sheep
have been spotted in Scotland and Germany.[83] Airlie Castle,
Angus, is occasionally visited by the 'Doom of Airlie Castle',
a ram that circles the walls as an omen of death or misfortune
for the Ogilvie family.[84] A pamphlet on a London haunting of
1661 described how the ghost of a baker could appear as a goat
and a black cat, as well as in human form, but always left the
hellish whiff of brimstone after it.[85]

Phantom pigs roam the Chiltern Hills, it is said. In some
places, the curious custom of burying alive a pig or horse in a

cemetery has resulted in the creation of a 'kirk-grim', a sort of spectral guardian. In the parish of Tillington, Sussex, a headless horse was joined by a headless pig.[86]

NATIVE WILDLIFE

The last bear to be killed in Sussex is said to haunt the ruins of Verdley Castle near Fernhurst where it was slain. Cornered in the Great Hall by hunters on Christmas Day, the bear's end is believed to replay every anniversary with growling and the shouts of the hunters.[87] A ghost said to be able to take the form of a lion or a bear was that of a young man of Stamford, murdered in 1679.[88]

The ruins of Knepp Castle near West Grinstead, West Sussex, are said to be haunted by a white doe. The story is a curious legend involving animal transformation by witchcraft said to date from the reign of King John (1167–1216).[89]

EXOTIC SPECIES

In 1898 O'Donnell met an old keeper in the Zoological Gardens, Regent's Park, who told him that he had often seen the ghosts of departed animals, particularly that of a young lion from East Africa. He had encountered this beast on the Broad Walk adjoining the zoo, apparently at the moment of its death, and its lifelike appearance at first led him to believe that the animal had escaped.[90]

The ghost of Topsy, a circus elephant, was said to haunt Luna Park, Coney Island, after she was electrocuted for aggressive behaviour.[91] Carew Castle, Pembrokeshire, Wales, is home to the spirit of Satan, Sir Roland Rhys's pet monkey.[92]

Vegetable

Creaking, rustling, twisted into fantastical shapes and strangely watchful, it should be of no surprise that haunted trees, even demonic trees, have been reported. O'Donnell, of course, told stories of a few: one he encountered on the north side of Hyde Park; another told to him by a tramp of an evil tree on Clapham Common; and a miner's account of a prehistoric forest deep underground. O'Donnell even claimed that trees can sense 'superphysical phenomena' themselves, shaking violently in alarm.[93]

Inanimate (manmade)
A human spirit agency is often assumed to be behind hauntings of these kinds. An unseen hand is usually attributed to the mysterious opening of a window, for example. However, to correctly identify the anomaly we must exclude assumptions.

Fixtures and furnishings
When investigating a haunting Elliott O'Donnell often asked whether the victim had recently bought or acquired any old items. It was a question that self-styled demonologist Ed Warren also asked. This need not be some well-polished antique; even a fragment of something from a haunted location appears to be able to transfer the haunting. For example in the 1960s, a woman in Edinburgh received some pieces of wood from the staircase of haunted Sandwood Cottage and reported that the ghost came with them.[94]

The bed was a traditional four-poster situated in a pleasant room overlooking the gardens, but it had the reputation of awaking sleepers with the sensation of being strangled. I regret to say that I spent a peaceful night under the covers.[95] Others have fared less well with supposedly haunted beds. A bed once slept in by Charles I now resides in Penkaet Castle, Pencaitland, and according to reports he still does. The four-poster bed with a gruesome reproduction of his death mask is frequently found in a state as if just slept in, and once creaking noises were heard to come from it, just as if someone were tossing and turning under the sheets.[96]

The grotesquely carved and blood-stained 'poltergeist chest' of Stanbury Manor, Morwenstow, Cornwall, caused its owner Mr T.A. Ley considerable trouble. Ley found that wherever the chest was placed, things would fall off the walls around it. The chest or whatever haunted it was playfully dubbed 'Old George'. Underwood recalled another haunted chest, described to him by a surgeon, that had contained the apparition of a man with his throat cut. The surgeon learnt that a man had committed suicide in the chest. Tony Cornell investigated a poltergeist case in a Cambridge antique shop that revolved around a George III tallboy.[97]

An old chair bought from an antique shop still had one of its former owners sitting in it – fortunately, a kindly old man – according to Barbara L. Barnes and one of her children who both claimed to have seen the apparition. Stella Metchling in Charlotte, North Carolina, had a rocking chair that rocked by itself, and from Asheville, North Carolina, comes a report of a haunted wheelchair that moved about by itself.[98]

Eric Russell recounted a news story from a local Surrey paper in January 1969. It was a classic antique furniture haunting with a twist. A table said to be a hundred years old had been purchased from an antique dealer. That evening, as the table stood in its new home, and the owner watched television, the apparition of an old woman appeared: 'The lady was wearing glasses, had lightish brown hair streaked with grey, and had blunt features. She was gazing at the television with an incredulous look.' The room was a comfortable 21°C, but the table's new owner felt chilled to the bone. A telephone call to the antique dealer revealed that the description matched that of the previous owner's grandmother. This case presents an interesting fusion of object and apparition with the additional suggestion that, as reported, the phantom could see the present world and apparently register a reaction to it.[99]

Andrew Green reported three cases of ghostly trousers haunting, respectively, a house in Surrey, a shop in Devon and a field in Gloucestershire. He suggested that they were either all that was left of old hauntings, or had been incomplete from the start due to some aspect of the ghost's creation.[100] A novel variation is said to occur in Room 419 of the Crescent Hotel,

Eureka Springs, Arkansas. Guests awake to find their clothes packed and their cases standing at the door.[101]

Clocks: violently rocking, whining, even speaking as omens of doom, and in one case Elliott O'Donnell described how a hooded head had appeared instead of the clock face. O'Donnell seemed to be obsessed by possessed clocks. In 2010 a woman called Rachel wrote in to *Paranormal* magazine claiming that her clock-radio was haunted, turning itself on for the national anthem on Radio 4 and then off again. In some cases unusual clock behaviour is taken as an indication of other paranormal activity. Ghost hunters in Bruce Castle, Tottenham, in 1949 on the anniversary of Lady Coleraine's death – the time when she traditionally put in her return appearance – noticed that an otherwise reliable clock failed to strike 1 a.m. despite striking the hours before and after, and that this coincided with an unexpected fall in temperate.[102]

Pianos playing by themselves are almost as much a staple of the ghost story as rattling chains. Mordecai House, North Carolina, has a haunted piano in the parlour, reputed to rattle out a tune when tour groups are passing through, although not during the 2005 TAPS investigation.[103]

A portrait of local shipping magnate, Pierre Le Fleur, hanging in the Red Room of Brennan's Restaurant on Royal Street, New Orleans, Louisiana, is said to change its expression – smiling, scowling, frowning, etc. – every time it is looked at. According to the story, Le Fleur arranged three funerals before killing his wife and son, and hanging himself from the chandelier in the Red Room. Financial difficulties are sometimes cited as the reason for the double murder and suicide. Portraits of all three hang on the wall, but only that of Pierre is said to change its expression.[104]

In fact, almost any sort of furnishing or decorative feature can end up becoming part of a haunting. Over the years people have reported seeing ornamental statues of lion-like animals sitting on the stone gate pillars leading to the vanished mansion house of Knighton Gorges, Isle of Wight, which then mysteriously disappear.[105] Spontaneously appearing and disappearing objects are often reported in poltergeist cases. One of the first poltergeist cases of the twentieth century involved the inexplicable appearance of small black stones 'falling, very slowly, from the area of the ceiling'.[106]

Vehicles

Ships, trains, cars, trucks, buses, motorbikes, bicycles, lifts, even farm machinery, have all made their way into the ghost story. A phantom cyclist and hence also his phantom bicycle terrorized Brighton, Sussex, in 1903, apparently colliding with several witnesses.[107]

HORSE-DRAWN TRANSPORT

Phantom coaches, like rattling chains, are another mainstay of the ghost story, but unlike the chains, the coaches are far better attested. Often the coach is driven by a headless coachman and sometimes, too, drawn by headless horses. Just such a one was witnessed by a terrified couple in 1915. According to the legend a traveller had been foully murdered at the seventeenth-century Fleece Inn, Elland, but now haunted the Westgate road in a phantom coach driven by a headless coachman with a team of headless horses – the traveller or the whole ghastly ensemble being dubbed 'Leathery Colt'.[108] The timing – midnight in January – the presence of horses and the significance of rushing wind in the story echo earlier legends of the Wild Hunt passed down since pagan times.[109] W.B. Yeats noted that among the Irish such a coach was known as the 'coach-a-bower' (from cóiste-bodhar) and the driver was called a Dullahan. This apparition was linked to the banshee and if you were foolish or curious enough to open the door after it rolled up to your house, then a bucket of blood would be thrown in your face.[110]

But it is not all phantom coaches; also to be included in this category is the phantom chariot. The ghost of Boudica, the first-century CE Queen of the Iceni tribe, reputedly still drives her chariot along Ermine Street, an old Roman road, where it passes near Cameringham, Lincolnshire.[111]

SEAFARING VESSELS

'At 4 a.m. *The Flying Dutchman* crossed our bows. She emitted a strange phosphorescent light as of a phantom ship all aglow.' The sighting was recorded off the coast of Australia on 11 July 1881 by a sixteen-year-old midshipman aboard HMS *Inconstant*. The young sailor was Prince George, later King George V of Great Britain, and along with him a total of thirteen other men witnessed the apparition that morning; and it has been sighted many times since. Another possible sighting occurred in 1925. As the P&O liner SS *Barrabool* passed South Africa en route from Australia to London, four sailors saw a luminous ship approaching and observed it for some time before it abruptly vanished.[112]

The schooner *Lady Lovibond* sank with all hands on 13 February 1748 and has reputedly appeared every fifty years to the day off the coast of southern England. A WWII landing craft flying the Cross of Lorraine, the flag of the Free French forces, was sighted in difficult weather off the coast of Devon in 1959, fourteen years after the end of the war.[113]

AEROPLANES

After the Wright Brothers' historic flight in 1903, it could only be a matter of time before the skies were filled with their share of ghosts, too. Bircham Newton aerodrome in Norfolk saw service through both world wars and, if accounts are to be believed, is still doing so despite being disused. A film crew there to shoot a management training video instead caught sounds of aircraft engines, human voices and machinery, in fact, all the noise and bustle of a busy hangar in active use. Other members of the film crew also saw ghostly figures in RAF uniform and enquiries revealed a history of hauntings. A lone spitfire can sometimes still be heard as it returns from a sortie to the famous Battle of Britain airfield at Biggin

Hill in Kent. Some witnesses even claim to have seen it perform a victory roll over the runway. The villagers of Hawk-
inge near Folkestone have heard the unforgettable drone of
a Nazi V1 'flying bomb' passing overhead decades after the
event.[114]

RAILWAY TRAINS

As one example among many, a ghost train was seen by five
people in Sweden, travelling noiselessly at high speed between
Orresta and Tortuna on the Västerås Railway. A newspaper
report noted that it had been seen several times before and
that it was believed to be an omen of some impending accident. Interestingly, the same report also gave an account of a
ghost train in Lapland, haunting a forested locale despite the
lack of a railway line.[115]

MOTORIZED ROAD VEHICLES

A 'phantom lorry' was claimed to be the cause of an accident
in 1930 on the A75 between Hyde and Mottram-in-Longdale.
The area was discovered to be a mysterious accident black
spot, despite being a straight stretch of well-maintained road.
More accidents were to follow. One even involved a pedes-
trian who was apparently run over by the phantom lorry.[116]
The 'Ghost Bus' of Kensington was cited at the inquest into
an accident at the junction of St Mark's Road and Cambridge
Gardens in 1934. Ian James Beaton had been killed when
his car collided with another being driven by George Pink,
chauffeur to the Hon. Samuel Vestey. The jury learned from a
witness that a ghost bus haunted the notorious accident black
spot. 'The legend of the phantom bus has been going strong
for years,' said a local resident. She continued that 'on certain
nights, long after the regular bus service has stopped, people
have been awakened by the roar of a bus coming down the
street.' The fully illuminated double-decker is seen 'without
driver nor passengers [. . .] careering to the corner of Cambridge Gardens and St Mark's Road and then vanishes'. Later

remodelling of the dangerous junction was said to have put paid to the apparition.[117] Other vehicles include a ghostly tractor which makes its way down a road outside the small town of Old Colwyn, Conwy, Wales.[118]

LIFTS

The old Palace Hotel in Southport once laid claim to a ghost-powered lift. Due for demolition, the 1,000-room building was unoccupied and without power, but workmen reported that the lift was still working, powered by some mysterious energy source of its own. North Wales Electricity Board investigated and confirmed that there was no electricity being supplied to the hotel. Despite this the lift would repeatedly travel up from the ground floor to the second. The workmen cut the cables in the main shaft and used sledge hammers to batter the lift into the cellars.[119]

O'Donnell also had a story about a ghostly lift, this one in a hotel in Boston, Massachusetts. The lift apparently re-created the last journey of a man found dead in it under mysterious circumstances. He claimed to have seen it himself, gliding up and down with no one inside to operate it.[120]

Fixed structures

Is the bridge witnessed in railway sightings, such as the ghost of the Tay Bridge disaster, a phantom bridge? The old bridge, the one that collapsed, was not rebuilt. Instead another was constructed nearby, so if it is seen as part of the anniversary train haunting, then it, too, must be considered paranormal. Here we see that we cannot differentiate between them. There are not two hauntings – one of a train and one of a bridge – but only a single anomaly involving multiple aspects.

The various encounters with apparently paranormal buildings and features of the landscape that have been recounted over the years have become known, after G. W. Lambert, as 'phantom scenery'. The most famous cases were the vanishing buildings or scenery of Boscastle, Bradfied St George,

Hailsham, Man Sands and Versailles. Members of the Society for Psychical Research managed to track down these alleged phantoms and establish that they were real. The Georgian house in Hadleigh that apparently appeared and disappeared one day in 1946 remained undiscovered until the late 1990s. Melvin Harris eventually found the house on maps of a local authority neighbouring those that had already been checked. The explanation was what Lambert called, 'mislocation': the precipients simply looked in the wrong places when searching for the original feature and, not finding it, assumed it must have been a paranormal experience.[121]

Sir Victor Goddard observed an airfield, complete with hangars, aircraft and personnel, about five years before it was built, although here we must note that this is much more in the nature of a premonition than a classic haunting.[122]

Luminescence

The appearance of unexplained lights is sometimes interpreted as spirits, as at Borley Rectory, Penkaet Castle, and the Church of St Nicholas in Pluckley, for example.[123] At 'The Farm of Spooks' in Fenny Compton, Warwickshire, 'ghostly lights' drew large crowds of spectators in the 1920s. Attempts were made to try and photograph them, but it is not known if they were successful.[124]

So-called 'death-lights' were 'once a common article of faith', according to folklorist Henry Penfold. He described them as being blue lights of about three feet in height. At the moment of death, the light would leave the house and take the road the funeral cortege would follow to the church and there occupy the spot where later the coffin would rest. After some space of time it would leave the church and find its way to the intended gravesite and there sink into the ground. Penfold heard the tale of someone who on returning home one evening saw a death-light and stood in its path to try and see what it was. The light evaded him by ducking between his legs and continuing on its way.[125]

Miscellaneous inanimates
In the literature of the Middle Ages – a report by a monk in Yorkshire around the year 1400 – there is curious mention of a haunted haystack. It was even more curious that the haystack was thought to be the shape assumed by the spirit of a deceased person, a sort of shape-shifting ghost, if you will. The same ghost had also taken the form of a horse, according to the story.[126]

Physical
In the PSH about one in ten (10.4 per cent) haunting phenomena involve some sort of physical interference, which could be either observed or unobserved at the time. Most often (30.21 per cent) this was related to doors opening and closing or locking and unlocking apparently by themselves, or the movement/manipulation of objects (25 per cent), but it could also involve electrical effects, non-electrical lighting effects and the appearance of writing or other visible traces. These objects or events are themselves not thought to be haunted, but their behaviour is taken to imply some invisible agency affecting them. Such phantom actions on physical objects we should term spectrokinesis or, better, nemokinesis (movement by no one), to differentiate them from tele- or psychokinesis whose results are attributed to human agency.

TAPS have come across a number of opening and closing doors: one in the DeVilles' house in 2005; at the Sutcliffes' home, also in 2005; at the old Rolling Hills Asylum, Batavia, New York, again in 2005; and at The Stanley Hotel, Colorado, in 2006. Other mysterious nemokinetic effects at The Stanley included a glass shattering as if from internal pressure, curtains repeatedly opening by themselves and a table and chair levitating.[127]

ELECTRICAL EFFECTS
Although there was only one reported instance of an electrical effect in the PSH, spontaneous equipment failures,

usually involving sudden battery drainage, are widely reported during investigations. Before beginning their investigation
of Culcreuch Castle, Scotland, a Ghost Club team discovered
that three batteries, all fully charged beforehand, were inex-
plicably flat.[128] A similar thing happened when CASPER UK
investigated the Waggon and Horses Public House, Doulting
Beacon, in August 2011.[129] Loyd Auerbach has experienced
every sort of equipment failure during investigations, often
finding that by simply leaving the 'haunted' location the
equipment starts working properly again.[130]

TAPS investigators Steve Gonsales and Mike Dion experienced abnormally rapid battery drainage during filming of
a possible poltergeist manifestation in the home of the Worthington family in Keene, New Hampshire, in 2005. The
same thing happened at The Armory, New Bedford, Massachusetts, shortly before sound technician Frank DeAngelis
was floored by an invisible assailant. Confronted by a 'dark
mass' in New Hampshire in 1997, Hawes reached for his
camera, only to find the freshly charged batteries were dead.
Investigations have also been hampered by computer crashes
occurring at the same time as possible paranormal activity.[131]

Electric lights mysteriously switching off and on is also
reported in poltergeist cases. The clinical psychologist Peter
McCue had a patient who had experienced lights apparently
switching themselves off and on in different parts of his flat
in Glasgow's East End during the 1990s. In poltergeist cases
electrical equipment is also reported to fail outright. During
a period of six years in the aforementioned haunted Glasgow
flat, the occupier went through two refrigerators, six hi-fis,
five or six vacuum cleaners, eight television sets and innumer-
able light bulbs. Electricians called out to investigate could
never find any wiring problems in the flat.[132]

LIGHT EFFECTS (NON-ELECTRICAL)
A flickering candle flame was once said to denote the presence of spirits, which, given the draughty nature of older

properties, must have led to the belief that spirits were in almost constant attendance. At other times a flame burning blue was held to betoken the paranormal.[133]

WRITING

'Marianne get help' read the writing scrawled on the wall: hauntings can also involve the spontaneous appearances of words or images. The most famous case is that of Borley Rectory when a supposed entity tried to communicate with Marianne Foyster.[134] 'The Great Amherst Mystery' of Amherst, Nova Scotia, in 1878–9 centred around a young girl called Esther Cox who was threatened several times in mysterious written messages, including one on the bedroom wall that read 'Esther Cox you are mine to kill'.[135]

A more recent case was reported by Rose-Mary Gower concerning events at her family home, a farmhouse in Mold, Flintshire.[136] At The Black Horse Inn, Cirencester, the apparition of an evil old woman in old-fashioned clothes was accompanied by the name 'John' being scratched on the window panes in an antiquated script.[137]

OTHER TRACES

Adult hand-prints and child-sized shoe-prints appeared on the walls and ceilings of a terraced house in East Park, Wolverhampton, during the late 1960s. The haunting, which included an apparition of a man in sailor's uniform and the presence of a child brushing past one of the witnesses, is attributed to a young sailor, Harry Parks Temple, who died while trying unsuccessfully to rescue two boys, who also drowned, from a pool in the 1920s. The correspondent, Ian Deakin, wrote that he had seen some of the prints himself in the front bedroom in the mid-1980s.[138]

Non-visual form

Emotional

A particular route that my wife and I often used to drive across the Ardennes took us through the Belgian town of Thieu and past the church with its old cemetery. Having met by chance in London's atmospheric Highgate Cemetery, we found that we shared an interest in visiting unusual, if not actually haunted, locations. So it was that we decided to stop off in Thieu and explore the old cemetery.

We walked up the steps and through the rusty wrought-iron gate and circled the church to the graveyard behind it. It was a plain churchyard, relatively speaking, and not of any great age. But there was an uncanny air lingering among the stones – tombstones, moreover, that appeared to have been visited by some violent force and lay cracked and with gaping black fissures to the charnel within. We, who had strolled leisurely round the overgrown and extravagant funereal architecture of Highgate, looked at each other and decided to get the hell out of there. Neither of us is nervous by nature and we usually take a delight in visiting supposedly haunted spots, but the churchyard of Thieu was an exception. There was simply that unaccountable feeling of something unpleasant.

The famous horror writer Dennis Wheatley often told the story of his encounter with the supernatural as a young soldier. He was building a lean-to in an old walled garden behind the lines at the Somme. It was night and he was working by moonlight when he felt a presence:

> I *knew* that something incredibly evil was watching me from behind – and it had suddenly become very cold. After a minute that seemed an eternity I panicked and fled in abject terror.[139]

There were few recorded emotional phenomena in the PSH: 19 cases or 2.06 per cent of the total. Terms used included 'an extraordinary atmosphere' and a 'strange atmosphere', as well as the feeling of being watched or a sense of unhappiness lingering in a place, but most often the report was of a feeling of 'presence'.

Auditory

Rattling chains à la Athenodorus's encounter might be a stock part of the ghost story, but they are rarely reported. In his *A–Z of British Ghosts* Peter Underwood mentioned three cases: one at Hastings Castle in Sussex; another in Amen Court bordering the site of the old Newgate Prison, London; and the final one at the Church of St Nicholas, Sandford Orcas, Dorset.[140] I dug up another, but it was a case of fraud persecuted by a villainous steward against his master.[141] However, the noise of chains is still reported in the field. A recent Ghost Club investigation at Alloa Tower, Alloa, reported 'the clanking of the chains' on the main turnpike stair.[142]

Phantom footsteps are one of the most commonly reported phenomena, but this category also includes voices and other sounds, such as bangs, creaks, clicks, raps, etc., that seem to have no physical origin. O'Donnell reported that unexplained noises in houses usually began in the basement before travelling to the upper stories.[143] In practice most noises attributed to ghosts can manifest in any part of the house and except in poltergeist cases tend to remain in that initial locality.

Percussive sounds – knocking, banging, thumping, drumming, etc. – are commonly noted in a haunting. From the PSH I found that the single largest group (34.89 per cent) of phenomena were auditory. Indeed, mysterious and apparently intelligent knocking sounds or raps started the whole Spiritualist movement. Whilst the Fox sisters who started it all in 1848 by apparently communicating with a 'Mr Splitfoot' eventually confessed to have produced the sounds themselves,[144] recent research has demonstrated an unusual acoustic signature to knockings associated with poltergeist phenomena.[145] In researching this book, I found it significant that the knocking sounds that attended the Epworth poltergeist case of 1716 were described as having a 'dead, hollow note'.[146]

Voices are sometimes heard when no speakers are visible. An instance occurred during the writing of this book. Whilst searching in the attic of our new home in Staudernheim, Germany – a sandstone villa from 1905 – my wife heard a croaky voice say 'I'm back'. Apart from our fifteen-month-old daughter who was fast asleep downstairs, she was alone in the house. Some minutes later I arrived home and called out 'I'm back!'. The Society for Psychical Research found that 'auditory hallucinations' of a recognized human voice were experienced by one in every ninety adults (1.1 per cent).[147]

The sound of clothing is sometimes also heard. Sir Charles Taylor, MP, was surprised by the swish of a long dress when staying at Capesthorne Hall, Cheshire. He turned and saw a 'lady in grey' rushing by the foot of the staircase.[148] A rustling of silk drew the attention of a guest at The Black Horse Inn, Cirencester, to the apparition of an evil old woman in old-fashioned clothes approaching the bed.[149]

Music is often heard for which there is seemingly no apparent explanation. This can be divided into martial, vocal and instrumental. Martial music is most often drumming and phantom drummers are a widespread phenomenon. The Drummer of Airlie, Kirriemuir, Scotland, portends the death of the head of the Airlie family with not just drumming, but also a sound like the wail of the bagpipes.[150] Vocal music is usually ecclesiastical chanting, or less frequently singing. Likewise, instrumental music tends to be organ music heard in and around church buildings. The PSH gave eighteen cases of music (1.95 per cent).[151]

Phantom bell-ringing is also often reported. Naturally, these cases are mostly churches, but off the coast of Forrabury, Cornwall, phantom bells are said to be heard ringing beneath the waves. There are several other such cases. At Llangorse Lake, Breconshire, the bells of a submerged cathedral are also reportedly heard; and the stolen bell of St David's

Cathedral, Pembrokeshire, lost at sea when the thieves were wrecked, is also heard. When grand houses used bell systems to summon the servants, these, too, could ring without apparent cause. One of the most famous cases was that documented by Major Edward Moor in 1834 at Bealings House, Great Bealings, Suffolk. From 2 February to 27 March, the Major, his family and staff witnessed a succession of ringing, at one time so violent that a bell hit the ceiling. After Langenhoe Church was demolished the old vicar gave Peter Underwood the Credence Bell that had so mysteriously rung by itself during the building's period of haunting.[152]

As we saw earlier, sounds of battle, including musical instruments, human voices and firearms, accompanied the phantom Battle of Edgehill. Cromwell's cannon are said still to be heard pounding the walls of Arundel Castle. Ghostly phenomena reported at Battlefield House, quite appropriately, include sounds of fighting.[153]

Olfactory

Strange odours, sometimes pleasant, sometimes not, whose origin is inexplicable are often considered supernatural. Smell can herald the appearance of an apparition or other phenomena, or simply linger mysteriously by itself. When I lived in Bacharach am Rhein in Germany, my study was frequently visited by a flowery scent. Previous research suggested that somewhere between 3 and 8 per cent of hauntings involved smell, although only 1.19 per cent of cases in the PSH did so.[154]

The fragrance of flower-scented perfume heralds the appearance of several ghosts. The headless woman who haunts the Blue Room of Bovey House in Devon is preceded by the scent of lavender. Peter Underwood and his wife Joyce smelt it 'faint but distinct' at 4.30 a.m. one morning.[155] Lilies are associated with the Grey Lady of Bramshill House; gardenias with the Grey Lady of The Gargoyle Club in Soho, London.[156] The Marquess of Bristol's Manor House at Bury St Edmunds has its Scented Lady.[157]

Dr James Gordon-Russell who rose to become a senior NHS psychiatrist was holidaying with his family in Devon. They were staying in an old hotel run by a retired colonel. On the first night Gordon-Russell was awoken by an intense smell like 'rotting leaves or graveyards'. This was accompanied by a sudden temperature drop that caused him to start, shivering uncontrollably, followed by the bedclothes being whisked off the bed. The colonel was unsurprised when they checked out in the morning.[158]

The smell of death was reported as part of wider phenomena haunting a private house in New Orleans investigated by TAPS in February 2005. Investigating a possession case in Falmouth, Massachusetts, they were told that some of the odd things going on in the house included the smell of dirty nappies even though the children in the house had been toilet trained for some years – one was nine years old, the other sixteen.[159]

The smell of opium wafts along Fisher Lane in Cambridge. This narrow medieval alleyway leads off Magdalene Street past the ancient Pickerel Inn, and people taking Alan Murdie's Cambridge Ghost Walk have reported 'a strong perfume, or sweet-smelling substance being burned'. Murdie's research has unearthed evidence of nineteenth-century opium smoking in the vicinity. According to local historian Enid Porter, one of the opium smokers set himself alight with his pipe and, being intoxicated to stupefaction by the drug, burned to death.[160]

Tactile
The landlord kept a fire burning in one of the bedrooms of the Crown Inn at Oxted, Surrey, for ten straight days. The resident ghost, 'Aggie', was associated with a 'cold spot' that made the bedroom 'one of the coldest rooms' that ghost hunter Andrew Green had ever visited. But the landlord's efforts were in vain. The room was still as cold as the grave.[161]

Strangulation, intense cold, electric shocks – hauntings can involve a range of phenomena directly sensed by the body. In some cases these have been known to leave lasting physical marks. In the PSH, 5.96 per cent of the reported phenomena were classified as 'tactile'.

The sensation of warmth or the lack of it is felt by the skin, even if we sometimes feel chilled to the bones, and so it is appropriate to file temperature drops and 'cold spots' under 'tactile'. These are one of the most commonly reported phenomena. Their apparently unaccountable nature readily leads people to a supernatural explanation.

As ghost hunters Jason Hawes and Grant Wilson sat with the Taylor family in their haunted home, psychic Bethany Aculade started trying to communicate with the spirit. Within moments the temperature dropped. The ghost hunters' EMF meters started picking up 'marked fluctuations'. Then the little girl Selena Taylor said she could see her grandmother in the room with them. Her grandmother had died only months earlier. On another occasion TAPS investigator Andrew felt something pass him by on a staircase and measured a sudden ten-degree drop in temperature during an early 1996 investigation in Massachusetts.[162]

It is also the case that heat can be reported in association with paranormal phenomena. TAPS document several instances of rising temperature in connection with alleged paranormal activity.[163] Staying at Ballygally Castle, County Antrim, BBC reporter Kim Lenaghan experienced a temperature rise she estimated to be at least ten degrees in conjunction with the smell of musty vanilla during a séance in the Ghost Room.[164]

A feeling of pressure in the ears has also been reported. When ghost hunters Jason Hawes and Grant Wilson conducted a vigil in the 'slave shack' at The Myrtles, Louisiana, in February 2005, they both experienced the sensation of increased air pressure in their ears at about the same time when camera footage later showed a lamp move fourteen inches across a table, apparently of its own accord.[165]

A generalized prickling sensation has also been attributed

to paranormal activity. As Jason Hawes writes, two of his investigators 'started to feel tingly' when in a reputedly haunted bedroom, which he explains is 'a sign that something or someone was in the room with them'. A similar sensation of ants crawling over one's skin was reported by an eye-witness to the hauntings at Frankenstein's Castle near Darmstadt, Germany. Dizziness and a sense of heaviness were also reported.[166]

When Dirk Bogarde lived at Bendrose House in Amersham Common, Buckinghamshire, he and seven other guests, without knowledge of the others' experiences, all complained of receiving a surge of pain like an electric shock while sleeping in one of the bedrooms.[167] In other cases blows are received but without any sensation of pain. As Sir Simon Marsden prepared to photograph an ancient earthwork in a field next to the church at Long Compton, Oxfordshire, he was physically thrown backwards by an invisible force. He fled the scene in understandable panic and later discovered a large but curiously painless bruise running from the top of his shoulder down his arm to the wrist.[168]

A survivor of the *Lusitania* sinking, a Miss Avis Dolphin, spent some years living at Penkaet Castle in the 1920s. One night in 1925, as she climbed the stairs in the dark, she felt the unmistakable touch of a finger drawing itself across her throat.[169]

A number of ghosts seem to enjoy pinching bottoms and groping behinds. Anecdotal accounts canvassed by www.bbc.co.uk include ghostly goosers at Rhyl Railway Station in Wales, on a stretch of road from Penycae to Rhos in Wales, at the Pwll Gwyn Inn, Afonwen, at an unnamed location in Cornwall and at another in California.[170] TAPS investigated a case of invisible groping that developed into supernatural rape in Newport, Rhode Island, which they attributed to an incubus drawn in by the victim's use of a Ouija board.[171]

The infamous Bell Witch case from Tennessee during 1817–21 involved a dramatic and alarming manifestation of tactile phenomena. John Bell, father of Betsy Bell, the girl at the centre of the haunting, was subjected to extreme bouts of violence as the entity expressed its intention to persecute him to his grave. Bell was afflicted by a range of symptoms that appeared to be connected with the haunting, such as speech-lessness, seizures and unconsciousness. He was also physically assaulted, experiencing, 'a blow on his face which felt like an open hand that almost stunned him'. This in turn precipitated a fit: 'Then his face commenced jerking with fearful contortions. Soon his whole body [. . .] I was terrified by the spectacle of the contortions which seized father.'[172]

Taste
The alleged haunting at Lowes Cottage in Upper Medley, Staffordshire, possibly involved the sense of taste when Josephine Smith described her mouth being filled with something that felt like cotton wool, although she did not say whether it tasted like cotton wool.[173] I have always wondered how physical mediums who extruded ectoplasm from their mouths, among other orifices, would have described the taste of this supposedly supernatural substance.

Other associated phenomena

Animal behaviour
It is a frequent feature of the horror film to find swarms of creepy crawlies as a prelude to the paranormal. It makes a good visual motif, but even though O'Donnell 'arrived at the conclusion that where there are hauntings, there are, more often than not, plagues of beetles', it is something rarely reported in ghost hunting today, although we are reminded of Montague Summers' possessed leg of mutton alive with maggots. In fact, an absence of insects was reported on the fairy hill by Aberfoyle in association with other allegedly paranormal phenomena. Other factors, such as the absence of birdsong, are sometimes reported. In general, the most often

reported behaviour of animals in association with supposed paranormal activity is that of domestic pets, such as cats and dogs.[174]

Human illness

Once a medical theory in ancient Babylon, there are still cases of human illness being ascribed to the actions of malevolent spirits. A haunting in Malaysia was held responsible for two illnesses and a death after exorcists claimed that 'the ghosts had to take another life in order for them to rest in peace'. After a previous owner committed suicide in a house called Balgownie in Prestwick, Ayrshire, it was said that every woman who lived in the house developed an acute illness with symptoms like appendicitis and died. Donald Crichton wrote in to the *Fortean Times* to tell of his mother's near escape from such a fate and of the 'presence' that could be heard walking up the stairs and into one of the bedrooms which frequently scared the family dog, a fierce Alsatian-Labrador mix.[175]

Even if modern medicine rejects such a diagnosis, it cannot be denied that in some instances the victims of haunting appear to be scared to death, or to the point of physical and mental collapse. The entity haunting 50 Berkeley Square, London, was held responsible for several deaths and cases of insanity.[176] The 'ratchety' ghost that terrorized a family living in Ferrestone Road, Hornsey, London, in January 1921 was believed to have scared the youngest child, Muriel, to death and caused the oldest boy, Gordon, to be hospitalized following a nervous breakdown.[177]

Behaviour

Apparitions represent themselves in three manners: purposeful, replay and crisis. As we have seen, Athenodorus's chain rattler was a purposeful ghost. A ghost is also purposeful even if that apparent purpose is not clear to the observer. The poltergeist, for example, seems to act with its own purpose, but the victim(s) and witnesses are usually at a

loss to discover what that is other than a general malevolence
or mischievousness. The crisis apparition takes two forms
– modern and traditional. The modern form was identified
and categorized by members of the SPR in the nineteenth
century and occurs at the moment of individual crisis. The
traditional is part of that folklore transmitted through
families of a particular spirit whose appearance is a warning or death token to a family member. Elliott O'Donnell
contrived the fanciful name of 'Clanogrian' for such family
apparitions. Here we also stray into the realm of fairy, for
the family ghost is somewhat akin to the Celtic banshee
whose wail would portend death or disaster to the hearer
or the hearer's kin and that likewise a banshee might attach
itself to a clan or family.[178]

Interactive

Few ghosts interact with witnesses. Wilson reported that it
was a 'widespread folkloric belief' that ghosts, like Victorian
children, could only speak when spoken to. In some parts of
the UK one must begin any conversation with a variation on
the formula 'In the name of God, why are you troubling me?'
Wilson was unable to say whether this had ever been used
successfully.[179]

However, even O'Donnell, whose stories were most often
of the spectacular kind, noted that 'On the few occasions
that I have spoken to a phantasm, I have received no reply, no
indication even that it has heard me'.[180] Other reports support
O'Donnell's experiences. The wife of a verger at the Church
of St Magnus the Martyr near London Bridge found that
every time she spoke to the strange priest kneeling in front of
the Blessed Sacrament in the Lady Chapel he disappeared.[181]
This typical behaviour has a long history. Aubrey noted in
his *Miscellanies* that in the year 1670 an apparition seen near
Cirencester 'being demanded, whether a good Spirit, or a
bad? returned no answer, but disappeared with a curious Perfume and most melodious Twang.'[182]

In some rare cases a certain responsiveness to the real world has been recorded. The ghost of John Cockburn, a former owner of Penkaet Castle and alleged murderer, has the reputation of being a 'perfect gentleman'. Mysterious rattling and tapping sounds that disturb the night hours in the castle usually cease when one calls out 'Now John, that's childish. Stop it.'[183] The owner of the haunted table in Surrey, mentioned earlier, noted that the apparition appeared to be amazed by the television set, clearly registering a response to its surroundings.

Purposeful

For most people their first and perhaps only encounter with a ghost is through fiction and fictional ghosts are always purposeful. The ghost of Hamlet's father returns to reveal his murder to his son and incite him to exact revenge in Shakespeare's *Hamlet* (*c.* 1599–1601); and the ghost of the murdered Banquo returns to confront his killer with the crime in *Macbeth* (*c.* 1603–7). The spirits in Charles Dickens's *A Christmas Carol* (1843) arrive to transform the character of Ebenezer Scrooge through grim and prophetic messages. With such precedents it is unsurprising that the purposeful ghost continues to be a theme in popular culture, as in, for example, the films *Ghost* (1990), *The Sixth Sense* (1999) and *Ghost Town* (2008). This is a technical requirement of the story: a ghost without a purpose is a poor plot device. But it is also a reflection of (and interaction with) popular belief.

As well as protesting against the improper implementation of funerary customs, such as Athenodorus's ghostly visitor, ghosts also return to right other wrongs. The dead have interceded in legal cases, as when the spirit of Sir Walter Long's (*c.* 1591–1672) first wife allegedly scared the wits out of a clerk who was preparing the legal papers enabling Long's second wife to disinherit her stepson. In 1660 the spirit of Robert Parkin supposedly appeared to Robert Hope of Appleby in the parish church, crying out 'I am murdered' over and over, which prompted the local Justice of the Peace to begin a murder enquiry. Borley's ghostly nun was likewise believed to have returned because of her cruel murder. The ghost of Sellis, murdered by the Duke of Cumberland, son of King George III, appears to simply make a visible deposition of the crime, lying on his deathbed, drenched in blood and a terrible wound gashed across his throat.[184]

The vengeful ghost has its counterpart in the repentant ghost. Remorseful murderers have been said to return to reveal their crimes. In other cases such criminal spirits appear to have no wish to do so. It is Charles Macklin, who murdered another actor in the Theatre Royal's Green Room, rather than his victim who has been seen haunting the scene and there seems to be little about his appearance or actions that suggests regret.[185]

Other ghosts appeared to mark the date of their death, especially in the case of suicides, whilst others simply continued to do what they had always done and followed their everyday routine. In very rare, but most interesting cases, spirits of the dead return to warn the living, make prophecies, or even to give evidence of the afterlife, a mix of purposeful and interactive.[186] For example, it is said that the Duchess of Mazarin returned from the grave to inform Madame de Beauclair, quite precisely, of her impending death.[187]

Repetitive

Replays often occur periodically, but just as easily sporadically. The replay is essentially the same on each occasion of its manifestation: the Roman soldiers walk through the wall again; the white lady glides along the corridor again; and so on. Particularly of note are the anniversary hauntings recurring on the date of the creation of the apparitional phenomena, encompassing suicide, murder, battle and disaster. As such, replays can also be non-human or inanimate in form. The Tay Bridge rail disaster, for example, is a classic inanimate anniversary haunting.

Living

Some years ago a certain Peter Burn of Brampton, Hereford-shire, asked his old nurse, Bessie Harding, about ghosts of the living: 'You believe in wraiths, Bessie?' he asked. 'Believe in wraiths; that I do, master,' she replied, adding, 'yer oan mother, hed she been to the fore, wad hae witnessed to my hevin' seen Esther Railton's wraith. Peer Esther dee'd next day, at the varra hour she meade her appearance to me.'[188]

Already well attested in folklore, as early as 1886, the SPR considered that they had proved beyond doubt the existence of crisis apparitions.[189] Famous examples include Queen Eliz-abeth I, who was supposedly seen prowling the corridors of the Palace of Richmond as she lay comatose and on the brink of death, which finally came on 24 March 1603. But even humble subjects are capable of producing the same effect, nor does impending death have to be a factor; any strong emotion will do. A furious farmer in Kent was still shouting obsceni-ties from his balcony two years after the event, for example.[190]

Several ghost hunters have been responsible for their own phantasms. O'Donnell apparently managed to project him-self arriving home at his house in St Ives, Cornwall. His wife distinctly heard him come in and call out some time before he actually arrived. In the early 1970s, the still living Andrew Green haunted the rockery he had built in his garden at Guild-ford after he had sold the house. Peter Underwood's wraith once popped in for coffee at a small coffee shop in Goodwin's Court, off St Martin's Lane, London.[191]

5

LOCATE (1): WHAT?

'Every house has its haunting spirits,' said Elizabeth Ellett, famous for a scandalous involvement with Edgar Allan Poe, to her gentle readers in *The American Review*.[1] But she was short of the full truth. Almost every conceivable type of property and place has its reputed ghosts, and not just houses. Everywhere has its haunting spirits, if indeed spirits they be. This means that ghost hunting can be conducted almost anywhere; however, there are patterns in the data.

For the Preliminary Survey of Hauntings (PSH), I analysed 263 reputedly haunted locations across the UK to draw up the following categorization and ranking of types of location reputed to be haunted. Most of these (85 per cent) were centred around buildings, including those now ruined.

Residential
By far the most commonly haunted property is a residential one. Given the nature of hauntings, especially apparitions, as the reported observation of non-physical people, this is

unsurprising. Both the event and the witness are much more likely to be found in a location where both spend (or have spent) the most time. The residential category is also perhaps the largest, encompassing everything from council houses to royal palaces, although I have not included temporary residential locations such as former coaching inns, hotels, halls of residence, etc., or religious buildings used as residences. Of all the types of residential property the country house was the most haunted, accounting for 52 per cent of all residences, or 23 per cent of the total. A country house is a vague concept and the term here embraces manor houses, i.e., those properties formerly serving a feudal function, and what are also called stately homes. Again it should not be surprising to find the country house looming so large in the figures; many of them are among some of the oldest inhabited buildings and their broad range of purposes has ensured their continuing use and value, and hence survival. While some can be relatively modest, little more than farmhouses with airs, others of these country houses, such as Knebworth House, rival palaces in their size and grandeur.

Most haunted types of location

Rank	Location type	Number	Percentage (%)
1	Residential	113	42.97
2	Religious	36	13.69
3	Recreational	27	10.27
4	Military	24	9.13
5	Transport	15	5.70
6	Workplace	9	3.42
7	Educational	6	2.28
8	Burial site	6	2.28
9	Coastal	4	1.52
–	Other buildings	3	1.14
–	Other locations	20	7.60
	Total	263	100.00

Investigation report: Michelham Priory

Many things happened on both occasions I visited, the most memorable being standing in the well of the staircase and looking up to see a scrap of black cloth apparently travelling up the stairs at some speed. I said 'Oh look!' but didn't say what I was seeing, and the organizer ran up the stairs, telling me not to say any more about what I was seeing (presumably not to bring suggestion into the event). When she came down, we compared notes, and she had seen a figure dressed in a black robe running up the stairs, apparently at the same speed and place as my scrap of black cloth. Of course, there was nothing there when she reached the top of the stairs (she was only a few feet away from the 'cloth').

At the end of the evening, when the other members had left and there was only me, the organizer and the editor left to pack up, the organizer said she would show me where the stairs to the Abbot's chamber used to be. We three squeezed into the little space where the foot of the stairs would have been and the walkie talkie that she was carrying (which had been switched off, along with all the other walkie talkies) came on and an elderly, male voice shouted out something that might (or might not) have been 'Get out!' The others certainly heard it as this. I couldn't be 100% sure, but it was a viable interpretation.

Max, Ghost Club member (GHS, 2012)

Religious buildings

Again this is a diverse category including not just places of worship but also the lodgings of ecclesiastical personnel. Borley Rectory is the most notable member of this category and it is remarkable that the vicarages, rectories and parsonages that housed the Church's army of clerics are frequently among the most haunted locations. Although we could construe these as simply 'residential' there is perhaps something worth noting about their religious ownership and incumbency. Here we also find the monasteries, nunneries, priories, friaries and abbeys, as well as the ubiquitous church and grander cathedral. Reports of ghostly monks and nuns feature prominently in the annals of the supernatural, so it unsurprising that their places of work, worship and domicile are among the most haunted. We should also consider that many country houses incorporate older ecclesiastical buildings, especially those seized after the Dissolution of the Monasteries, or indeed feature their own chapels and vaults, as well as 'priest holes' for the concealment of Catholic clergymen. These special considerations aside, religious buildings account for almost 14 per cent of the total, placing them ahead of many other types of property.

Recreational

The places of human recreation are multitudinous, from vile drinking dens to magnificent opera houses with cosy country pubs somewhere in between. The survey included twenty-seven such places, being a little over 10 per cent of the total. Formerly there was a distinction between drinking establishments and inns, which offered accommodation in addition to food and drink, but the rise of 'bed and breakfast' and modern hotels, and the demise of coaching, which required numerous staging posts given the duration of the journeys involved, has brought the two nearer in meaning: a place for recreational drinking. These pubs and inns formed the largest sub-category, accounting for over half (59 per cent) of all recreational venues with alleged hauntings.

After having enjoyed a pint in the decidedly chilly haunted corner and quizzed the barman about witchcraft rituals that reputedly took place upstairs, I was a little disappointed to find that Nicky-Tams Bar & Bothy, Stirling, oft proclaimed as Scotland's 'most haunted pub', did not make the list. In general, this

Most haunted pubs in the UK by reputation[2]

Rank	Name	Location	Score
1	The Red Lion	Avebury, Wiltshire	39
2	The Mermaid Inn	Rye, East Sussex	38
3	The Grenadier	Wilton Row, London	35
4	The Devil's Stone Inn	Shebbear, Devon	33
5	The Bucket of Blood	Phillack, Hayle, Cornwall	28
6	The Ostrich Inn	Colnbrook, Buckinghamshire	27
7	The Skirrid Inn	Llanfihangel Crucorney, Wales	23
8	The Hyde Tavern	Winchester, Hampshire	18
8	The George and Dragon	West Wycombe, Buckinghamshire	18
9	Jamaica Inn	Bolventor, Cornwall	17
10	The Ancient Ram Inn	Wotton-under-Edge, Gloucestershire	15
10	The King's Arms	Monkton Farleigh, Wiltshire	15

reflected an English bias in the published top ten listings of haunted pubs. The Skirrid Inn, Wales, only makes the listing by virtue of having won the Strongbow campaign to find the most haunted pub in 2004, judged by Richard Jones.[3]

After his experiences at the Ferry Boat Inn, Holywell, in the 1950s, psychic researcher Tony Cornell advised against investigating public houses: 'No serious investigation of alleged psychical phenomena is ever likely to produce worthwhile results in a pub.'[4]

The recreational category also comprised three theatres, two cinemas and one place of 'other entertainment'. London's once famous Gargoyle Club in Soho had its spooks, mingling with the clientele who have included the likes of Dylan Thomas and then latterly with the strippers who worked there. Worth mentioning in this vein is Liquid Assets at 118 New Market Ave, South Plainfield, New Jersey, another reputedly haunted strip club, still frequented by the ghost of mobster 'Mad Dog' Vincent Coll.[5]

Also included here were hotels, as much of their usage depends on recreational travel and many also offer public bars. However, as a temporary residence they form their own subset, being not entirely recreational nor yet completely residential, combining the qualities of being a holiday location to some and a workplace to others. The five hotels covered accounted for 1.9 per cent of the total, or 18.5 per cent of this category.

Military

Foremost in this category are the ancient castles, towers, fortresses and other fortifications that still dominate much of Britain's landscape. 'Military' is a modern term to describe these structures, but their purpose undoubtedly fits the description. Serving as garrisons and strategic defences, castles were also administrative power bases in the feudal period, governing, as well as enforcing. In less troubled times their military aspects were tempered by the requirements of the people who lived there and many old castles were remodelled as primarily residential buildings, but with a lingering martial air. The castle could range from an imposing edifice like Windsor Castle, Britain's largest castle, to a simple fortified farmhouse or pele tower. Less commonly haunted than one might think, or simply less common, they accounted for under 10 per cent of haunted places.

Modern military installations

Airfields, bunkers, and bases of various kinds also feature in reports of paranormal activity. A good example of the modern military installation is Fort Chaffee, outside Fort Smith, Arkansas. A WWII-era military camp, it has served as a training camp, German POW camp, refugee camp and film location. It is also reputedly haunted and was featured on *Ghost Adventures* in 2010.

Most haunted castles in the world by reputation[6]

Rank	Name	Country	Location	Score
1	Edinburgh Castle	Scotland	Edinburgh, Lothian	67
2	Castle Bran	Romania	Near Braşov, Transylvania	63
3	Chillingham Castle	England	Chillingham, Northumberland	49
4	Dragsholm Slot	Denmark	Odsherred, Zealand	36
5	Berry Pomeroy Castle	England	Berry Pomeroy, Devon	29
6	Belcourt Castle	USA	Newport, Rhode Island	26
7	Tamworth Castle	England	Tamworth, Staffordshire	21
8	Warwick Castle	England	Warwick, Warwickshire	20
8	Burg Eltz	Germany	Near Münstermaifeld, Rheinland-Pfalz	20
8	Ballygally Castle	N. Ireland	Ballygally, County Antrim	20
9	Predjama Castle	Slovenia	Near Postojna	19
9	Bodelwyddan Castle	Wales	Near Rhyl, Denbighshire	19
10	Tower of London	England	London	18
10	Leap Castle	Ireland	Near Roscrea, County Offaly	18
10	Newcastle Castle Keep	England	Newcastle-upon-Tyne, Tyne and Wear	18

Transport networks

Ghost trains whistle over phantom bridges, spectral vehicles speed down haunted highways, phantom coaches are pulled by headless horses along midnight roads, ghost ships ply their

Investigation report: Coalhouse Fort
In one of the tunnels, there were quite a few of us, and I was acutely aware of someone having moved and standing next to me. I turned to look and see who it was, but there was no one there. I was then very aware of two figures in my mind's eye standing at the back of the room, and I got the feeling they were angry and a bit nasty.

Iain Lister, East Anglia investigations co-ordinator,
Ghost Club (GHS, 2012)

old trade routes, even an Egyptian mummy lingers on one London Tube station platform: the arteries of communication over land, sea and air are filled with their quota of restless spirits. Streets alone accounted for a little under 6 per cent of haunted places, but there was only one bridge in the survey.

In 2006 the roadbuilding company Tarmac produced a list of the most haunted highways in Britain. The M6 motorway came top with ghostly Roman soldiers, a female apparition and a lorry that drives up the wrong side of the road, but Scotland's A9 appeared twice on the list with haunted stretches in the Highlands and on The Mound near Dornoch. Tony Simmons, responsible for co-ordinating the research, said that 'We compiled the top 10 on the basis of the clarity of the sightings rather than just the number of experiences . . . it's easy to mistake swirling mist for something more sinister.'[7]

Workplace

Our places of work are as diverse as the places we live in; sometimes they overlap, but, on the whole, they seem to be much less haunted. The category 'workplace' had to be narrow in meaning to avoid including buildings that were better listed separately. So whilst a castle was (and sometimes still is) a workplace to its garrison, a hospital is a workplace to nurses and doctors, a hotel is a workplace to its staff, a public house is a workplace to its landlord, and so on, we usually think of these locations as other than workplaces. Included in the survey was a fire station, a police station, a shop and several mills, accounting for less than 4 per cent of the total.

Educational establishments

From the PSH, three Oxbridge colleges, one university, one school and one museum all claim their ghosts. Such places often provide a long history and quaint traditions, as well as a transitory and intense student body, that may or may not be conducive to ghost stories. Most of these places are also unlikely to want the adverse publicity that goes with rumours of haunting, and establishments in current use will

Most haunted highways in the UK (Tarmac survey)

Rank	Road	Haunting
1	The M6	Roman soldiers, woman, lorry
2	A9, Highlands	Coach, horses and footmen
3	Platt Lane, Leigh, Manchester	Eyes watching from bushes
4	High Street and Suffield Road, Great Yarmouth	Dog
5	Gloucester Drive, Finsbury Park, London	Playing children
6	B4293 at Devauden, Wales	Voice of a guardian angel
7	B3314 near Tintagel, Cornwall	Victorian woman
8	A9, The Mound between Dornoch and Golspie	Victorian man
9	B1403 near Doncaster, South Yorkshire	Marching soldier
10	Drews Lane, Ward End, Birmingham	Overturned cars

be difficult locations to investigate for both practical and political reasons. In all, places of education or edification account for a fraction over 2 per cent of the total.

The *Telegraph* newspaper produced its own top ten list of haunted universities in the UK. St Andrews topped the list, with Durham and Southampton coming second and third.[8] However, Christ's College, Cambridge, and Oxford's Merton and St John's colleges were the places mentioned in the PSH. In the USA, Ohio University and Penn State University are frequently described as the most haunted colleges, with the University of Illinois and Boston University also featuring prominently, although on looks alone Hower House of the University of Akron, a colonial Gothic fantasy, would win any prize.[9]

Burial sites

It is a trope of the horror genre that the haunted house is built over an old Native American burial ground, invoking desecration of a sacred site multiplied by a nameless heathen horror and propped up by the logic of 'they're more spiritual than we are' – remember all the Red Indian spirit guides of yesteryear – hence more deadly when dead. But the reason it is a regular plot device is because it is sometimes true. Going one better than the stereotype, Forest Park (Pinewood) Cemetery, Troy, New York, lovingly dubbed 'the Gateway to Hell', is reputed to have been laid out over an Indian burial ground: a cemetery on a cemetery.[10]

All places associated with the dead are associated with their spirits. These include Christian graveyards and catacombs, pagan burial grounds, Jewish cemeteries and those of other religions. The Singapore Ghost Hunting Club found a haunted Muslim cemetery, Pusara Abadi, in Choa Chu Kang, Singapore's largest cemetery, and final resting place for people of many different faiths.[11]

Some ghost hunters, such as Troy Taylor, believe that cemeteries are 'spirit portals' or 'doorways', but there is no evidence for such a theory.[12] However firmly the haunted graveyard is lodged in our collective imaginations as a location connected with reports of paranormal phenomena, it comes low on the list. On analysis, only six locations or just over 2 per cent of cases in the UK were burial sites. These were mostly formal Christian cemeteries.

We could, of course, add other places to bolster the numbers. Churches, with their vaults full of mouldering bones, and many an old mansion or castle with a skeleton in its walls, could come under the purview of 'burial site' in the broadest sense, but their inclusion would only complicate the category.

Some of the best-known cemeteries are worth a visit in their own right, including Prague's Old Jewish Cemetery, Paris's Père Lachaise Cemetery, Greyfriars in Edinburgh and London's justly renowned Highgate Cemetery.

Coastal

The most common coastal phenomenon reported in the PSH was the ringing of submerged bells, as at St Ives, Cornwall, and Aberdovey, Merionethshire. There was also the apparition of a sailor reputed to haunt Sandwood Bay, Cape Wrath, in Scotland, and a whole phantom boat and crew at Forrabury near Boscastle, Cornwall, again with ringing bells.

Other buildings

There was only one hospital on the list, but hospitals, nursing homes and other care facilities have their fair share of the supernatural. Ghost hunter Troy Taylor found from his own experience that such places were generally reluctant to broadcast their ghosts and rarely welcomed investigators. Even New Zealand's former hospital turned haunted attraction, Spookers, does not like to discuss the odd things that go on there for fear of overly scaring the staff.

Operational prisons, like working hospitals, can be difficult places to investigate, but again prisons have their ghosts. A history of incarcerated criminals, harsh penalties, suicides, murders

Most haunted cemeteries worldwide by reputation[13]

Rank	Name	Country	Location	Score
1	St Louis Cemetery No. 1	USA	New Orleans, Louisiana	28
2	Highgate Cemetery	UK	London	27
3	Père Lachaise	France	Paris	25
4	Catacombes de Paris	France	Paris	18
5	Catacombe di Roma*	Italy	Rome	16
6	Stull Cemetery	USA	Stull, Kansas	15
7	Resurrection Cemetery	USA	Chicago, Illinois	11
7	Garden of Hope Cemetery	USA	Gautier, Mississippi	11
8	Greenwood Cemetery	USA	Decatur, Illinois	10
9	Rookwood Cemetery	Australia	Sydney	9
10	Westminster Hall and Western Burial Ground	USA	Baltimore, Maryland	8

*The 'catacombs' are not a single location, but refer to many underground burial sites around Rome. None of the sources consulted specified which was meant, but the largest, oldest and best preserved site is the Catacombe di San Domitilla.

and executions leaves its mark on the psychic fabric, so to speak, and many old jails, despite having released their last prisoners, cling on to their spirits. There were only three 'other buildings' in the survey, comprising just over 1 per cent of the total.

Other outside locations

Death by violence has long led to the belief that such souls linger on earth. Battlefields and murder scenes are obvious locations. Where the life blood soaks the ground, the stain of death remains. However, only two battlefields were surveyed: Edgehill, Warwickshire, scene of the Civil War clash of 1642, and the less well-known Slaybrook Corner, Saltwood, Kent.

In general, the range was diverse, including fields, wood-
land, a sports pitch, two race tracks, an execution site, a body
of inland water and a number of unidentifiable places. Other
outside locations accounted for less than 8 per cent of the total.

6

LOCATE (2): WHERE?

It is not in one volume that the authentic examples of haunted houses could be collected. It is rather in ten or twenty volumes.[1]

When the French astronomer Flammarion wrote the above it was 1923. Since then, to say that ten or twenty more volumes have been added to the shelves of paranormal investigation is to grossly underestimate the situation. When researching his book *The Haunted Realm*, Sir Simon Marsden compiled a list of over 2,000 locations in Britain and Ireland alone. He visited about 1,500 of them, but only fifty ended up in the book.[2]

Instead of attempting to cram a gazetteer into these pages, I have taken a different approach and asked which are the places believed to be the most haunted. For it is surely in these places that the ghost hunter stands the greatest chance of success. It is also the case that this tells us something about our social world. It reveals the beliefs and expectations that people have of these places. Because this is a book on ghost hunting, it is also useful to discover which locations have been the most ghost hunted. As we will see, 'most haunted' and 'most hunted' are not always the same thing.

Analysis

Most haunted locations worldwide by reputation
To find the places reputed to be the most haunted I analysed twenty-nine 'top ten' listings online and in printed sources. There was a total of ninety-five different locations mentioned, ranging from Alcatraz to Woodchester Mansion. Many of these locations received only one vote, even well-known sites such as Chillingham Castle and the Jamaica Inn. There were many interesting locations on the lists, even if some of them would not immediately spring to mind in connection with ghosts. Nick Redfern drew attention to the fact that there were more than just aliens rumoured to haunt Roswell, New Mexico.[3] It is particularly notable that both Edinburgh and London had two locations ranked in the top twenty. Of them all, the Tower of London received the highest score and number of votes.

However, some curious quirks in the data emerged. Looking only at castles reputed to be the most haunted worldwide, Edinburgh Castle came out the clear winner, but considered as a worldwide location it only came second. Considered as a UK location, it did not even make the top ten. In contrast, the Tower of London, bottom of the castles list, came out top as a worldwide location. It seems that people think of different things when they are considering the most haunted castle, or the most haunted place in general.

We can also see from the table that despite accounting for few of the 263 locations surveyed, military locations (castles) featured prominently on reputation ranking, although in line with the general trend most (54 per cent) were residential properties. In some regards, people's perceptions of what a haunted location should be clearly affected the rankings,

Most haunted locations worldwide by reputation (1 to 10)

Rank	Location	Country	Category	Score	Votes
1	The Tower of London	England	Military	119	17
2	Edinburgh Castle	Scotland	Military	90	15
3	The Myrtles Plantation	USA	Residential	73	12
4	The Whaley House	USA	Residential	71	13
5	The White House	USA	Residential	63	13
6	RMS *Queen Mary*	USA	Transport	60	12
7	Bhangarh Fort	India	Military	53	8
8	The Winchester Mystery House	USA	Residential	51	7
9	Raynham Hall	England	Residential	48	8
9	Monte Cristo	Australia	Residential	48	7
9	Catacombes de Paris	France	Burial Site	48	7
9	The LaLaurie Mansion	USA	Residential	48	7
10	Borley Rectory	England	Religious	37	8

although both The White House and RMS *Queen Mary* go against type. Different sources admit different biases: most of the worldwide listings were American, for example, surely accounting for the fact that almost 45 per cent of the top twenty are in the USA.

Most haunted locations in the UK by reputation
As might be expected, opinion on which is the UK's most haunted location is sharply divided. Blickling Hall, Norfolk, is considered to be 'the most haunted country house in Britain' by *Country Life* magazine, a view shared with the National Trust,[4] whereas the official tourist website Visit Britain hands the prize to Highgate Cemetery, London.[5] Meanwhile, the *Guardian* newspaper decided that Knowlton

Most haunted locations worldwide by reputation (11 to 20)

Rank	Location	Country	Category	Score	Votes
11	Waverly Hills Sanatorium	USA	Hospital	32	7
11	The Stanley Hotel	USA	Recreational	32	7
11	Eastern State Penitentiary	USA	Other	32	6
11	The Amityville House	USA	Residential	32	5
12	Rose Hall Great House	Jamaica	Residential	30	5
13	Bran Castle	Romania	Military	26	4
14	Coliseum, Rome	Italy	Recreational	25	4
14	Auschwitz-Birkenau	Poland	Other	25	4
15	Aokigahara Forest	Japan	Outside	22	4
15	Edinburgh Vaults	Scotland	Other	22	3
16	Gettysburg	USA	Outside	21	6
17	50 Berkeley Square, London	England	Residential	19	3
18	The Bell Farm	USA	Residential	18	5
19	Pluckley	England	Mixed	17	2
19	Changi Beach	Singapore	Other	17	2
20	Alcatraz Prison	USA	Other	16	2

Church in Dorset should have this honour.[6] Clearly, we need to find a way round these differences.

To find the most haunted location in the UK by reputation a total of fifteen different sources were analysed, ranging from the *Guardian* newspaper, to the official tourist website www.visitbritain.com, to niche paranormal websites such as Richard Holland's www.uncannyuk.com. This gave a surprising diversity of opinion. A total of ninety-one different locations were mentioned. The list was also quite different from the worldwide reputation ranking. To an extent this was

Most haunted locations in the UK by reputation

Rank	Location		Score	Votes
1	Borley Rectory	Essex	44	6
2	The Tower of London	London	42	8
3	Pendle Hill	Lancashire	40	5
4	Blickling Hall	Norfolk	37	4
5	The Ancient Ram Inn	Gloucestershire	35	7
6	Glamis Castle	Angus	34	5
7	Pluckley Village	Kent	31	4
8	Chillingham Castle	Northumberland	25	4
9	Highgate Cemetery	London	20	2
10	The Jamaica Inn	Cornwall	18	2

unsurprising since the sources were not the same and, apart from one, were all UK-based sites.

Despite having been burnt down and demolished, Borley Rectory still enjoys its reputation as not only 'the most haunted house in England', but in the UK overall. As Paul Tabori and Peter Underwood found, 'there is reasonable evidence that inexplicable happenings took place and still take place at Borley'.[7] The Tower of London received more votes, but scored slightly less, coming second in the ranking. Blickling Hall and Highgate fared less well, but still received respectable rankings of fourth and ninth respectively. However, the *Guardian*'s choice of Knowlton Church failed to make the top ten, coming 18th.

The most hunted

To find out the most investigated locations in Great Britain and the Republic of Ireland I examined the investigations of twenty-three individuals, groups and television programmes from the UK and USA, including old-school ghost hunters Andrew Green and Peter Underwood, and established organizations such as the Ghost Club, as well as the recent wave of paranormal reality TV such as *Most Haunted*, *Ghost Hunters*

Most investigated locations in the UK

Rank	Location	Investigations
1	Edinburgh Vaults (Blair and Niddry Streets)	10
2	Mary King's Close, Edinburgh	7
3	Morecambe Winter Gardens, Lancashire	6
4	The Ancient Ram Inn, Gloucestershire	5
5	Coalhouse Fort, Essex	4
5	Jedburgh Castle Jail, Scottish Borders	4
5	Samlesbury Hall, Lancashire	4
5	Tutbury Castle, Staffordshire	4
5	Woodchester Mansion, Gloucestershire	4

International and the rest. In total there were 571 separate locations and 702 investigations. Most of the locations were in England (80 per cent), with only 10 per cent in Scotland, 5 per cent in Wales, 3 per cent in Northern Ireland and 2 per cent in the Republic of Ireland. Most of the investigations were single investigations (85 per cent), a further 11 per cent had been investigated twice, but for the purposes of this study I was interested in the remaining 4 per cent that had been investigated three or more times. None of the locations in the Republic of Ireland was investigated more than once, and so the following results can be considered as limited to the UK.

The results were surprisingly different to the general perception of the most haunted locations worldwide and in the UK. Notably, Edinburgh Castle, number two on the worldwide reputations list, only had one investigation to its name. Similarly, the Tower of London has only been investigated once. Despite their high tourist volumes, both locations are still the headquarters of British Army regiments and are the guarded repositories of historic and extremely precious artefacts. These factors undoubtedly make official ghost hunting on the premises a challenging proposition. One could not imagine Derek Acorah, bathed in *Most Haunted*'s trademark

Most investigated UK towns and cities

Town/city	Locations	Investigations	Ranking
London	30	34	1
Edinburgh	9	25	2
Liverpool	10	12	3
Glasgow	7	11	4
Derby	8	10	5
Pluckley	7	10	6
Manchester	8	9	7
Stratford-upon-Avon	6	8	8
Lancaster	6	6	9
Bristol	4	6	10

green glow, having a chat with spirit guide 'Sam' in the Tower's Jewel House, for example. For the ghost hunter, the most investigated locations are important for the greater wealth of data they provide, as most of the investigation reports are available from those responsible.[8]

Selected locations

London
With thirty locations and thirty-four investigations, London heads the list of ghost hunted cities in the UK. Given its ancient history and sprawling size, this is, perhaps, of no surprise, but that should not usher in complacency. The capital of the UK, is also the capital of hauntings. Highlights include The Grenadier, third most haunted public house in the UK by reputation, but certainly not the only one in London. Other haunted pubs of note are The Blind Beggar in the East End, and The Spaniards Inn, said to be haunted by the infamous highwayman Dick Turpin; both featured on *Most Haunted Live!* The Queen's House, Greenwich, was the scene of one of the most famous alleged ghost photographs: a figure (or figures) ascending the Tulip Staircase captured by a Canadian

tourist, and considered by Peter Underwood to be 'the most remarkable and interesting ghost photograph I have come across in fifty years of serious psychical investigation'.[9] At the top of the list (worldwide and UK) are the Tower of London and 50 Berkeley Square.

THE TOWER OF LONDON

'The Tower is the most haunted ground in London,' said Charles Dickens, adding, 'and it would be strange if it were not, remembering the tragedies that were acted there during many successive centuries.'[10] His opinion is not unusual. To see the broken tooth of the White Tower blanched by sharp sunlight and framed by blue-black thunderous skies, a millennium of earthwork and stonework as buttress against the changing world around it, is to gaze upon what Dickens called 'the stronghold of ghosts'. That was how this most famous of London landmarks presented itself to me on my last visit: dramatic, 'background of all the darkest scenes of English history', supercharged with history, and perhaps also with the supernatural.[11]

Although the Tower of London chalked up only one investigation among those I analysed for the 'most hunted' list, it does not mean that no other ghost hunter has ever set foot within its walls. Several paranormal groups have entered the Tower as tourists and have written up their visits, such as Canada's Montreal Paranormal Investigations and Paranormal Explorers.

However, the first and so far only officially condoned investigation was orchestrated by BBC Worldwide and Galaxy Productions in 2001. *Ghostwatch Live!* was, as the name suggests, a live broadcast from the Tower with simultaneous webcast on UK Horizons. Presented by actors Paul Darrow (*Blake's 7*) and Claudia Christian (*Babylon 5*), the show featured Ross Hemsworth and Andy Matthews fielding what were described by the BBC as 'temperature gauges, "black cameras" which turn night-time into day and infrared light', as well as minicams, DV cams and EMF meters to cover Sir Walter Raleigh's study in the Bloody Tower, the Bell Tower, the Chapel of St Peter ad Vincula and the Beauchamp Tower.[12]

Asked whether the investigation had been a success, Matthews pointed out that the EMF meters were 'useless with all that equipment about', and as for the night-vision cameras, 'all they caught were dust orbs'. At that point in time the prosaic nature of orbs had yet to be realized and EVP was not considered by the BBC. The live nature of the broadcast also caused its problems. As Matthews explained, 'constant interviews on camera, screen set-ups, re-takes for trailers, etc., etc., make it very difficult to get anything done'. However, at one point Matthews 'sensed something standing before me'. A photographer was on hand to snap a shot. Matthews felt it move and the photographer took another shot. The film later revealed a strange blue light moving in front of him.[13]

So far, my investigations have turned up fifty-four instances of haunting phenomena ranging from the smell of incense, to footsteps, to shadows, to full-blown apparitions reported in twenty-two separate locations in the castle. Areas of particular activity are St Thomas's Tower, the Bloody Tower, the Queen's House and the Martin Tower. When Patrick Zakhm of Montreal Paranormal Investigations visited the Tower in 2009, staff told him that the Salt Tower was the most haunted.[14]

The tales of haunting begin at the very gates of this ancient fortification. A Medieval procession bearing a headless corpse with its head tucked under its arm was witnessed by a sentry during WWII in the Tower entrance. Two painters in 1977 were alarmed by the sound of footsteps coming from the deserted battlements of the Middle Tower which stands over the entranceway. Proceeding inside, the Outer Ward between the outer and inner walls has seen a doughty Scots Guardsman panicked by being followed by phantoms on his beat between Byward Tower and Traitors' Gate in 1968. Further

Types of haunting at the Tower of London

Type		Count	Percentage (%)
Visual			
	human	21	38.9
	non-human	2	3.7
	animal	1	1.9
	inanimate	1	1.9
	luminescence	1	1.9
	physical interference	3	5.6
Non-visual			
	emotional	2	3.7
	olfactory	3	5.6
	auditory	13	24.1
	tactile	6	11.1
	unidentified	1	1.9
	total	54	100.0

up in Water Lane another sentry was scared witless by a headless figure in a cloak. And that is just the beginning.[15]

In total, there have been twenty-six apparitions recorded at the Tower. These have been mostly human, but also include what has been described as a bear-like apparition outside the Martin Tower, as well as a bluish form hovering in Tower Green over by the Queen's House, and a bizarre tube of swirling bluish white liquid seen in a room of the Martin Tower in 1817. The more famous human apparitions have included Henry VI who haunts Wakefield Tower where he was murdered in 1471, Sir Walter Raleigh and the two princes in the Bloody Tower, and a procession led by Anne Boleyn in the Chapel of St Peter ad Vincula, not forgetting poor Margaret Pole who is said to still be seen being chased by the axe man on Tower Green. The next most commonly reported type of haunting was auditory phenomena – sounds of footsteps, gasping, chanting, screaming and even a baby crying. Other incidents have involved poltergeist-like activity, such as objects being moved by unseen hands in the Beauchamp Tower, and sentries being pelted with stones from the Wakefield Tower by invisible assailants. All in all, the Tower is a rich store of supernatural encounters; a fertile field for the ghost hunter, but one that is likely to remain closed to further officially sanctioned investigation for the time being.

50 BERKELEY SQUARE

No. 50 Berkeley Square is a modest eighteenth-century townhouse in the most genteel district of Mayfair, the polar opposite of the forbidding Tower of London. Yet this neat four-storey brick building has the reputation of being 'the most haunted house in London' with 'at least one room in which the atmosphere is supernaturally fatal to mind and body'.[16] Here, where Augustus Hare said 'the best trees of any square in London' stand and the nightingale sang in the dark days of WWII, is 'that gloomy pile', 'grim and gaunt' where 'ghosts and ghouls should have their way'.[17]

In 1872 a small notice appeared in *Notes and Queries* asking for further information about the haunting of No. 50. George William, Lord Lyttelton, replied, confirming that the house was reputed to be haunted, and hinted at 'strange stories' which he refused to divulge.[18] This inspired a certain E.M.P. to undertake his own investigations. 'I took the trouble to ring the bell,' he said, but got no information from the surly old woman who answered. He asked around the square and was told that strange noises were heard by those in neighbouring houses and at a shop he learned of a woman who had lost her reason after spending a night there.[19]

Lady Dorothy Nevill, who had been born at No. 11 in the square in 1826, later recalled that No. 50 'used always to be known as the haunted house'.[20] A tenant called Myers was said to have lost his reason after being jilted on his wedding day and lived a reclusive, shadowy existence in the building. In consequence the building fell into disrepair and Myers's nocturnal habits gave rise to rumours of ghosts. There was talk of a gang of coiners using an underground tunnel to access the building for their nefarious purposes and making all sorts of ghoulish din to frighten away anyone who might discover them. Screams were reputedly heard by pedestrians as they passed by at the dead of night.[21]

Perhaps picking up on a story in *Mayfair* magazine in 1879 about a room being used for hours on end for some unnamed purpose, the Revd Frederick Lee suggested that a 'French adept' (Eliphas Levi) and the novelist Edward Bulwer-Lytton (1803–73) had been involved in séances and magical rituals in the self-same haunted room.[22] In 1907 it was said that a 'Mr Du Pré of Wilton Park' imprisoned his lunatic brother in the attic. This brother, on account of his frenzy, could only be fed through a hole in the door and alarmed the neighbours with his shrieks and howls, until Du Pré ended the wretch's life with a bullet.[23]

Elliott O'Donnell could not resist the story and added his own unique embellishment. In the 1870s, he said, two sailors – Charlie and Bert – had broken into the unoccupied building to shelter for the night, but one of them never left, driven to destruction by the unnamed thing.[24] By 1945 Harry Price could add a number of other accounts of the haunting or hauntings at No. 50, including further apparitions, suicides, insanity and poltergeist-like activity involving ringing bells, thrown objects and smashing windows.[25]

A whole host of new characters enter the scene in the late twentieth century. Sir Robert Warboys becomes the foolhardy adventurer who stays in the haunted room, armed with gun and bell, to be found dead of fright. Lord Lyttelton – and there is some confusion over which one – also spends a night in the haunted room with a gun loaded with silver sixpennies and survives to tell the tale.[26]

Gone now is all the grimness and gauntness. No. 50 is a smart, well-cared-for building in a smart, well-cared-for square. Even by 1880 it was noted that the previously unkempt façade had been spruced up with a taste of 'soap, paint and whitewash'.[27] Since 1938 the building has been occupied by the far-famed antiquarian booksellers Maggs Bros, Ltd.[28] When in 1969 they issued their catalogue of books on witch-craft and magic they sought to calm potential customers, noting 'as the "ghost" in question was exorcized by a Bishop, no one need fear a visit to 50 Berkeley Square now'.[29]

Dennis Bardens made some enquiries in the 1960s or ear-lier, but the then proprietor told him that he himself had never encountered anything out of the ordinary. In 2008 the Hampshire Ghost Club applied to Maggs Bros to conduct an investigation of the premises. 'I'm afraid we're not terribly keen on the topic,' was the reply.[30]

Edinburgh

Helped by the efforts of the city's hauntrepreneurs, the fame of Edinburgh's ghosts has grown considerably over the years. We find the vaults being touted in the German newspaper *Rheinische Post* as the most haunted location in the UK, for example. So much have ghosts become a part of Edin-burgh that Lonely Planet's guide to the city has a section on 'Haunted Edinburgh'.[31] When compiling volume three of *Ghosts Caught on Film*, Gordon Rutter was bemused to find that Edinburgh cropped up time and again in his research, so much so that he was led to wonder whether it was the world's most haunted city. He is not the only one.[32]

In 2001 Professor Richard Wiseman led a ten-day investi-gation into haunting with a team that included Drs Caroline Watt, Ciarán O'Keeffe and James Houran, and over 200 vol-unteers. He chose to come to Edinburgh, picking the castle, the vaults and Mary King's Close as his locations. Asked why, he said 'We decided to come to Edinburgh because it has an amazing reputation for being haunted. What better place to come if you want to carry out an investigation into ghosts?' Wiseman launched his 2001 investigation in the dungeons of Edinburgh Castle.[33]

EDINBURGH CASTLE

The extinct volcano that rears its stony head as Castle Rock
is the keystone of Edinburgh. A manmade lava of streets and
buildings flows from it to condense in the distinctive dragon's
tail of the High Street (Royal Mile), jagged with tenements,
and the interminable sweep of the Mound as it descends into
the imprisoning grid of the New Town. It is a town of snakes
and ladders, constantly rising and falling away. Overlooking
it all, a crown of battlements and cannon on the Rock, is Edinburgh Castle, the reputed world champion of haunted castles.

A history of war, siege and destruction has remodelled this
crown many times, leaving a utilitarian defensive work, lacking any of the frills so customary among the Gothic towers of
Europe. Angular gunnery platforms girdle a group of buildings dominated by the dismal block of the New Barracks, the
horseshoe of the Royal Palace, Great Hall and Queen Anne
Building and the brooding bulge of the Half Moon Battery.

Over a million tourists march through the Portcullis Gate
every year, despite the fact that the castle is still the regimen-
tal headquarters of the Royal Regiment of Scotland. The garrison guards the precious Honours of Scotland and armed
sentries flank the gatehouse. Another continuing presence is
the seven or more ghosts believed to haunt the castle.

The castle's best-known legend concerns a phantom piper
and a secret passageway to Holyrood Palace. Numerous tunnels are believed to honeycomb the laval foundations of the
castle, snaking secret ways here and there, and especially
to the Palace of Holyrood at the bottom of the Royal Mile.
Excavations in 1912 discovered some of these hidden burrow-
ings, believed to date from the time of King David II (1329–
70). According to the story, it was decided to send a solitary
explorer – a piper – into the darkness to find the route to the
Palace. He played his pipes so that those above ground could
follow his progress, and follow they did, for a while. Suddenly, the pipes stopped playing. The piper was never seen again,
alive. Sometimes when the roar of the traffic is stilled and the

crowds have quitted the streets, the faint wail of bagpipes can be heard drifting up from the uncharted tunnels below. Various versions of the legend are in circulation, each with their own embellishments.[34]

Perhaps a different phantom piper has been seen and heard in a narrow close near the Scottish National War Museum in the castle precinct and on the battlements. The sound of drumming has also been heard echoing round the lonely battlements. Sometimes the drummer himself is seen. He is reputed to have first put in an appearance in 1650, beating the 'Old Scots March' to raise the alarm that the parliamentarian forces of Oliver Cromwell were about to attack.[35] The drumming was again heard in 1960 by a soldier on patrol. He followed the rat-a-tat-tat to discover a man standing on the battlements. As the soldier approached he realized that the drummer was headless. With awful deliberation the figure turned round, only to disappear. Perhaps he has some connection to an exhibit in the castle. The sleeve of a nineteenth-century soldier's tunic on display in the building now used as a restaurant has been seen moving as if beating a drum.[36]

Others imprisoned in the dungeons and rumoured never to have left include Jacobites from the 1745 Uprising, such as Thomas Alexander Erskine, the Sixth Earl of Kellie, and POWs from the Seven Years' War (1756–63) and the American War of Independence (1775–83). Another Jacobite story, this time from the first uprising, concerns the crisis apparition of John Graham of Claverhouse, the famous 'Bonnie Dundee', appearing at the moment of his death at his great victory at Killiekrankie (1689) before Lord Balcarres, then being held in the castle on suspicion of his sympathies. Finally, a black phantom dog has been seen in the area of the Pets' Cemetery.[37]

In 2002 Historic Scotland, which runs the castle, attempted to gain an entry in the *Guinness Book of Records* by staging, with Mercat Tours, the world's biggest ghost hunt in the castle with upwards of 2,000 participants. However, the Ministry of Defence is adamant that the castle is not haunted, and thirty years of guard reports investigated in response to a freedom of information request were devoid of anything relating to the paranormal.[38]

THE VAULTS

Standing on South Bridge today one could be forgiven for thinking it was just an ordinary street. Cars fume and snarl their way up and down the road, flanked by shops and offices, but underneath is another, hidden world. In the late eighteenth and early nineteenth centuries a total of five bridges – North Bridge (1772), South Bridge (1788), Regent's Bridge (1818), King's Bridge (1833) and George IV Bridge (1836) – were built to overcome Edinburgh's geographical handicaps. Due to the town's chronic shortage of space these were not freestanding structures. Tenements and other buildings were built fast up against them, and use was made of the space under the arches of the bridges themselves, turning them into a warren of vaults and chambers. Originally intended as artisanal workshops and storage rooms, the cold, damp, airless conditions drove business out and in their place came the city's poorest and most desperate, happy for anywhere to call their own. This underground city was rife with poverty, disease and crime, a living tomb from which few escaped. The vaults were eventually abandoned and closed off. They had already passed into legend when building work in 1985 accidentally uncovered the remains of this dark labyrinth.[39]

When work was originally finished on the South Bridge linking the Old Town's High Street with Edinburgh University, the bridge's 1,000-foot span and twenty-two arches created the largest complex of vaults in Edinburgh. Today these can be accessed at two points: Niddry Street and Blair Street.[40]

When *Most Haunted* visited the Niddry Street Vaults, tour guide Frances Hollinrake told viewers that 'We've had figures being seen. We've had people feeling somebody breathing on their necks. We've had voices whispering in people's ears. [. . .] We've had the whole range of paranormal experiences.'[41]

During his investigation here, Mark Turner of Ghost Finders Scotland found that an EMF meter fluctuated apparently in response to questions asked. 'Never before,' he said, 'have I witnessed such readings on my EMF meter.' During this 'conversation' the group heard what sounded like heavy footsteps coming down one of the darkened passageways towards them.[42] Interestingly, Australian Paranormal Investigators also claimed that an EMF meter registered fluctuations at the same time as questions were asked. They too heard loud footsteps in the corridor.[43]

In comparison to the higher Niddry Street Vaults, the Blair Street Vaults are three levels under the street above. This is the haunting ground of 'Mr Boots'. According to *Most Haunted*'s historian Richard Felix, 'he's been seen pushing people; standing, glaring at people; and actually been recorded shouting, telling people to "get out".' Hollinrake was candid enough to admit that 'I wouldn't spend the night in the vaults,' adding, 'In Blair Street, I won't even go down there by myself.' Most of the *Most Haunted* team felt physically sick during their vigil here. Strange odours were smelt, mysterious thumping sounds were heard above them and Yvette Fielding claimed to have felt her arms being pulled. Ghost Finders Scotland recorded fourteen EVP during their investigation, including what sounded like a spirit giving its name in response to a question.[44] Australian Paranormal Investigators experienced mysterious battery discharge.[45] 'This place was terrifying,' Fielding said, 'and I honestly couldn't wait for this investigation to be over.'[46]

Ireland

Ballygally Castle (Northern Ireland)
Ballygally Castle is a seventeenth-century Scottish baronial tower house built by James Shaw. The BBC have described it as 'one of the most haunted places in Northern Ireland'. It features in both Jeff Belanger's *World's Most Haunted Places* and Lionel and Patricia Fanthorpe's *The World's Most*

Mysterious Castles. Ghosts here include that of Lady Shaw, wife of James Shaw, a suicide or murder victim, a child who wakes sleeping guests, laughing and running about the room, poltergeist-like activity in the Dungeon Room, showers that turn on by themselves and mysterious knocking on guests' doors in the middle of the night. The castle has now been turned into a forty-four-room hotel, complete with a Ghost Room. Despite an initial scepticism, manager Olga Henry said, 'I think there's definitely something in this hotel.'[47]

LEAP CASTLE (REPUBLIC OF IRELAND)

For Washington DC Metro Area Ghost Watchers, Leap Castle, County Offaly, is one of the scariest places they have ever investigated and they rank it their personal second most-haunted place in the world. The team experienced panic attacks, equipment failures and even reported seeing some of the ghosts: they did not last past midnight.[48] Sir Simon Marsden called it 'the most haunted castle in all Ireland'. Certainly, its reputed ghosts are numerous and varied, from the 'Bloody Chapel' where Teige (or Tadgh) O'Carroll murdered his brother in the sixteenth century to the skeletons found in the dark, rat-infested dungeons.[49]

Mildred Darby, lady of the castle in the early twentieth century, held several séances here and believed she had conjured up a terrible demonic entity reeking of decomposition.[50] Derek Acorah claimed to have seen it during *Most Haunted*'s investigation.[51] Other visitors have described it as having a sheep's skull for a head and a body covered in shaggy black fur.[52] A recent guidebook numbered the castle's ghosts at twenty.[53]

During a visit in 2002, Dr Bob Curran noted a number of inexplicable occurrences: a mysterious scream heard in the dungeons; the sensation of a cold hand at the base of his spine; the recording of voices in empty rooms; dragging sounds; equipment failure; small items going missing; and, most disturbing of all, an urge to throw himself from a window in the

Bloody Chapel. At the end of his investigation Curran said, 'I was glad to leave Leap Castle behind me.'[54]

Europe
  Arrête! C'est ici l'Empire de la Mort
  (Stop! Here is the Empire of the Dead)

The words are chiselled in stone above a narrow passageway. Dark, winding tunnels have led to this point. Darkness lies beyond. The intrepid explorer who crosses the threshold steps into the final resting place of the mortal remains of some six million people. Their bones are stacked in walls. Racks of femurs, tibias, fibulas and the rest are punctuated with skulls, here forming a cross, here a heart shape. 'Some people go down and they are very afraid after seeing the bones,' said one security guard, 'Some say they hear things. Voices.'[55]

The Catacombes de Paris, France, heads the list of European locations with a worldwide ranking of ninth and a worldwide cemeteries ranking of fourth. Macabre curiosity has drawn many distinguished tourists in its day, including Napoleon III and his son, as well as modern-day ghost hunters, such as the Tuscaloosa Paranormal Research Group.[56]

Also worth visiting is Père Lachaise. Although unlisted in the worldwide tables, this Romantic Parisian cemetery comes third in the worldwide cemeteries ranking. Covering 44 hectares (110 acres), this is the largest cemetery in Paris, at least above ground. Here among the one million graves the visitor will find Isadora Duncan and Oscar Wilde, as well as Felix Nadar, noted for his photographs of the Catacombes and experiments in ballooning, and of course Jim Morrison.

The only book to cover French hauntings in English is Sir Simon Marsden's *Ghosthunter: A Journey Through Haunted France*. Illustrated with his trademark photography, the book features Père Lachaise, as well as many other lesser-known locations.

High grey walls and steep red roofs pierce the green tree

line, giving wide views of the verdant valley below and craggy mountains beyond. Here the Teutonic Knights built their fortress against the Mongol hordes; others rebuilt it against the later Ottoman hordes. After the Tower of London, *Castelul Bran*, Bran Castle, known to the world as Dracula's Castle, is the second most-haunted castle in the world. Despite that, it has less connection to either Bram Stoker's novel or the historical leader Vlad Tepeș – the infamous 'Impaler' – than is often assumed. Romanians themselves are 'frequently bewildered about how this myth came to be attached to Bran Castle'.[57]

However, its picturesque position and rich history lend it the necessary charm to overcome such shortcomings. Among the 450,000 visitors per year, it has been observed that Western tourists often improvise their own Dracula 'history' in relation to the castle. UK Shadow Seekers made a visit in April 2012, purporting to capture evidence of 'a strange moan and a weird mist'.[58] It seems that Bran Castle is haunted more by our expectations than by anything else, giving it a worldwide ranking of thirteenth and a worldwide castles ranking of second.

But there is more than just Bran Castle to this country. The ghost hunter reality shows have made visits to Bonțida Bánffy Castle (*Ghost Hunters International*, 2008), Poenari Castle, ranked twenty-second for castles worldwide (*Ghost Hunters International*, 2008), and the citadel of Râșnov (*Most Haunted*, 2007; *Ghost Hunters International*, 2008). As Alan Murdie noted, 'Romania is the spiritual home for people interested in ghosts, vampires and the paranormal.'[59]

Rome has two major haunted locations: the Coliseum, ranked fourteenth worldwide; and the Catacombs (*Catacombe di Roma*), ranked fifth for cemeteries worldwide. The shattered monolith of the Coliseum, where once mock sea battles, animal hunts, executions, mythological dramas and gladiatorial contests were held, has also witnessed demonic invocations and Catholic rituals. Built in the first century

CE, the Coliseum was the largest amphitheatre in the Roman Empire, capable of seating 50,000 people. To celebrate his conquest of Dacia (now modern Romania), Emperor Trajan held a grandiose and gory spectacle over 123 days involving 10,000 gladiators and the slaughter of 11,000 animals.[60] There is a belief that the Coliseum is haunted by the many who died there, and there are unverified reports of a range of phenomena, which are, unfortunately, too dubious to repeat.

The Roman catacombs are not a single location, but refer to many underground burial sites around Rome. There are around forty different sites, dating back to the second century CE, but the largest, oldest and best preserved is the Catacombe di San Domitilla, stretching over nearly ten miles.[61] Again, whilst undoubtedly spooky, there are few if any reliable reports of haunting in any of these locations. *Ghost Hunters International* have instead investigated Lucedio Abbey and the Fort of Fenestrelle in Turin, Malaspina Castle, the Palazzo Ducale in Genoa and Pisa's Villa di Corliano.

Given its rich cultural heritage, it is surprising that Germany does not have more of a reputation for haunted places. Only *Ghost Hunters International* have visited the country, choosing to investigate Burg Reichenstein on the river Rhine, Burg Frankenstein near Darmstadt and Burg Fürsteneck in Hessen where a knight supposedly walled up his unfaithful wife alive.[62] There are vague reports of 'wailing voices' and 'hooded apparitions' at the castle of Heidelberg.[63] Picturesque Burg Eltz in Rheinland-Pfalz, still owned by the same family that built it in the twelfth century, is recognized as the eighth most-haunted castle worldwide.

Neighbouring Austria has two locations on the ghost hunting radar: Moosham Castle, Unternberg; and Schloss Porcia, Spittal an der Drau. *Ghost Hunters International* visited both in 2009. Moosham, known as Witches Castle after its role in the area's witchcraft persecution, is believed to be haunted by the spirit of 'Toni'. This would be so-called Schörgen Toni of legend, a man infamous for his cruelty, said to have been carried off by the Devil in a phantom coach drawn by four coal-black horses.[64] The *GHI* team captured some EVP, breathing sounds and the feeling of touch during their investigation.[65] Probably due to *GHI*, Moosham has the reputation of being the seventeenth most-haunted castle worldwide.

Eastern Europe is brim-full with promising locations for the ghost hunter. Slovenia's Predjama Castle, dramatically built into the rock face, is reputed to be the eleventh most-haunted castle worldwide and scene of a *Ghost Hunters International* investigation in 2008. *GHI* have taken their gadgets to Poland, visiting the Wolf's Lair (*Wolfsschanze*), Hitler's bunker on the Eastern Front, and Reszel Castle, another fortress of the Teutonic Knights. But it is the former concentration camp of Auschwitz, where, according to the official plaque, 1.1 million died during WWII, that has the reputation of being the fourteenth most-haunted place in the world, although there have been no investigations conducted here and no verifiable reports of haunting.

USA

Locations reputed to be haunted in the USA are, as elsewhere, a diverse lot. In the top ten by reputation we find a battlefield, a prison and a graveyard, as well as the more common residential properties. The state of California features most often with three top ten locations, followed by Louisiana with two. Again we see that worldwide and country listings produce slightly different results. Notably, RMS *Queen Mary* has a better worldwide reputation (sixth) than it does at home (twenty-second) and is probably a more interesting location than The Myrtles Plantation, which nevertheless features prominently both worldwide (third) and at home (fourth). Other sites such as Bachelor's Grove Cemetery are better known at home (eighth) than they are worldwide (forty-ninth).

Both the Whaley House and the Winchester Mystery House are also widely reported as, rather improbably, US Department of Commerce 'certified' haunted houses.[66] Matt

Most haunted locations in the USA by reputation

Rank	Location	State	Score	Votes
1	The Winchester Mystery House	California	67	9
2	The LaLaurie House	Louisiana	56	7
3	The White House	Washington DC	53	8
4	The Myrtles Plantation	Louisiana	49	9
5	Gettysburg Battlefield	Pennsylvania	44	7
6	The Whaley House	California	42	6
7	Alcatraz	California	37	8
8	Bachelor's Grove Cemetery	Illinois	37	7
9	Lemp Mansion	Missouri	36	8
10	The Lizzie Borden House	Massachusetts	36	5

Schulz, Technical Director of San Diego Ghost Hunters, contacted the US Department of Commerce regarding the certified claim. It turned out that the US Travel Service, part of the Department of Commerce, had released a brochure aimed at promoting travel to the US abroad in the late 1960s or early 1970s. Called 'Who's Whooooo', the brochure gave details of some thirty allegedly haunted locations in the US, including the Whaley and Winchester Houses.[67]

The locations I have chosen to discuss in a little more depth are those that balance both their worldwide and country reputations, and are particularly significant to the history of modern ghost hunting. The first on the list almost ended the career of two of today's most famous ghost hunters.

THE MYRTLES PLANTATION
Behind a rotten wicket fence an unkempt gravel path struggles through the grass to reach an old unpainted, clapboard shed, and steps lead up to a small veranda, just large enough for a table and two chairs. This is the so-called 'slave shack', and,

inside, one of the most controversial events in the recent history of ghost hunting took place one summer's night in 2005.

The slave shack stands on land belonging to The Myrtles Plantation, an eighteenth-century building in the style of the Old South, low with a long veranda, set in extensive grounds. The intricate ironwork throws complex patterns in the shade of the veranda and Aphrodite's sacred myrtle dapples the southern sunlight falling on the terrace. It is undoubtedly picturesque and at first glance a haven of tranquillity, but a dark shadow lies over The Myrtles. According to one source, it 'holds the dubious record of more ghostly phenomena per square inch than anywhere else in the country.'[68] For the paranormal plumbers Hawes and Wilson, it is 'every paranormal investigator's dream to check the place out'.[69]

Hawes and Wilson brought their team here to shoot *Ghost Hunters* in July 2005 and left with what they believed was indubitable evidence of the paranormal, but this evidence may have cost them their reputation. At least twenty different sorts of paranormal phenomena have been stated to occur at The Myrtles, ranging from footsteps to full-blown apparitions. Until Hawes and Wilson investigated, there appear to have been no alleged paranormal occurrences connected with the slave shack.

It was after 2 a.m., and Hawes and Wilson were sitting in the shack, discussing whether ghost hunting in general had been a wise investment of their time and energy. It sounded like they were having a dark night of the soul, perhaps even on the brink of giving up ghost hunting.

Watching the video footage later, the team were amazed by what they saw. Behind their backs as they talked a lamp moved 14 inches across a table. It was possible, they conceded, that Wilson may have inadvertently caught the lamp cord with his foot and caused it to move. They went back to check the room by daylight and ruled out the cord theory. There was only one other explanation possible: 'the place was haunted'. But better than that, they had caught it on camera.[70]

Alleged paranormal activity at The Myrtles[71]

Visual (human)

1. The ghost of a black slave called Chloe (also Cloe, Cloey or Cleo).
2. The ghost of the plantation owner's wife, murdered by Chloe.
3. The ghost of a girl or girls:

   (a) one who died in 1868

   (b) two murdered daughters of the plantation owner, who may or may not be:

   (c) the ghosts of two blonde-haired girls seen by a guest.
4. The ghost of a girl who only appears before storms.
5. The ghost of a French woman who moves from room to room.
6. The ghost of an American Civil War soldier in the grounds.

Visual (human body parts or indications of them)

7. Handprints on or in the mirror in the hallway.
8. Bloody handprint on wall next to painting or on painting seen in infrared.

Auditory

9. The footsteps of the ghost of William Winter are heard on the stairs as far as the seventeenth step.
10. The sound of children playing heard in the grounds.
11. A piano that repeatedly plays the same chord by itself.
12. Banging sounds.

Tactile

13. Tug felt on sleeve by manager Hester Eby, but no one there.

Physical

14. Bedclothes are repeatedly disarranged in the Room of the Rumpled Bed.
15. Doors opening and closing by themselves.
16. Paintings re-arranged during a Murder Mystery Weekend in 1985.

Other

17. Lights must be kept burning in the house to prevent paranormal occurrences.
18. Haunted painting on the first-floor landing.
19. 'Orbs' caught on film.
20. High EMF readings.

One TV critic characterized the ensuing debate as 'the biggest online controversy over paranormal show footage', reporting that 'upon close inspection, fans concluded the lamp was being pulled by its own cord'. Worse still, night-vision camera footage appeared to show 'the cord extending from behind the table to Mr Wilson's hand'. Joe Nickell later added to the controversy, arguing that the so-called slave shack was a 'structure of recent vintage that never held a slave', throwing doubt on who or what might have been haunting it in the first place. Despite executive producer Craig Piligian's defence of Hawes and Wilson, 'some fans declared the ghostbusters busted'.[72]

Events reported by TAPS at the Myrtles[73]

Report	Location	Witness(es)	Instrumentation
'A flitting shadow'	the grounds	Steve Gonsales	–
Barking dog quiet on command	the grounds	Steve Gonsales	–
Moving warm mass	staircase	Hawes, Wilson	thermal camera
Human-like shadow	house interior	–	unspecified camera
Pressure felt in ears	slave shack	Hawes, Wilson	–
Moving lamp	slave shack	–	night-vision camera

The murder of William Winter seems to be the only documented homicide at The Myrtles, but over the years the tales of murders committed here have swollen to around ten in total, and with them the number of ghosts.[74] The most abiding legend concerns the slave Chloe and her murder by poison of her owner's wife and two daughters, all of whom are now said to haunt the property. There appears to be no historical basis for this story, or for any of the others told about the property. Nickell believed that much of the unexplained phenomena could be accounted for by banging shutters and doors hung off balance.[75]

Billing itself as 'one of America's most haunted homes', The Myrtles is now run as a guesthouse and operates its own evening 'Mystery Tours', sometimes with crowds of over a hundred. For Paul and Hilary of the Paranormal Research Society of North America, the 'chatting and screams of the guests throughout the night' severely hampered their own investigation. Coming away with only a few 'orb' photographs, they nonetheless reported that there is a 'heavy feel to the place'.[76] Natchez Area Paranormal Society (NAPS) reported more success. Using a Panasonic RR DR60 they captured what they consider to be their best EVP. Standing in the grounds near the woods, the recorder picked up 'what sounds like a little girl coming right up [. . .] and saying "Hi" to us'.[77]

THE WHALEY HOUSE

Candlelight faintly illuminated the group of people sitting round the large wooden table. Paranormal investigator Michael Kouri of the Orange County Society for Psychic Research spoke calmly: 'open your mind, don't be scared, hold hands [. . .] if anyone [gets] scared, they should just leave the room, preferably not screaming'. He then asked the spirits 'to communicate by raising or lowering the flame of the middle candle or by moving the table or other objects in the room'. The Convocation of Souls had begun.[78]

The group asked their questions. The flame flickered in response. Soon a rapid tapping sound seemed to come from the middle of the table. It started to travel around the table. The sitters could feel it vibrate as the tapping increased in intensity. Then the table began to lift up. Was it the former occupants of California Historical Landmark No. 65 – the Whaley House – trying to communicate from beyond the grave?

When Thomas Whaley struck a great deal on a parcel of land in San Diego in 1855, he already knew it was the site of the former gallows. He had seen James Robinson, 'Yankee Jim', strangle slowly to death years earlier after the executioner failed to adjust the rope to account for the man's 6-foot 4-inch stature. Perhaps he was no believer in ghosts, but events would change his mind.

Reported hauntings at the Whaley House[79]

Category	Description
Visual: animate (human)	
	Thomas Whaley
	Anna Whaley
	Violet Whaley
	George Whaley
	Francis Whaley
	Whaley's great-granddaughter
	unidentified woman
	unidentified girl
	Annabel/Carrie Washburn*
Visual: animate (animal)	
	dog (fox terrier)
Visual: inanimate	
	mysterious fog
Non-visual: auditory	
	organ/piano music
	Yankee Jim's footsteps
Non-visual: tactile	
	cold spots
Non-visual: olfactory	
	perfume
	tobacco smoke

*Dismissed as an 'urban legend' by the museum.

The house that still stands on this plot is the original that Whaley designed and built in 1856–7, a square Greek Revival building with a colonnaded portico and balcony over the front. At the time it was hailed as the 'finest new brick block in Southern California'.[80] A hundred years later, the popular paranormalist Hans Holzer would describe it as 'one of the most actively haunted mansions in the world today'.[81]

In the mid-nineteenth century San Diego was a small town with, Whaley estimated, some 250 to 300 inhabitants. The climate he compared to Italy and 'healthier than San Francisco'. He came during the Gold Rush, but made his money through several different enterprises. He owned a brick foundry, for example, where he made the bricks for his house, dealt in real estate, and operated several general supplies and hardware shops during his career.[82]

The house has always been more than a house. It served in its time as a courtroom, an off-licence, a place of worship, a theatre with seating for 150 people, and a ballroom, and it had a supply store and granary. It is now run by Save Our Heritage Organisation as the Whaley House Museum with 100,000 visitors a year, and is one of California's legendary 'certified' haunted houses.

It has had its share of tragedy, too. Thomas Whaley, Jr, died here in 1858 aged just 18 months. In 1885, following a failed marriage to a dowry hunter and the ensuing social scandal and personal depression, twenty-two-year-old Violet Whaley shot herself through the heart. Her father Thomas had risen from the breakfast table to look for her when he heard the gunshot outside. He rushed out and carried her into the back parlour where she died. She left a poignant suicide note:[83]

> *Mad from life's history,*
> *Swift to death's mystery*
> *Glad to be hurled,*
> *Anywhere, anywhere, out of this world.*

The lines are from Thomas Hood's poem 'The Bridge of Sighs', inspired by the suicide of a fallen woman who plunged to her death from London's Waterloo Bridge. Violet had first tried to kill herself by drowning. Her father's .32 calibre revolver was more suited to the task. The shock must have been terrible. Thomas Whaley took his family to a new house at 933 State Street where he himself died in 1890 after some years of failing health.[84]

Robin Sweeton, a guide at the house since 2002, says, 'I think Mr Whaley just kind of went downhill emotionally. When he died, maybe his daughter was here and he thought, "Well, I've got to stay here with her and protect her".' [85]

More famous for his investigations at the Amityville house, Hans Holzer brought witch Sybil Leek and TV presenter Regis Philbin to the Whaley House in the 1960s. They supposedly encountered the ghost of Anna Whaley. Philbin, a novice in paranormal investigation, lost his nerve. As Holzer told the story, 'the older woman, she appeared – it was a very white figure, and Regis got excited and turned on the flashlight, and of course that was the end of the phenomenon.' It was something that Holzer would never let Philbin forget. Philbin returned to the Whaley House for *Celebrity Ghost Stories* in 2011.[86]

When asked about the hauntings, Rob Wlodarski, who with his wife Anne wrote *The Haunted Whaley House*, said, 'On a scale of 1 to 10, this house is probably a 15.' Today, San Diego Ghost Hunters run regular 'Paranormal Investigation' tours at the house to raise money for the upkeep of the historic property.[87]

THE WHITE HOUSE

> When I turned the light on one morning, he was sitting there outside his office with his hands over top of each other, legs crossed, and was looking straight ahead.

Tony Savoy, White House operations foreman in the 1980s, recognized Abraham Lincoln immediately. Savoy had been watering the plants on the second floor when he chanced to see a lean figure wearing 'a gray, charcoal pin-striped suit' and 'a pair of three-button spats turned over on the side with black shoes'. Savoy was stopped in his tracks: 'when I blinked he was gone'. The spell broken, he raced down the stairs to tell assistant usher Nelson Pierce what he had seen. Pierce shrugged and told him he was 'just one of the other ones that had seen him throughout the house over the past years'.[88]

Reported hauntings at the White House

Haunting	Location	Principal witness(es)
Abigail Adams	East Room	William Howard Taft
David Burns	Yellow Oval Room	unidentified valet
Andrew Jackson	Rose Room	Mary Todd Lincoln
		Lilian Parks
Abraham Lincoln	Lincoln Bedroom	Grace Coolidge
		Claudia 'Lady Bird' Johnson
		Eleanor Roosevelt
	Yellow Oval Room	Grace Coolidge
	East Room	Unknown
	Queen's Bedroom	Winston Churchill
		Queen Wilhelmina of the Netherlands
William Lincoln	2nd-floor bedroom	Lynda Johnson Robb
	Living Room	Mary Todd Lincoln
Edward Lincoln	Living Room	Mary Todd Lincoln
Alec Lincoln	Living Room	Mary Todd Lincoln
Thomas Jefferson	Yellow Oval Room	Mary Todd Lincoln
John Tylor	Yellow Oval Room	Mary Todd Lincoln
music	2nd-floor bedroom	Jenna Bush
British soldier	2nd-floor bedroom	unknown
William Henry Harrison	Attic	unknown
'demon cat'	basement	unknown
Dolley Madison	Rose Garden	gardeners (period 1913–21)
Anne Surratt	North Portico	unknown
British soldier	North Portico	unknown

Abraham Lincoln still gets around despite the fact that he died in 1865. It is said that his ghost has been seen at his tomb in Springfield, at Fort Monroe in Virginia, at Ford's Theatre in Washington where he was assassinated, and most famously at the White House, especially in the 'Lincoln Bedroom'.[89]

If Abraham Lincoln ever slept in the Lincoln Bedroom, then it was with his head on his desk. The second-floor room now called a bedroom was, during Lincoln's presidency, his office.[90] But it is here where his ghost is most often seen or felt. Lincoln actually slept in what is now the Master Bedroom; his wife Mary slept in an adjoining room currently used as a private living room.

In the room now called the Queen's Bedroom, formerly the Rose Room, Churchill met Lincoln in 1941, or so the story goes. Churchill had just emerged from his bath and wearing nothing but the smoke from his ever-present cigar walked into the room to find Abe leaning on the mantelpiece. 'Good evening, Mr President,' he supposedly said, 'You seem to have me at a disadvantage.' Whether he used that witty retort or not, Churchill asked for a different room.[91]

The 'demon cat', which also allegedly haunts the US Capitol in Washington DC, is said to be an omen of doom for the USA. According to some, the black cat is first seen as a small kitten, but when approached it grows to a menacing size. It is said that a White House guard saw the cat before the stock market crash of 1929 and it was again seen days before the assassination of John F. Kennedy in 1963. There is also the belief that the cat appears before elections at which the current incumbent will fall – the so-called 'demon cat prophecy'.[92]

At a dinner party in 1986 Ronald Reagan entertained guests with the story of how their dog Rex often behaved strangely, once barking furiously in the Lincoln Bedroom before backing out and refusing to cross the threshold again, and at another time barking at the ceiling in their room as they watched television. However, as Reagan revealed, it was his daughter Maureen and her husband who actually saw a ghost.

Both claim to have seen a transparent figure while staying in the Lincoln Bedroom on different occasions.[93]

George W. Bush's daughter Jenna Bush Hager reported hearing ghostly music coming out of the fireplace in her bedroom when she lived here during her father's administration from 2001 to 2009.[94] Former First Lady Hillary Clinton admitted the house 'can be a little creepy'.[95] The White House Chief Usher, Gary Walters, revealed that 'the presidents that I have worked for have all indicated a feeling of the previous occupants of the White House'.[96]

None of this would have surprised President Harry Truman. After hearing footsteps up and down the hallway and knocks on his bedroom door at 4 a.m., he wrote to his wife, saying, 'Damned place is haunted, sure as shootin'!'[97]

Unsurprisingly, other than Mary Todd Lincoln's séances, no paranormal investigations have been conducted inside the White House. As one of the most haunted locations in the USA it remains tantalizingly out of reach for the ghost hunter, but conveniently open for public tours arranged through one's Member of Congress for US citizens, or through one's embassy. Note that cameras and camcorders are not allowed, and O'Donnell would not have made it through the door with a revolver in his pocket.

Canada

THE MACKENZIE HOUSE

An unassuming three-storey Victorian townhouse at 82 Bond Street, Toronto, has the reputation of being the most haunted house in Canada. At least three apparitions have been reported, as well as the sounds of footsteps, a piano playing and a printing press in operation. Cold Spot Paranormal Research and Investigating Unit also report that a noose has been seen over the stairwell, that taps turn on by themselves, a toilet flushes itself and an empty rocking chair rocks with no one in it.[98] Mrs Charles Edmunds, the caretaker's wife in the late

1950s, is said to have once been given a black eye by one of the ghosts, although, according to Ontario group ParaResearchers, there is no evidence of haunting prior to 1960. The house takes its name from William Lyon Mackenzie (1795–1861), newspaper publisher, revolutionary leader and Toronto's first mayor. Mackenzie died in the house and many believe that he haunts it now. His youngest daughter, Isabel Grace King, also died here. Supposedly listed in the inventory is the entry 'One Ghost (exorcized)' in reference to the exorcism performed by Archdeacon John Frank of the Holy Trinity Anglican Church on 2 July 1960. The building is now a museum and open to the public.[99]

South Africa

Although ghost hunting is not one of the top ten reasons to visit South Africa according to the official tourist website, the country is nevertheless rich with ghosts, from murderers to their victims and battlefield phantoms to poltergeists. South African Tourism does, however, give a list of the top ten hauntings.[100]

Heading the list is the Castle of Good Hope, Cape Town. This former Dutch East India Company fortress, dating from the seventeenth century, is haunted by a Grey Lady. It is now the headquarters of the South African National Defence Force, but the Castle Military Museum is open to the public. Second are the Southern Seas off the Cape of Good Hope, haunted by *The Flying Dutchman*. Claimed to be 'one of the world's most famous ghosts' is the Uniondale hitchhiker: drivers who stop to pick up a female hitchhiker find that she mysteriously vanishes. The Old Gaol in Grahamstown is said to be haunted by Henry Nichols, the last man to be executed there.

Kimberley has the reputation of being South Africa's most haunted city, with a total of 158 haunted buildings. The city has two entries in the top ten: fifth is the former public library (now the Africana Museum), haunted by the first librarian who committed suicide by drinking arsenic; and at ninth is Rudd House, the haunt of at least eight ghosts, including Percy Rudd, the first owner. Another haunted library is that of Port Elizabeth, still being looked after by janitor Robert Thomas who died in 1943. Seventh is the village of Matjies-fontein, Central Karoo, which also claims to be South Africa's most haunted place. While filming for *The Story of an African Farm* was taking place here in 2004, several security guards were startled by a woman in Victorian dress, believed to be the ghost of Louisa Margaret Green who died in 1860. The Lord Milner Hotel, the town's only hotel, is haunted by an invisible party, laughing and playing billiards. The Nottingham Road Hotel, KwaZulu-Natal, is believed to be haunted by a former barmaid or prostitute called Charlotte who defenestrated herself. Last on the list is Doornkloof in Irene, southeast of Pretoria. Here the former home of General Jan Christian Smuts, now the Smuts House Museum, is haunted by a Royal Hussar and a 'little grey man'. As Arthur Goldstuck put it after ten years working on his book about the paranormal in this country: 'the South African ghost is a complex character that reflects a turbulent history and a harsh experience.'[101]

Australia

'Don't worry, it will be all right,' she said before vanishing. The stunned couple continued looking at the spot where moments before a young woman in white had been standing. With several apparitions, lights mysteriously turning themselves on and off when no one is at home, strange forces blocking people on the staircase, phantom footsteps, and a case of possession, Monte Cristo Homestead has the reputation of being Australia's most haunted house and there are plenty who believe it. Responding to a poll on a newspaper website, almost two thousand people (49 per cent of the total) voted that they believed in ghosts.[102] According to the Australian Ghost Hunters Society, the homestead has between ten and twelve ghosts in residence. It comes ninth on the worldwide reputations ranking.[103]

Paranormal Australia (October 2001) and *Ghost Hunters International* (13 January 2010) have both investigated here, as well as other groups. The Homestead is also open to the public and runs regular ghost tours, but anyone looking to conduct a serious investigation will be charged Aus$700 per day plus tour costs.[104]

Other places of note in New South Wales are the Victorian-era Lisnagar Homestead, Sydney's atmospheric old Quarantine Station with its own ghost tours, and 'Australia's most haunted gaol', according to Paranormal Australia, Maitland Gaol, also with its own 'psychic tours'.

HM Gaol Adelaide in South Australia was home to 300,000 prisoners during its 147-year history, including the murderess Elizabeth Woolcock, and the scene of forty-five executions. It is reputed to be haunted by its first governor William Baker Ashton along with hangman Ben Ellis and executed prisoner Frederick Carr. The Gaol runs its own ghost tours after sunset.[105] Another atmospheric Victorian prison worth visiting in South Australia is Gladstone Gaol, Gladstone, where investigators have heard ghostly whispering and singing, experienced temperature drops and seen shadowy figures.[106] Australia's largest re-created pioneer village, Old Tailem Town, is also home to its share of ghosts. 'Old Tailem Town,' said Alison Oborn of Paranormal Field Investigations, 'can get a bit scary.'[107] According to Adelaide's Haunted Horizons who run ghost tours here, Old Tailem is South Australia's most haunted town, an accolade shared with Kapunda.[108] Paranormal activity here centres around the cemetery and site of the now demolished St John's Reformatory, once run by an insane priest.[109]

Queensland Paranormal Investigators have teamed up with Ghost Tours Pty Ltd to offer tours in and around Brisbane. Warning that 'ghosts have been seen, heard and felt on tours', locations include Toowong Cemetery, South Brisbane Cemetery, Ipswich Cemetery and Boggo Road Gaol.[110] Other places that have drawn Queenland's ghost hunters are Brisbane's Arts Theatre, Goomeri's Grand Hotel, the late Victorian Woodlands of Marburg mansion house, and St Helena Island Prison. Ryan Turnbull, owner of the Criterion Hotel, Maryborough, called in 'Australian Psychic of the Year' Charmaine Wilson in 2009 to try and lay the ghost of a troublesome chambermaid, but ghost hunters still find that there is something to investigate in this old Victorian property.[111]

Tasmania's Port Arthur Penitentiary and Hobart's Supreme Courthouse have been featured on *Ghost Hunters International*. Also worth mentioning is the island's abandoned Royal Derwent Hospital (also known as Willow Court), New Norfolk, former home of the criminally insane and now reputed to be haunted.[112]

An unlikely new addition to Australia's most haunted list is the IGA supermarket in Brompton, Adelaide. In March 2012 three security cameras working on motion sensors filmed a packet of sweets falling to the floor. The shop was closed at the time and none of the burglar alarms was activated. Speaking to journalists, owner Norm Hurst said, 'I think the ghost has a sweet tooth.'[113]

Some places, however, are best left alone. A security patrol investigating mysterious lights seen in the derelict and reputedly haunted Swanbourne Hospital, Mount Claremont, Western Australia, did not find any evidence of the paranormal, but instead apprehended four would-be ghost hunters illegally trespassing.[114]

New Zealand
Ghost Hunters International reached New Zealand's shores in 2008, but the island has several home-grown ghost hunting groups and its own TV show investigating the darker side of their country's history. From 2005 to 2006 Brad Hills, Michael Hallows and Carolyn Taylor took TV show *Ghost Hunt* round what they considered to be the most haunted locations.

New Zealand's only 'castle', Larnach Castle, would not be complete without a ghost. Although the 'castle' is, in fact, an eccentric Victorian mansion, *Ghost Hunters International* claim to have filmed an apparition in the ballroom. Many members of staff have heard footsteps, felt ghostly fingers on their necks, and experienced doors mysteriously opening and closing. Following claims that a tourist was pushed by some unseen entity a spokesman said 'reports of ghosts were not uncommon at the castle'.[115] Waitomo Caves Hotel is known as 'New Zealand's most haunted hotel' with reports of temperature drops, presences, the sound of a maid's trolley rattling along empty corridors and bathtubs dripping blood.[116] The Fortune Theatre, Dunedin, began life as a Methodist Church, and now the Gothic Revival building is known for twenty-seven sightings of the *unknown*. Technician Cory Anderson thought he saw someone on stage reading lines. When he turned up the lights there was no one there.[117] Riccarton Racecourse Hotel, Christchurch, is thought to be haunted by the spirit of Donald Fraser, murdered in one of the bedrooms. According to *Ghost Hunt* there have been fifteen reported sightings at Riccarton House, Christchurch. Whatipu Lodge, former home of the Gibbons, is haunted by a Pink Lady believed to be Matilda Gibbon, but the whole area has the reputation of being, in the words of Bob Harvey, former mayor of Waitakere City, a 'coast of ghosts', with sixteen reported sightings according to *Ghost Hunt*. The Vulcan Hotel is a single-storey stone house in the old gold-mining town of St Bathans. The town's population of six is rivalled by the reputed number of ghosts, also six, headed by the succubus spirit of Rose, a prostitute murdered in the hotel. There have been forty-four sightings in and around Auckland's Waikumete Cemetery, site of a mass grave for over a thousand bodies following the 1918 influenza epidemic and the nineteen unmarked graves in Murderers' Grove. Kinder House and Ewelme Cottage are two reputedly haunted Victorian properties lying on Ayr Street in Auckland's Parnell suburb. During recording at the cottage the *Ghost Hunt* team picked up an EVP they interpreted as 'Please . . . go away'.

South of Auckland in the small town of Karaka is Kingseat Hospital, a former psychiatric hospital and now home to Spookers theme park. The location boasts over a hundred ghosts, enough, perhaps, to win it one of Spookers's coveted 'O'Scares Awards'. The most commonly reported apparition is the 'Grey Nurse', reputed to have died in one of the rooms. Over the years staff have reported numerous unusual experiences including mysterious doubles, voices, unexplained noises and flying objects. Every year, Spookers's Director, Beth Watson, arranges a Maori blessing for the building. Visitors are warned that 'the Spookers Haunted House may well be the last thing you ever do.'[118]

Asia

BHANGARH FORT, INDIA

It is not just the ruined fort but also the surrounding ruined town of Bhangarh that are rumoured to be haunted. Standing before the tumbled masonry and roofless walls is a signpost from the Archaeological Survey of India prohibiting anyone from entering Bhangarh after sunset. Much has been made of this battered blue placard. According to Australian website www.news.com.au, 'Bhangarh Fort is so spooky the Indian Government prohibits entry after sunset'. Tourists who flout the law are rumoured to have disappeared.[119] The ruined fortress is treacherous enough by daylight, and certainly it is more so after nightfall, particularly as it lies on the borders of the 866 km² Sariska Tiger Reserve. Legend has it that a black magician called either Guru Balu Nath or Singhia cursed the place soon after it was built in the sixteenth century.[120]

The Indian Paranormal Society's investigative team – Ghost Research and Investigators of the Paranormal (GRIP) – slipped past the nightwatchmen to conduct a vigil in the ruins. Equipped with EVP recorders, cameras, trigger objects,

Frank's Box and an ELF meter, the group found plenty of wild animals, empty bottles, used condoms, cigarette butts and 'Tantrik materials', such as candles and skulls, but no evidence of paranormal activity. Interviewing local villagers, GRIP documented at least ten different ghost stories and a common belief in the ruins being haunted.[121]

AOKIGAHARA JUKAI, JAPAN

Known as Suicide Forest, Japanese authorities recover as many as a hundred bodies a year from this dense tangle of evergreens at the foot of Mount Fuji. A large sign stands by the public path as it wends its way into the densest part of the Jukai – 'the sea of trees'. It reads 'Your life is a precious gift from your parents' and gives contact details of the Suicide Prevention Association. Tape and string, like Hansel and Gretel's trail of bread crumbs, wind deep into the forest as a lifeline for those uncertain whether this will be their last journey. Nooses hang like vines from the branches. On one tree a macabre doll is nailed upside down, its face torn off. On another a small figure of the Virgin and Child is tied with wire. Skeletons litter the forest floor like fallen branches. Here a moulding pair of shoes, here a whited skull. Elsewhere, 'strange fruit' swings in the air.

The forest is anciently associated with demons – an impression reinforced by the inability of compasses to function properly here – but Seicho Matsumoto's 1961 novel *Nami no To* (Tower of Waves), in which the beautiful but doomed heroine kills herself in the forest, is often blamed for the popularity of Aokigahara as a suicide spot. The forest is also recommended in the notorious *Suicide Manual*. Japan has one of the highest suicide rates in the developed world, over 30,000 per year, and here in the silent forest is a grim testament to that fact. According to Kyomyo Fukui, a Buddhist monk who prays for the lost souls of Aokigahara, 'the spirits are calling people here to kill themselves, the spirits of the people who have committed suicide before'.[122]

CHANGI BEACH, SINGAPORE

This idyllic crescent of golden sand was once the scene of a massacre. During WWII, the Japanese invaders rounded up thousands of Chinese men and executed them at several locations, including Changi Beach and nearby Punggol Point – the so-called Sook Ching ('a purge through cleansing') massacre. A plaque commemorates the sixty-six Chinese who were killed by firing squad here. According to reports, British and Australian prisoners of war were also executed on the beach. Today, among the tree roots small statues of the elephant-headed god Ganesha, placed there by Hindu worshippers, watch the waves break on the shoreline.[123]

Singapore Paranormal Investigators have documented several ghost stories and urban legends connected with the beach. These include witnesses apparently hearing crying and screaming, seeing dead bodies 'flying everywhere', as well as headless bodies walking on the beach, and a full-blown replay of the execution with blood staining the sand.[124] During their full moon night vigil SPI attempted to summon the spirits of those massacred. They believed that they were successful, although much of their evidence was based on the appearance of 'orbs' caught on film.[125] The *Singapore Haunted* show on the Singaporean web TV broadcaster R3Load Network also investigated the beach in 2011.

7

CONTACT

Emergency. Which service do you require?

Harry Fuller was a used car dealer. He had his enemies. Maybe his fondness for flashing cash about made him a bit of a spiv, a bit of a wide boy. Perhaps something of a gangster.[1] He always liked to say how much he had on him, sometimes thousands of pounds. He had a younger wife, Nicola. There was an age difference of almost twenty years between them. Perhaps people thought she was a trophy, but they liked her more. She was quiet and sensitive. They had been married for less than six months. People talked of a 'whirlwind romance'. Together they lived in a cottage in the small market town of Wadhurst, East Sussex.[2]

But now Harry was lying face down with a bullet hole in his back. The round had penetrated his heart and killed him outright. Nicola had been shot three times and left for dead. The emergency telephone operator who took her call could not understand her. In spite of having her jaw smashed by a bullet, Nicola was desperately trying to get help. The operator decided it was someone being silly and did not route her call to the police. It was logged as 'child on line'. Her murderer had heard her making the call. He knew it was not a prank. He came back and finished the job with a shot to the back of the head.[3]

Stephen Young had been Harry Fuller's insurance broker. He was described as 'a very responsible family man', well liked by the people who knew him. But Detective Chief Superintendent Graham Hill said 'there was a totally different side to him'. Like everyone else, he knew all about Fullers's money. Unlike most people, Young had debts totalling over £100,000. He was also a gun enthusiast with an 'arsenal of unregistered and unregisterable weapons'. And the evidence put him at the scene of the crime.[4]

The evidence was circumstantial: a telephone call the day before the murder agreeing to meet and video footage from a security camera showing his car entering and leaving Wadhurst around the time of the murder. Young protested his innocence. He admitted that he had been there. He had seen the dead bodies, but fled and had been too scared to tell the police. On 23 March 1994 the trial jury found him guilty. There were cheers from the public gallery. The judge passed down two life sentences. Young was on his way to Wormwood Scrubs. But the jury had had access to more than just the police evidence.[5]

A month later Young's lawyer received an anonymous note from one of the jurors. It alleged that several members of the jury had used a Ouija board to contact the spirit of Harry Fuller. Unable to reach a decision, the jury had been accommodated in a local hotel for the night. Drinking together in a hotel room, four jurors had rested their fingers on an upturned wineglass, using scraps of paper with letters of the alphabet printed on them as an improvised board. They believed that whatever it was that had seemed to guide the glass was the murdered man communicating from beyond the grave.[6]

The Ouija board

Ray then asked, 'Is anyone there?'

The glass went to 'yes'.

Ray said, 'Who is it?'

The glass spelt out 'Harry Fuller'.

When I say the glass spelt it out, I mean it went to each letter. I realised Fuller was the subject of the evidence we were hearing.

Ray said, 'Who killed you?'

The glass spelt out 'Stephen Young done it'.

Ray said, 'How?'

The glass spelt 'shot'.

Ray said something else and the glass spelt 'shotgun and pistol'.

Ray said, 'Where is the gun?'

The glass spelt 'Police'.

Ray also asked who killed Nicola, and the glass spelt out 'Stephen Young'.

[. . .]

It continued, 'Vote guilty tomorrow'.[7]

The secrecy of a jury's deliberations is sacrosanct. It is also protected by law. But now the truth was out. The jury had come to their decision based on directions given by the dead victim. Young's representation appealed. When it was heard at the Court of Appeal in the Victorian Gothic Royal Courts of Justice on the Strand, London, his conviction was quashed and a retrial ordered.

This time the trial was at the Old Bailey. Presented with all the evidence, a new jury also found Young guilty. The judge sentenced him to two consecutive life terms. He continued to profess his innocence and lodged a further appeal, which was denied.[8]

Young's trial made legal history. The use of the Ouija board was described as a 'material irregularity', allowing the court to look into the jury's deliberation process. It is routinely cited in the press and by lawyers. On giving his reasons for ordering a retrial Chief Justice Lord Taylor of Gosforth said:

> Although many, perhaps most, people would regard attempts to communicate with the dead as futile, there can be no doubt that the four jurors were going through the motions of asking questions to that end and apparently receiving answers. It seems to us that what matters is not whether the answers were truly from the deceased, but whether the jurors believed them to be so or whether they may have been influenced by the answers received during this exercise or experiment.[9]

Everyone has heard of the Ouija board. The layout is familiar: an arc of the letters of the alphabet in two or more rows above the numerals one to nine plus zero with 'yes', 'no' and 'hello', 'goodbye' printed at strategic points. A planchette, usually a triangular wooden fingerboard, is used to point to the symbols. But can it really be used to contact the dead? Should legal decisions be based on it? And can the ghost hunter use it in paranormal investigations?

Among the wild theories abounding about the Ouija board's history is that it can be traced back to the Greek philosopher Pythagoras around 540 BCE and a 'mystic table moving on wheels' that glides over 'signs inscribed on the surface of a stone slab'. It is, unfortunately a red herring. It is also grossly incorrect that the planchette used with the Ouija board is named after its inventor, 'a well-known French spiritualist, M. Planchette', as the much-referred-to encyclopedist of the occult Lewis Spence wrote. Monsieur Planchette never existed and the word itself comes from the French meaning 'little board'.[10]

What we do know is that on 28 May 1890, Elijah J. Bond of Baltimore, Maryland, applied for a patent on 'certain new and useful Improvements in Toys or Games' for what he proposed to call the 'Ouija or Egyptian luck-board'.[11] Even before the patent was granted, the Kennard Novelty Company trademarked 'toys known as talking boards' under the name of

Ouija.[12] Later that year Charles Kennard patented his 'Talking Board' – an adapted Ouija-board-style layout with a fixed planchette moving on a wheel about a pivot. It was specifically described as an improvement over the Ouija design, but time has shown it to be far less popular than the original.[13] Both designs were specifically intended to be games. Bond made no mention of contacting spirits. Questions were 'answered by the device' and nothing more.

That Bond considered his Ouija board to be an improvement demonstrates that there must have been some sort of pre-existing device or method. Since starting the Spiritualism movement in 1848 with rapping sounds purporting to come from the spirits, the Fox sisters had already found that calling out the letter of the alphabet to which the raps could reply proved a more useful method than the simple yes/no and counting method they started with. The Ouija board made this far easier with a printed alphabet and other useful symbols and words, working in combination with a movable pointer similar to already existing designs.

The planchette had been in independent use some years before the Ouija board appeared. Developed in France, it was being sold in the USA from 1868 onwards. The heart-shaped board has changed little since, except that, used on its own, it was pierced with a hole to accommodate a pencil for taking messages from the spirits. It had been popularized in the 1850s by the French spiritualist Allan Kardec (pseudonym of Hippolyte-Léon-Denizard Rivail), perhaps the Monsieur Planchette of the joke Lewis Spence never got.[14]

Bond did not explain where the word Ouija came from or what it meant, leaving room for considerable speculation over the years. Nellie Walters had the novel idea of asking the Ouija board itself what the name meant. 'The reply,' she wrote, 'was that the word sprang from the Greek of the ancients, and means "The Master's Hand" '.[15] Of course, it means nothing of the sort. It is most plausibly a construct comprised of two words for 'yes': the French *oui* and German *ja*.

Sunker Abaji Bisey came up with his patented 'spirit type-writer' in the 1920s, claiming that its design would make it possible to find out if messages were really from a source other than the operator's own mind. A mechanical type-writer mechanism was constructed in a circular layout so that the unmarked keys could be struck by a planchette moving across the top of the device. A printout of the messages was produced at the side. It was claimed that by not seeing the markings on the key, the operator would not be able to sub-consciously influence the result.[16]

It is not known what happened to Bisey's 'spirit typewriter', but it was not the first such machine. Hereward Carrington recounted having witnessed a medium use a typewriter to produce spirit messages. Standing some distance from the machine, the medium nonetheless was able to demonstrate the typewriter keys moving apparently of their own accord to type out messages. Carrington remarked 'the effect is cer-tainly most uncanny'. The whole thing was a fake, of course. An assistant behind the scenes operated the typewriter using invisible thread and a pulley system.[17]

Other non-mechanical attempts were made to prevent the operator from seeing what messages were being delivered by the board. Sir William Barrett's experiments in 1913 using blindfolded operators and frequently rearranged letters still produced meaningful messages, in one case involving infor-mation unknown to the operators.[18]

Other systems were devised on the same principle as the Ouija board. In the 1890s several methods were then known: the psychograph, the espirito, the daestu, 'the oracle', Freder-ick Ayres' Pytho and Chrao, and the elaborate Spiritoscope of Professor Hare.[19] Pearl Curran of St Louis used a planchette with a pencil attached to take dictation from the spirits. A housewife with minimal education, she nonetheless wrote several novels as the spirit of 'Patience Worth', a seventeenth-century Englishwoman. The novel *Tekla* was said to contain no word of English that had entered the language later than

1700 and her poetry was compared to that of Wordsworth. This technique is more properly automatic writing and many mediums have used it without the assistance of a planchette.[20]

Whilst Barrett and other early investigators were using the Ouija board in a séance setting, Ada Goodrich-Freer (aka 'Miss X') pioneered its use in actual ghost hunting. The experiment took place during the investigation of Ballechin House near Strathtay, Perthshire, in 1897:

> In the afternoon [of 6 February] an experiment was made with the apparatus known as a Ouija board, and this, as is very often the case, resolved itself, after a time, into automatic writing. There is in the library a portrait of a very handsome woman, to which no name is attached, but which shows the costume of the last century. Her name was asked, and the word 'Ishbel' was given several times. [. . .] In reply to questions as to what could be done that was of use and interest, the writers were told to go at dusk, and in silence, to the glen in the avenue, and this, rightly or wrongly, some of those present identified with what had been called Scamp's Copse.[21]

'Scamp's Copse' was a small plantation of young fir trees so named because it had caused the dog – 'Scamp' – to bark at it in alarm. Goodrich-Freer and her companions followed the instructions. Although it was by now dark, 'the snow gleamed so white' that they could find their way:

> Against the snow I saw a slight black figure, a woman, moving slowly up the glen. She stopped, and turned and looked at me. She was dressed as a nun. Her face looked pale. I saw her hand in the folds of her habit. Then she moved on, as it seemed, on a slope too steep for walking. When she came under the tree she disappeared – perhaps because there was no snow to show her outline. Beyond the tree she reappeared for a moment, where there was again a white background, close by the burn. Then I saw no more. I waited, and then, still in silence, we returned to the avenue.[22]

Goodrich-Freer first made the connection between the woman in the portrait and the name 'Ishbel', but now seeing the 'nun' she decided that this must be 'Ishbel'. She then found evidence that the former owner's sister, Isabella Margaret, had entered a convent and died in 1880. She obtained a photograph and was satisfied that it matched her own sighting. The previous theory concerning the lady in the portrait was dropped entirely. The two men with her that night saw nothing. Frank Podmore, reviewing the case for the Society for Psychical Research, was not impressed.[23]

The White Lady talks
'Who are you?'
  'I am Juliet.'
  'Where did you die?'
  'Here.'
  'How did you die?'
  'Hanged.'
  'Why were you hanged?'
  'Because I loved Thomas.'
  'When did you die?'
  'Ten fifty.'
  'Is your grave in this room?'
  'Yes.'
  [. . .]
  'Can you tell us how much I have won on the football pools?'
  'Twenty-five shillings.'
          The 'White Lady' of The Ferry Boat Inn, Holywell,
             responding to questions put by Tony Cornell and
          colleagues during an improvised Ouija board session
             (Cornell, *Investigating the Paranormal*, pp. 65–7).

On 17 March 1953 Tony Cornell and three friends were sitting in The Ferry Boat Inn, Holywell, awaiting the annual appearance of the White Lady. According to the legend, the White Lady would appear in front of the fireplace and point dramatically to the spot on the floor where her final resting place was said to be. The flagstone covering the spot, normally sound, would become loose and could be rocked to and fro.[24]

The barman and the few locals enjoying a pint that night must have been bemused to see Cornell and group – his girlfriend Betty M., Roy and his wife Brenda, and David Wright – taking it in turns to rock the flagstone. Growing bored with the flagstone, the group borrowed a tin tray from the bar and chalked out a Ouija board on it and used an upturned wineglass as their planchette. Other than cracking a few jokes, the locals took their experiment in good stride, but as it neared closing time Cornell and his friends decamped to the Blue Boar in Cambridge and continued there.

During the two sittings they obtained a wealth of information from the White Lady. She called herself Juliet Tewslie and said that she had died at the age of nineteen on 17 March 1050. She confirmed that her grave was under the flagstone. She had been hanged for loving Thomas Zoul, a married man and woodcutter by profession, she said.

Cornell and his group left it at that until being invited back next year by the owner of The Ferry Boat Inn. Cornell now interviewed most of the older inhabitants of Holywell, but could find no one who had seen the ghost, nor could he find any written records of the haunting. As for Juliet Tewslie and Thomas Zoul, he again found no evidence of their having existed.

Cornell despaired as the story gathered momentum in the media, and try as he might no one was interested in hearing the results of his investigation. 'Ghost Hunters Get Extra Hour for Drinks' reported the *Daily Mail* the day before the big event, stating that 'the White Lady (aged 900) has

positively promised to try and materialize'. Every room in
the inn was booked up by journalists. The car park was full
and the police were turning vehicles away a mile up the road.
People jostled to look through the windows. The local vicar
hovered outside.[25]

The lights were periodically turned off. Ultraviolet and
infrared light flooded the bar. Photographs were snapped.
But there was no sign of the White Lady. Cornell and his
team resorted to the Ouija board – this time a purpose-built
octagonal wooden board. The glass flew round it at 'break-
neck speed'. At 12.35 a.m. it spelt out 'I am Juliet'. After more
questioning Juliet informed them 'I am trying to materialize'.
She never did.[26]

Cornell concluded that Juliet had been the imaginative
product of the minds of he and his fellow Ouija board sitters.
As a side note we might remark upon a retrial of the experiment. Members of the Ghost Club, including Tony Cornell,
convened at the inn on the half centenary of Cornell's famous
contact with the spirit of the White Lady. Just before midnight the Ghost Club seated themselves round a Ouija board
and, as Alan Murdie recounted, 'entities claiming to [be] Juliet
and Thomas came through messages on the board'.[27]

Despite dismissing his encounter with Juliet, Cornell and
his group continued experimenting with the Ouija board.
At Brookside, Mill Lane, Histon, the board was out almost
every night and soon Cornell and others started to notice a
nauseating odour that seemed to appear after using the board
or discussing psychic matters.[28] Cornell could not call it a
typical poltergeist nor even a haunting, but 'the smell' as it
became known was 'decidedly annoying'. 'It was,' he said,
'like old socks in dire need of washing.'[29]

The smell became so intense that they took up the floorboards to search for decaying rodents. The rooms were
thoroughly cleaned. Boxes of silica gel were strategically
positioned to try and absorb it. Cornell even tried to Hoover
it up. But it remained. The smell seemed to be concentrated

in a column that stretched from floor to ceiling. And it could move around. Sometimes it was in one room, sometimes in another, often it appeared to try and block the doorway. During one Ouija board session it passed under the noses of the sitters in succession. They asked it to go away. Instead the glass tore round the board spelling out a succession of swear words. Finally, Cornell slammed a crucifix down on the board and commanded it go. Things seemed to calm down and they decided to retire to The Blue Boar. But the smell followed them in the car. On another occasion Cornell awoke at 3.30 a.m. to find that the smell had settled, suffocatingly, on his face. In total fifteen different people experienced 'the smell', including an electrician unconnected with Cornell's Ouija board group and unaware of his experiments.[30]

It is an understatement to say that the Ouija board has acquired an evil reputation. For many it is the mouthpiece of the Devil. The self-styled demonologist Ed Warren said, 'the Ouija board has proven to be a notorious passkey to terror'. He estimated that 40 per cent of the 3,000 cases he had then investigated involved 'individuals who have raised inhuman spirits using a Ouija board'. 'When you use the Ouija board,' he says, 'you give permission for any unknown spirit to communicate with you.' Warren calls it the 'Law of Invitation': open the door and something will come in.[31] Jason Hawes of TAPS believes something similar, saying that using the board 'can give demonic spirits an excuse to enter a house'.[32]

'If you are Satan what do you want us to do?' Some people are just asking for trouble. One of the most shocking cases involving a Ouija board to hit the headlines was that of the so-called 'Ouija Killer'. Michael McCallum was described as a 'Devil worshipper' who had turned his flat on Portland Street in Walworth, south-east London, into a 'shrine to the Devil' with Satanic symbols and an altar on which he sacrificed frogs to appease 'the demon madness'. In 1995 he asked two teenage boys – Michael Earridge and Stephen Curran – if they would like to come back to his place to watch films. Instead they would be plunged into a real-life horror story that could have come straight from a slasher film plot. When McCallum got out his Ouija board it seemed the obvious thing for him to ask the Devil for direction. The three watched as the word 'kill' was spelt out. McCallum immediately took a large combat knife and stabbed Earridge repeatedly in the chest and neck while Curran, horrified, looked on. When the police arrested McCallum, he told them, 'I am still buzzing.'[33]

It is not the only case of Ouija-inspired murder on record. Nancy Bowen, a Native American woman living on the Cattaraugus Reservation near Buffalo, used a hammer to beat Clothilde Marchand to death in 1930 after the purported spirit of her deceased husband communicated via a Ouija board to tell her that Clothilde had killed him.[34] Mattie Turley shot and killed her father in the infamous 1933 'Ouija Murder'. Her mother was also convicted after it emerged that she had encouraged Mattie to carry out the board's instructions to kill.[35] More recently, Carol Sue Elvaker stabbed her son-in-law to death after God, speaking through her Ouija board, told her he 'was evil' and she should kill him. She afterwards tried to kill her daughter and granddaughter.[36]

> *Viewpoint: the Ouija board*
> Ignoring the occult tradition that holds that use of a Ouija board can open a gateway to undesirable spirits, the only times I have used them they seem to be an opportunity for people to create evidence, even if unintentionally.
>
> Max, Ghost Club member (GHS, 2012)

Given its reputation it is not surprising that few ghost hunters take a Ouija board along with them. The Ghost Club, for example, has only reported using the board three times during investigations in over ten years. Andrew Green included it in his list of equipment, but without any comment. Joshua P. Warren was ambivalent about the board, leaving its use and interpretation up to the reader. Whenever John Fraser has used the board he found that 'the results have been basically meaningless', but did suggest using it as a 'back-up', if only to keep tired investigators awake in the wee small hours. Yvette Fielding and Ciarán O'Keeffe thought it was 'best avoided'. Loyd Auerbach does not take a board with him on investigations, either. Not even Zak Bagans recommends using one. Some locations have also banned their use, such as Australia's most haunted house, Monte Cristo, Junee.[37]

It is at least inadvisable to involve people who are not part of the investigative team. During some Ouija sessions, investigators have reported evidence of the glass being consciously moved by one or more of the participants who were not part of the team. For example, Fielding and O'Keeffe conducted a Ouija board séance at the Hex nightclub in 2005 that involved members of staff. The result was a fiasco with people deliberately pushing the glass and ended in 'chaos, hysteria, argument and tension'.[38] Of course, the Ouija board is just one of the ways in which one can purportedly communicate with the other side.

Dowsing and divining

> At first I suspected he had a compact with the Devil, but when I observed no incantations nor sorcery, I suspended my judgement, as there are many things we know to be true, but cannot explain.[39]

This was how the seventeenth-century Jesuit mathematician Claude Dechales described his reaction when he first observed the remarkable facility of 'a certain noble person' for finding fresh water springs using a forked twig.

Ghost hunter Andrew Green experimented with a divinatory device known as the Omni-Detector Kit to try and find what he called a 'missing' well in his garden. Despite not finding the well, or lost coins for that matter – he did not use it in hunting ghosts – Green still thought that some people might have a gift for using such tools.[40] The kit contained two angle rods, a forked spring rod and two pendulums.[41] All of these devices are used in divining or dowsing – a purported technique for finding things using non-physical means, which may in fact be caused unconsciously by the ideomotor response. Angle rods (L-rods) are short lengths of metal wire bent to form a handle at one end. Held in both hands, or within a casing, the movement of the rods is believed to indicate the presence or absence of almost anything the dowser wishes to search for. This is a variation on the classic forked stick (Y-rod), usually of hazel, whose movement upwards or downwards was likewise said to indicate something meaningful, typically the presence of underground water or mineral lodes.

Again the movement of the pendulum is also taken to indicate answers to questions posed by the operator. The pendulum can be used in the field, like dowsing rods, but it can also be used with maps or alpha-numeric charts allowing it to function like a Ouija board. Pendulums were traditionally constructed from a ring and a length of thread, but today are usually custom-designed crystals suspended on a fine-link chain. Tests at the Duke Parapsychology Laboratory in the 1990s used a simple button on a string.[42]

Almost anything can be used for dowsing or as a pendulum. Over the years dowsers – who have included the Ministry of Defence, the US Marine Corps in Vietnam and the US Army Corps of Engineers – have tried out scissors, pliers, crowbars, tongs, candle snuffers and even German sausages for what has been variously called water witching, doodlebugging (for oil), rhabdomancy, radiesthesia, divining and, of course, the most common and most obscure term, 'dowsing'.[43]

Other than being able to hold a stick, no special skills are required for divining, but estimates vary as to who can use dowsing rods effectively, from 20 per cent at the low end to as much as 80 per cent at the other. Prior intention is a prerequisite of the successful operation of any divining apparatus, which is to say, the dowser must hold in his mind the object of his search.[44]

Since being used primarily for finding water and minerals, dowsing rods are now used for finding practically anything. T.C. Lethbridge was a pioneering researcher in the further uses of dowsing. Developing his theories through several books, he argued that everything had an invisible field around it, that fields could be imprinted with emotions and events, and that tools such as the rod and pendulum could detect and measure such fields.[45] Experimental researchers have used water, electricity, photographs, money, lengths of pipe, megalithic sites, minefields and even horse races as targets in their studies,[46] to name only a few, but it was Lethbridge who suggested that spirits could be dowsed. Lethbridge's writings were not well received (nor much read) at the time, and Alan Murdie argues that it was the influence of Colin Wilson that created his posthumous popularity.[47]

The rods can also be used in questioning, with yes/no responses being indicated by their movement, such as during a 2002 Ghost Club investigation of the Union Inn in Rye. Standing in the cellar at 4 a.m., the ghost hunters had a bizarre conversation with an unknown 'presence'.[48]

Dowsing is a controversial method in ghost hunting. Harry Price may have been the first to use dowsing to search for missing church plate at the site of Borley Rectory in the mid-1940s, but he used the technique in the traditional sense: to discover lost or hidden objects. An early reported use of the pendulum in ghost hunting appeared in the 1950s, but precise details of this investigation in Shoreham, Sussex, are lacking.[49] TAPS team member Heather Drolet has used brass dowsing rods on investigations with mixed results.[50] During the Adam Zubrowski investigation her 'rods crossed a bit, indicating some ambient energy'.[51] In searching for or trying

> *A dowsing conversation with a ghost*
> 'Are you a man?'
> 'Yes.'
> 'Are you a seaman?'
> 'No.'
> 'Do you mind us being here?'
> 'No.'
> 'Were you in the toilets earlier?'
> 'No.'
> 'Were you responsible for slapping me on the head earlier and pinching Shirley?'
> 'Yes.' Emphatically.
>
> Conversation with an alleged spirit using dowsing rods during a Ghost Club investigation of the Union Inn, East Street, Rye, 23 November 2002.

to make contact with supposed spirits we find that just under a third of Ghost Club investigations have used dowsing rods for this purpose.[52]

Attitudes to dowsing in the ghost hunting literature tend to be mixed. Warren listed dowsing rods, even giving directions on how to make simple angle rods, and suggested that they worked by detecting magnetic/electromagnetic fields.[53] During the Ghost Club investigation of the Union Inn, Rye, Kathy Gearing specifically used non-magnetic phosphor bronze dowsing rods to try and rule out any mundane magnetic interference and was able to conduct a conversation with an alleged spirit. Although they mention dowsing rods, Yvette Fielding and Ciarán O'Keeffe do not include them in their equipment list and state that their use is not widespread.[54] This may be more of a personal preference, as Alan Murdie claims that today 'many, if not the majority' of ghost hunters will use rods and pendulums in their investigations.[55]

As it no doubt operates on the same principle, paranormal or otherwise, pendulum divining is also controversial. Although largely ignored in books on ghost hunting, the pendulum has been more popular with ghost hunters in the field than the dreaded Ouija board. For example, just over a quarter of Ghost Club investigations have used a pendulum.[56] During their investigation of Alloa Tower, Ghost Club members used a pendulum after one investigator, Marco Piva, thought he heard a female voice calling out the name 'James' in the Great Hall. Joan Green asked, 'Is anyone there?' The pendulum swung in reply: 'Yes.'[57]

The fact that many dowsers appear to be successful in locating water is generally explained by geology rather than parapsychology. Water rarely flows in underground rivers as the dowser would have one believe, but instead, where it is accessible, is found in an extended area of water-saturated stratum. In such an area boring a well almost anywhere will allow the water to collect and be drawn off.[58] The ideomotor response triggers the movements of the dowsing device, which is unrelated to the presence of the water itself.

Sir William F. Barrett was the first person seriously to investigate dowsing, doing so on behalf of the Society for Psychical Research. Barrett considered that the ability to read the landscape could lie behind the success rate of experienced dowsers, but ultimately decided that some sort of 'peculiar instinct or faculty' for dowsing was the cause, which was effectively picked up by the dowsing apparatus and transmitted as a visual signal.[59] His later experiments used radium salts to discover whether radioactivity could be responsible – it was not – and coins hidden under things on chairs to discover whether psychic ability was responsible. It was; at least that was the conclusion Barrett now came to.[60]

Barrett had forty-five chairs set out in a large room – the Council Room of Caxton Hall, Westminster – and hid a sovereign under an item lying on the seat of one of them. The subject, a Mr J. F. Young of Llanelly, located the coin five times in a row. Barrett calculated that the odds against chance were 80,000,000 to 1. Unfortunately, Barrett did not understand probability theory. The odds were still only 45 to 1 each of the 5 times, assuming that each chair had an equal probability of being chosen, because each instance of finding the coin was statistically independent from the others.[61]

Experimenters have recorded heightened sensitivity to electro-magnetic fields and physiological reactions – notably changes in skin conductivity, but also becoming dizzy or physically sick – in dowsers. Attempts have been made to physically locate 'dowsing sensors' in the body, placing it anywhere from an area between the ribs, around the kidneys to the pineal region of the brain.[62]

So far most experiments have found no significant evidence of psi (see p. 259) as a possible mechanism for dowsing and those that did were often methodologically flawed. Dowsing for physical objects has proven no more successful than chance,[63] so whatever is believed to lie behind the mysterious movements of rods and pendulum, they are unlikely to be of any use in detecting spirits.

Mediums and sensitives

I stood in the centre of the room, watching my breath fog in the cold air. The house was over two hundred years old, beautifully half timbered, but the heart of it was cold, ice cold, and dark despite the bright sunny day outside. No one had lived here for years. The house was abandoned. Unwanted. Something tugged at the back of my mind: a sense that something was not right here. The dog had been behaving strangely, spooked you might say. At one point she had even run out of the house and down the street. Now, as an elderly neighbour told me about the deaths that had occurred here – one man had fallen off the roof, another had been crushed by the piano he was carrying downstairs – a sense of foreboding came over me.[64]

Almost everyone has had, at one time or another, a strange feeling about a place. Most of the Ghost Club investigations that I have analysed have involved members receiving psychic impressions, ranging from emotional feelings about a place to 'sensing' the presence of supposed spirits.[65] Rosie Murdie even received a 'psychic kiss' when investigating The Old Swan, Cheddington.[66] Many of Elliott O'Donnell's cases involved his ability to see and sense things that others could not. Likewise most of Ed and Lorraine Warren's ghost hunting, as opposed to demon baiting, involved Lorraine's ability to sense spirits. In many cases this vague sense of unease or more particular sense of presence constitutes the entirety of the haunting.

The term 'sensitive', as in psychically sensitive, has been used of people able to receive impressions or information about a place or people through supposedly paranormal means since at least the nineteenth century, although it seems more popular now.[67] The medium is distinct in being able to allow the supposed spirit to possess and so speak through them, or clairaudiently to them, sometimes with accompanying phenomena, such as the levitation of objects or materialization. The term 'psychic' encompasses the whole range of ability in this regard. Whilst many people claim to be able to pick up on certain impressions, it is rarer to find a medium capable of directly channelling communication.

Despite professing some mediumistic powers himself, O'Donnell poured scorn on the professional mediums of his day. 'There must be at least a hundred shades of Dickens,' he wrote, 'for there is hardly a spiritualistic meeting or séance that I hear of at which Dickens is not alleged to be present.'[68] Even Sir Arthur Conan Dyle had been in touch with Dickens' alleged spirit, discussing his unfinished novel *Edwin Drood*. Apparently, Dickens rather liked the idea of Sherlock Holmes solving the mystery.[69] Unsurprisingly, the fraudulent spirit photographer Edouard Isidore Buguet managed to snap a picture of Dickens in 1874, four years after his death.[70]

For much of its history psychical research has shut itself up in the séance room with supposed mediums and after years of investigation the results remain mixed, if not actually disappointing. Most of the 'successes' have been the unmasking of fraudsters.

Living TV's *Most Haunted* brought ghosts and mediums to many people's front rooms for the first time during its nine-year run from 2002 to 2010 (with a 2011 one-off special). Despite using historians and parapsychologists on night vigils in reputedly haunted locations, a central feature of the show was the use of mediums to channel psychic information about the case, including the supposed spirits of the deceased. From the beginning and for most of the early years (2002–5) Derek Acorah was the show's star medium until dramatically exposed by resident parapsychologist Ciarán O'Keeffe.[71]

O'Keeffe's suspicions had been roused during an investigation of Castle Leslie, County Monaghan, in 2004. According to the legends a seventeenth-century four-poster bed has the reputation of levitating. Entering the bedroom, Acorah put his hand on the bed and proceeded to give highly accurate information about the alleged haunting. O'Keeffe later recalled that 'it was the wrong bed'. Suspecting that Acorah had had prior knowledge of the location chosen for filming against the show's production protocols, O'Keeffe devised a simple plan.

While shooting an episode at Bodmin Gaol, O'Keeffe invented Kreed Kafer, a deceased South African gaoler. He wrote the name down and requested a crew member to mention it to Acorah before filming. 'I honestly didn't think Derek would take the bait,' said O'Keeffe, 'but during filming he actually got possessed by my fictional character.' The name Kreed Kafer is an anagram of 'Derek Faker'.[72]

At the Elizabethan mansion of Prideaux Place, Cornwall, O'Keeffe came up with another invention, Rik Eedles, a supposed highwayman. During the show Acorah made contact with the spirit. Rik Eedles is an anagram of 'Derek Lies'.[73]

At Craigievar Castle, Scotland, O'Keeffe took the theme of *The Lion, The Witch and The Wardrobe* to concoct a story involving Richard the Lionheart, a witch, and the king's ghost walking through a wardrobe. It was as ingenious as it was impossible. Richard I (1157–99), known as 'the Lionheart', had reigned 500 years before the castle was built in 1626, but Acorah mentioned all of the stories.[74]

In the final case, O'Keeffe's powers of invention were spared. During the programme supposedly broadcast live from a Victorian madhouse (the former Manchester Royal Lunatic Asylum, now called Cheadle Royal Hospital), Acorah, O'Keeffe recalled, 'was communicating with spirits that sounded as if they'd been in an asylum'. Unfortunately, the film location was not Cheadle Royal, nor even an asylum, but actually the derelict Barnes Convalescent Home in Cheadle, Greater Manchester.[75]

The show had made Acorah Britain's best-known medium. The year before the sting he was voted TV Personality of the Year by the Variety Club. O'Keeffe told the *Mirror* newspaper that 'In my professional opinion, we're not dealing with a genuine medium – all we are seeing is showmanship and dramatics.' Questioned by reporters, Acorah said in his defence, 'I believe that I am a genuine medium'.

'I don't believe any of them,' said Fielding in an interview with comedian Justin Lee Collins, before offering '£200,000 to the medium who can prove to me that they are genuine and that they are real.'[76] Despite the controversy, the *Sun* newspaper still described Acorah as the 'UK's foremost medium', until he fell out of favour over claims about missing girl Madeleine McCann.[77]

Necromancy
Why hast thou disquieted me, to bring me up?

The aged figure stood wrapped in a mantle. He was the prophet Samuel, dead these many years, and now raised by the strange incantations of 'a woman that hath a familiar spirit', the infamous 'Witch of Endor'. Saul, King of Israel, bowed to the ground before the apparition and answered, 'I have called thee, that thou mayest make known unto me what I shall do.' The Philistines had gathered a great army against Saul, and Saul felt his smaller force was no match for them. He had tried asking God for advice, but 'the Lord answered him not', and so he had turned to necromancy. Unfortunately, Samuel had only bad news to impart. Saul and his sons would be killed and Israel would fall to the Philistines.[78]

It is but a short step from mediumship to necromancy. Generally understood as raising the dead, necromancy is technically divining by the dead (from the Greek *nekrós*, 'dead', and *manteia*, 'divination'), although the net effect is the same: the spirits of the departed must be summoned from wherever they are before communication can begin. Spiritualism was dubbed 'modern necromancy' by its detractors and they were not so far off the mark.[79] The distinction, if there is one, might be thought to lie in the assumed location of the spirits one wishes to communicate with. The classic necromancer raises the spirit from the otherworld – hell, heaven or whatever other name has been given to the abodes of the dead – whilst the medium communicates with spirits that are thought to be earth-bound or otherwise still near to the physical realm. Even more importantly, the necromancer summons the spirits to appear before him; the medium invites them to appear within through possession by the spirits. The necromancer uses the arcana of high magic and all its fantastic trappings; the medium prefers a séance round the dining-room table. It is not a hard-and-fast definition – exceptions are plenty – but it does capture something of the differences between the terms. But the essence of each procedure is the same: communication with the dead.

Necromancy is dangerous magic. Debate has raged over the interpretation of Saul and the Witch of Endor, but the biblical message was clear. Saul had already banished 'those that had familiar spirits, and the wizards', and his turning to the witch in desperation was only another sign of having lost

God's grace.[80] Christian writers have generally denied that the spirits of the dead can actually be raised through necromancy, stating instead that their appearances are the illusions of the Devil; and any sort of dealing with the Devil, illusory or not, is black magic. As such, necromancy was catalogued by the medieval German writer Johannes Hartlieb as one of 'the forbidden arts'. The medieval poet Johannes von Tepl talked of necromancers using 'the sacrificial fingers of the dead and sigils (talismans)' and Hartlieb was clear that they 'must make various offerings to the Devil . . . vow to him and be in league with him'.[81]

The *Fourth Book of Occult Philosophy* – a late sixteenth-century grimoire posthumously ascribed to Heinrich Cornelius Agrippa von Nettesheim – gave some gory instructions for performing necromantic operations:

> In raising up these shadows, we are to perfume with new Blood, with the Bones of the dead, and with Flesh, Egges, Milk, Honey and Oile, and such-like things, which do attribute to the Souls a means apt to receive their Bodies.[82]

According to the theory expounded, 'Souls do still love their relinquished Bodies after death', especially the souls of those who have died violently, have been improperly buried or have not been buried at all, or 'whom we know to be evil'. These souls 'wander in a liquid and turbulent Spirit about their dead carkasses'. Consequently, graveyards, places of execution and those reputed to be haunted were the best sites for conjuration.[83]

In his *Three Books of Occult Philosophy* Agrippa added that the stone 'synochitis' and the herb 'aglauphotis' both had the magical properties of being able to call up the ghosts of the dead. A more specific incense for raising spirits was composed of spermaceti, lignum-aloes, red storax, pepperwort, musk and saffron mixed with the blood of a lapwing. However, Agrippa himself stated that only God, not any necromancer, could raise the dead, limiting his belief in the powers of magic to within the bounds of the already strained and grudging toleration of the subject evinced by the theocratic powers of his day.[84]

Not everyone was willing to be put off the subject by pious proscriptions. In seventeenth-century England an unnamed individual heard an incredible story of 'deeds of darkness' from his servant and shortly before he died told it to the antiquary and poet John Weever. It concerned Edward Kelley (1555–97), alchemist, adventurer, convicted forger, and, at one time, Dr John Dee's 'scryer' or medium. The servant had been there with Kelley and his then master Peter Waring in the cemetery that night. They were gathered round the grave of the most recently deceased, a poor man buried that day, in St Leonard's churchyard adjoining the park of Walton-le-Dale in Lancashire. Spades in hand, they set to and exhumed the body. With 'black ceremonies' and 'incantations' they caused the body to speak and reveal 'strange predictions'. Weever had the story confirmed by the servant himself.[85]

In the nineteenth century the influential French occultist Eliphas Levi raised the spirit of the Greek philosopher Apollonius of Tyana on several occasions. At his first attempt in 1854 in the private magical oratory of a wealthy patron in London he described the materialization of the spirit:

> I recommenced the evocations, and placed myself within a circle which I had drawn previously between the tripod and the altar. Thereupon the mirror which was behind the altar seemed to brighten in its depth, a wan form was outlined therein, which increased, and seemed to approach by degrees. Three times, and with closed eyes, I invoked Apollonius. When I again looked forth there was a man in front of me, wrapped from head to foot in a species of shroud, which seemed more grey than white; he was lean, melancholy and beardless.[86]

Levi factored in the trappings of the ritual – 'the probations, the perfumes, the mirrors, the pentacles' – as causing 'an actual drunkenness of the imagination'. However, he was adamant that 'I did see and that I did touch, that I saw clearly and distinctly' the spirit of Apollonius. He regarded the result as 'the voluntary dream of a waking man', but also concluded that it was 'sufficient to establish the real efficacy of magical ceremonies'. After being touched by the spirit of Apollonius, Levi lost the power of his arm for several days afterwards.

It is worth noting that during an investigation of Sutcliffe House, Harrisville, Rhode Island, in 2005, TAPS member Dustin Pari also claimed to have been touched by a paranormal entity and that afterwards his hand felt as if it had been 'bathed in ice'. Jason Hawes claimed that this was a common side effect.[87]

Lisa Lee Harp Waugh is the founder of the American Ghost Hunters Society and a modern necromancer. She reputedly began summoning spirits at the age of twelve in Scotsville Cemetery, Texas. According to her website:[88]

> She dresses in ceremonial white robes, draws magical circle and triangles on the floor and commands spirits from Heaven, Hell and all places in between to appear before her and communicate with the living.

Levi avoided being merely credulous, wary of deluding himself, and yet was compelled to admit that something did happen that was to all intents and purposes against the laws of nature. Certainly he took necromancy seriously and warned others against its 'destructive and dangerous' practice. Saul would no doubt have agreed.[89]

8

EXPLAIN

Following the curious dogma that what we don't understand
can't exist, mainstream science has dismissed psychic phenomena as delusions or hoaxes simply because they're rarer than
sleep, dreams, memory, growth, pain, or consciousness, which
are all inexplicable in traditional terms but are too common to
be denied.[1]

Surely ghosts are also 'too common to be denied'? The more
one reads about ghosts, the more difficult it becomes to decide
the matter. On one level the sheer number of reports across
time, continent and culture seems irrefutable. But as one
investigates each story so many of them unravel into fantasy
and fabrication. Piles of double exposures passing for genuine ghost photographs can be consigned to the waste bin. All
those images of 'orbs' can now be safely deleted. Excluding
cold reading and prior research, the testimonies of mediums
seldom match the known facts when there are known facts and
are frequently admitted only in the absence of anything more

concrete. Eyewitness testimony is generally so unreliable that it cannot be taken as proof in itself. The scientific explanations sometimes work and sometimes do not. The ghost remains elusive, yet each night there will be those, crouching in the dark, who hope to catch them. And there will be those, not always the same people, who will see them. Sometimes ghosts are delusions or hoaxes, as we will see, but sometimes they are not and that remains the insolvable problem.

The dead

Ghosts are supposed to be spirits of the dead. This is the time-honoured and traditional interpretation. A figure is seen of someone who no longer appears to have any earthly life. It appears, it disappears. It walks through walls. It cannot be touched. It is clearly not of this world. Sometimes the apparition is even recognized by people who knew the person whilst still living. Apparitions very often look like real people – a complete figure is seen (89 per cent), vividly (37.5 per cent) and described as 'real' (22 per cent).[2]

When Athenadorus was interrupted in his studies by a pale visitor, bound in chains, he seems to have shown no doubt that this was a ghost. When the children of Revd Bull saw a nun walk down the infamously haunted 'nun's walk' in the grounds of Borley Rectory, the first and simplest explanation that came to mind was that this was the spirit of a dead nun. Most people are satisfied with this explanation. After all, it seems like common sense. You see someone who should be dead and conclude that it must be their spirit.

Most of the reputedly haunted locations considered in this book have seen murder, suicide, tragic death, sometimes all three, and at the very least human suffering in its more extreme forms. Since ancient times the spirits of those killed violently have been considered to be particularly prone to becoming ghosts. So far the evidence has been mixed. When Bozzano analysed 532 cases of things that go bump in the night in 1929 he found that of the 374 he considered to be 'phénomènes de

Explanations of haunting

Traditional	Physical	Psychological	Para-psychological	Behavioural
Spirits of the dead	Geology	Misperception	Telepathic hallucination	Fraud
Devil/demons	Structure	Suggestibility	Psychokinesis (RSPK)	Maliciousness
	Animal	Expectation		Publicity
	Vibration	Agency		Illegal occupancy
	Infrasound	Fantasy proneness		Criminal activity
	Electromagnetism	Multiple personality		
	Multiple universes	Mental illness		
	Quantum physics			

hantise proprement dite' ('phenomena of hauntings properly so-called') the majority also involved a reported death at the location. On the other hand, Eleanor Sidgwick, sifting through the cases that had been brought to the attention of the SPR, decided that there was 'extremely slight' evidence for supposing that apparitions were connected with 'some crime or tragedy'.[3] In support of Bozzano, Hart and his colleagues found that 59 per cent of apparitions of people dead for less than twelve hours and 44 per cent of apparitions of people at the point of death involved demonstrating the death of that person to others. This would suggest that death itself, rather than the manner of it, can be a predictive factor.

However, this same finding could lead us to suppose that it is death and only death, not the survival of personality after it, that creates the apparition. Whilst they may look real, apparitions seldom behave as real. They rarely speak (12.5 per cent) and are infrequently seen by two or more people at the same time (9.6 per cent).[4] Their actions have a strange mechanical aspect – a general inability to interact with the living or adapt to changes in the physical environment – and this is one of the main arguments against them being the spirits of the dead. Another prominent SPR member, Myers, noted that the 'frequent, meaningless recurrences of a figure in a given spot' – the typical ghost – suggested, not a personality surviving death and performing new actions, but rather that the past actions of the figure whilst living created the 'ghost'.[5]

The Church has all the answers: ghosts are the work of the Devil. On one level it is a convincing explanation, since it explains everything. The Devil is there, pretending to be some spirit of the dead, so that he can follow his mysterious plan to pervert the work of God. According to the self-styled demonologist Ed Warren 'ghosts are often called "angels of the Devil"', and he estimated that half of all apparitions are demons projecting themselves in human form.[6]

But then again, what is the evidence for the existence of the Devil or his demons? Other than faith in the scriptures, it comes down to things like ghosts, poltergeists and possession. The reasoning is circular. It goes nowhere.

If hauntings were truly the product of diabolical intervention, then exorcism should be a sure-fire method of eradicating them. However, the inconsistency of exorcism was noted by Elliott O'Donnell as early as 1916.[7] More recently, TAPS suggested that Sam Dillon, manager of a reputedly haunted warehouse in New Jersey, get his building blessed and exorcized, but noted that afterwards there were still reports of paranormal activity.[8] In another case TAPS documented what they believed to be paranormal activity in the former home of Dr Ellis, Eureka Springs, Arkansas, confirming the current owner's feeling that the property was haunted, despite a previous attempt at exorcism.[9]

Elliott O'Donnell remained convinced that ghosts, if they were not demons, were the spirits of the dead.[10] But many other ghost hunters have, after years of investigation, come to different conclusions.

The world

There have been a number of attempts to provide a purely natural explanation for supposed supernatural effects. Many of these do indeed seem to account for certain observed conditions in particular instances, but none of them easily explains all of the phenomena all of the time. This could point to there being simply multiple causes for events interpreted as paranormal, or it could suggest that the real mechanism is not yet understood. For the ghost hunter, it is necessary to understand what natural factors can be behind apparently unnatural activity because more often than not the causes are disappointingly mundane.

Geology

In the dark dungeons of Hastings Castle voices are heard. But the hearer stands alone, surrounded only by shadows. The dungeons are carved out of the solid rock; how could sound penetrate here? Are the dungeons haunted by the souls of those unfortunates imprisoned and perhaps tortured in this smothering darkness? But the voice is only that of the tour guide. Here a word whispered in one of the cells can be clearly heard many yards away. The castle is built with and stands on sandstone, the so-called Hastings sandstone found in this region of southeast England. It also contains ironstone, rich in iron pyrites, that has the curious property of being able to conduct sound. It is a particularly noticeable phenomenon in the dungeons.[11]

The clock had already struck midnight as Mr John May made his way through the gravestones in Borley churchyard one September evening in 1947. Faint music disturbed the autumn air. May recalled later that he heard 'soft notes and chords from the organ' but all in 'a jumble of atonal chords'. From 1946 to 1970, seven out of thirteen dated events recorded by seven different witnesses at Borley Church occurred on or within twenty-four hours of the full or new moon. The village of Borley is some way from the sea, too far to be subject to any tidal effect of the River Stour, but it does lie at a geophysically unstable point where the London Clay and its associated beds gives way to chalk. Vibrations arising from such instability could conceivably cause physical effects above the surface, similar to atonal organ music.[12]

As reported to the Geological Society of Glasgow, earth tremors can cause noises sounding like such unlikely things as 'the dragging of heavy furniture across the floor', 'the fall of heavy objects', 'the falling of a load of stone', and so on.[13] These are in the range frequently reported at allegedly haunted locations. In particular, it has been suggested that the many phantom drummers of Scottish legend may be the result of Scotland's seismic activity.[14] When significant haunting phenomena – including clanging, banging and crashing sounds – were reported at Ballechin House in Perthshire, in the late nineteenth century, it was also observed that there was considerable seismic activity at nearby Comrie, possibly accounting for the mysterious noises.[15]

Looking at fifty-four poltergeist cases with sufficient detail for analysis, Lambert found that a large proportion, 'nearly half', were within three miles of tidal water. Lambert also found a seasonal bias in his data with most cases occurring in the 'wet and wintry half of the year'. He theorized – his so-called 'geophysical theory' – that tidal action in subterranean rivers, particularly where the flow was temporarily blocked, inundated with sudden winter spates could cause sufficient hydraulic force to move objects, indeed a whole house above the surface, and produce much of what is attributed to poltergeists.[16] In a later paper, Lambert also drew together the seismic and hydraulic as related factors, noting that the action of water can cause earth tremors, which again can produce the necessary sounds and vibrations to be mistaken for poltergeists.[17]

Lambert's comparison of paranormal and earthquake effects[18]

Poltergeist and haunting effects	Earthquake effects (Mercalli scale)
Feeling of uneasiness or fear	I. Some birds and animals show uneasiness
Lamp swinging and suspended bell ringing	II. Delicately suspended objects may swing
'Footsteps', noises like a carriage or lorry	III. Vibration like the passing of a truck (lorry)
Electric lights turning on and off	IV. Dishes, windows, doors disturbed
Knocking sounds	Walls make cracking sounds
Breaking of windows	V. Dishes, windows etc. broken
Movements of small free objects	Unstable objects overturned
Stopping of pendulum clocks	Pendulum clocks may stop
Shaking of beds and disturbance of bedclothes	VI. Some heavy furniture moved
Movements of heavy furniture	Some falling of plaster and damage to chimneys

Building structure and related issues

A property can develop structural problems, or it can have them built in. Poor workmanship is often the source of apparently paranormal activity. Badly fitted windows cause 'mysterious' draughts, cold spots and noises, such as sighing and moaning sounds. Writing in the 1970s, Green particularly noted that the trend to install double glazing, especially DIY efforts, had led to an upsurge in such reports. Gaps in the frame or the wrong materials can all generate unexpected effects. Badly fitted doors can also cause effects frequently mistaken for the paranormal, such as doors that will not open or doors that repeatedly open 'by themselves', as well as doors and frames that split or crack. These can all be caused by using inadequately seasoned timber.[19] It is often noted, as it was back in 1882 when the Committee on Haunted Houses made its first report, that structural changes to a property result in the termination of the haunting.[20]

PLUMBING

John Fraser was in a haunted hotel, standing in front of the 'secret' compartment. Strange noises came from within. Was it a gateway to Hell, or some portal to quantum dimensions of staggering bizarreness? He had permission to unlock it. A crowd had gathered, the air was full of 'excitement and awe'. He opened the compartment. Inside was a bathroom cistern. As they watched, the solution became clear. Every time someone flushed a toilet in the hotel the cistern would rattle.[21] As Jason Hawes and Grant Wilson will tell you, sometimes being a plumber in your day job is indispensible training for a ghost hunter.

CONDENSATION

One of the supposed evidences of haunting at Lowes Cottage was the appearance of water on one of the walls. Described as 'weeping', the wall had been observed to be wet by the Revd Mockford and had been a factor in his deciding that the cottage was haunted.[22] In some newspaper reports the water had trans-mogrified into 'oozing slime'.[23] What was then Manchester's Anomalous Phenomena Investigation Team (MAPIT) and Tameside and Oldham Paranormal Research Association (TOPRA) conducted a joint investigation. They discovered beads of water on one of the cellar walls at about 5 a.m. The team wiped the water away, but noted that after about an hour it was again visible. The cellar being underground and the wall in question backing on to earth, it was concluded that moisture in the air was condensing on the cold wall surface. When they questioned the Smiths it was found that this was the wall that had been weeping water in an allegedly supernatural manner.[24]

CARBON MONOXIDE POISONING

Depression. Footsteps heard in empty rooms. A feeling of being watched. The children began to grow pale and listless. Bells were heard ringing when none was rung. The sound of doors slamming and the crashing of pots and pans disturbed the night hours. The plants began to die. The family had just moved into a large, rambling and ramshackle house dating from the 1870s. Even in 1912 the new occupiers noted that it was still lit by gas, not electricity. Heavy carpeting through-out stifled all sound and an eerie stillness lay over the house. Finally, one day the ghost was seen.[25]

The woman who saw it, the lady of the household, and she saw it several times, dismissed it as a trick of the light. But the children, the children's nurse and the governess were all con-vinced that the house was haunted. Luckily a visitor recog-nized the symptoms and the family called 'Professor S.'. After examining the household, the professor's assistant – 'Mr S.' – examined the building. He discovered the aged furnace to be in very poor repair. Fuel was not being properly com-busted, and, instead of exiting through the chimney, carbon monoxide was being pumped into the rooms. Mr S. advised them not to spend another night in the building, or it could be their last. When investigating a haunting where physiological symptoms are described, the ghost hunter should get out his CO detector.

ACCIDENTAL FACTORS

In the basement of a house in Roselle Park, New Jersey, something kept tripping the motion-detector alarm when the room was empty. The owner feared it was a ghost. After tripping the alarm themselves and accidentally summoning the local constabulary, TAPS investigators Jason Hawes and Grant Wilson discovered the real reason behind the alarm's paranormal activity. When the heating system came on in the basement it blew a draught of air strong enough to set the decorative Yuletide lights of the faux icicle type swinging in the breeze. That was what the motion detector was sensing.[26]

In some cases unusually cold rooms are found to have quite logical explanations. Tour guides at Beechwood, the former mansion of the Astor family in Newport, Rhode Island, complained that the ballroom was always cold even on warm, sunny days. A TAPS investigator found that the heating ducts had been blocked up with rags.[27]

Flora and fauna

Writer and paranormal researcher Peter Haining thought that his sixteenth-century home Peyton House might have yet another ghost when he began hearing mysterious tapping sounds from the library below his study. Cautiously climbing down the stairs, he could find nothing to account for the sound. This continued for several days, and each time Haining – throwing caution to the wind – dashed down the stairs. Each time he found the library deserted. Then, finally, he saw something. A movement at the window caught his eye. Turning round to confront the phantom, he discovered a bird knocking at the window with its beak. When it caught sight of Haining it flew off in alarm. Haining reasoned that the bird had been pecking at its own reflection thinking that it was a territorial rival.[28]

Haunt-type effects caused by carbon monoxide poisoning[29]

Category	Range of effects described			
Psychological presentations	depression	listlessness	feeling of being watched/followed	
Auditory hallucinations	footsteps	doors slamming	crashing of pots and pans	bells ringing	hearing name being called
Visual hallucinations	human figures			
Physical sensations				
(a) Imaginary	feeling of touch	being sat upon	strangulation	shaking of bed
(b) Physiological	feeling ill	loss of appetite	heavy sleep	headache	visual impairment

Vermin can often be the cause of otherwise mysterious sounds, even fires. Old wiring still to be found in many properties used fabric for insulation. Rats and mice, finding this a useful material for nest building, have been known to chew it off, causing short circuits and electrical fires. Rats scuttling about behind the wainscoting is a common feature in many ghost stories, but they can also cause pianos and harpsichords to apparently play by themselves by eating the felt pads from the wires. Running up and down bell ropes, they can also cause the bells themselves to start ringing.[30] In another case, rats rolling apples from their storage place in an attic down a cavity in the wall 'produced the spooky sounds' being reported.[31] In North America, a family of racoons nesting in an attic was discovered to be the source of a supposed haunting.[32]

Ticking sounds can be produced by a number of insects, notably death watch beetle (*Xestobium rufovillosum*). In one case of a supposedly phantom clock the sound turned out to be *Trogium pulsatorium*, a small species of bookworm.[33]

Nocturnal screams and crying can, in many cases, be attributed to cats, night birds and foxes. Mewling cats can sound horribly like crying human infants and a fox can fool anyone into thinking that murder most foul is being committed outside one's bedroom window. In many cases one would think that country folk would be used to such noises and therefore able to distinguish the natural from the supernatural, but at the dead of night with an overwrought imagination working on a full stomach or an empty head anything is, as we shall see, possible.

Infrasound

Vic Tandy called it 'the ghost in the machine'. He had already heard the rumours that the laboratory was haunted. He had already dismissed them, despite the fact that the laboratory made he and his colleagues depressed, sometimes even sending cold shivers down their spines. It was all noticeably worse one evening when he sat working alone into the night. He had the strange feeling that he was being watched. Out of the corner of his eye he could see a grey figure materializing. When he turned, it vanished. Understandably, Tandy decided to go home.[34]

The next day he was back to do some repair work on a fencing foil before a coming competition. He clamped the blade in a vice and went to look for some oil. When he returned he was astonished to see the free end of the blade waving up and down. With the benefit of broad daylight he began thinking of mechanical rather than supernatural explanations. He reasoned that there must be something providing sufficient energy and at the correct resonant frequency to move the blade. After some tests Tandy was convinced that a low frequency standing sound wave was the culprit. Making some quick calculations, he discovered that it had a frequency of 18.98 Hz ± 10 per cent. According to research, this frequency could also resonate parts of the human body, notably the head, causing a feeling of discomfort, and the eyes, causing a smearing of vision. Such effects could account both for the feelings of depression and the visual impression of a non-existent human figure.

When Tandy talked to the foreman he learnt that a new air conditioner fan had been fitted about the time that the haunting had started. When they switched the extractor fan off, the standing wave was no longer evident. Some adjustments were made to the fan housing and the infrasound 'ghost' was seen no more.

The sources of infrasound are almost limitless, encompassing both the natural and manmade, from ocean waves and tectonic movement, wind and waterfalls, volcanoes and violent storms, to transformers, heavy traffic, machinery, domestic appliances and, of course, extractor fans.[35] Considerable research has been done on the psychological and physiological effects of infrasound. As the table on p. 239 shows, fatigue and depression/apprehension are the most commonly observed reactions. Although the UK government's Health

Protection Agency says there is no consistent evidence of the effect of infrasound, the US Army is known to be pursuing an infrasonic weapons programme.[36]

Electro- and geomagnetics
It was 1975, and a flat in Sudbury, Canada, was being haunted. People experienced cold spots, they saw things that should not have been there, things were broken by invisible means. Some weeks after it began, the city experienced a surge in UFO reports. The paranormal had come to town. Two young researchers at Laurentian University were called in to investigate. Michael Persinger and R.A. Cameron had been working on physical theories of the paranormal and brought with them an array of sensitive equipment designed to detect slight vibrations and electromagnetic fields.[37]

The equipment had been running for ten days with nothing to report, before the monitors burst suddenly into life showing an intense signal lasting just ten seconds. Moments later 'Miss B.' jumped out of bed. She was afraid, more afraid than she could imagine possible. She ran out of the house. Analysing the data, Persinger and Cameron stated that 'the event was considered to be electromagnetic-like in nature' and to have come from Miss B.'s room.

In 1996 an anxious mother called Persinger. Her daughter was being visited by the Holy Spirit. She also said that she felt the presence of an invisible baby sitting on her left shoulder, heard footsteps and a humming sound, and complained that the bed vibrated. Even more alarming, the girl said that the Holy Spirit had impregnated her. The seventeen-year-old had sustained mild brain damage in early childhood, but this was not thought to be the principal cause. Persinger got out his equipment. He discovered electromagnetic pulses measuring 40 mG emanating from an area close to where the girl slept. The pulses were in the range known to trigger epileptic seizures.[38]

Electromagnetic fields are extremely popular among ghost hunters, especially since the TV hunters have started waving

Demonstrated biological effects of infrasound[39]

	Mohr (1965)	Gavreau (1968)	Stephens (1969)	Karpova (1970)	Lidstrom (1978)	Moller (1984)	Tandy (1998)	Chen (2004)	Hansen (2007)
Ear pressure	x			x		x		x	
Headache		x				x	x	x	
Fatigue		x		x		x		x	
Unable to concentrate					x				
Uncomfortable				x		x		x	x
Heart rate				x				x	
Blood pressure				x				x	
Respiratory rate	x			x					
Imbalance			x						x
Disorientation									x
Incapacitation									x
Nausea	x		x						x
Vomiting									x
Depression/apprehension		x	x	x			x	x	
Time perception					x		x		
Visual effects	x		x						

their EMF meters around like light sabres at a Star Wars convention. EMF meters make good television. Their lights flash. They make beeping noises. They appear to be doing something. They *are* detecting the unseen, but are they detecting ghosts?

At first glance it is not obvious why electromagnetics should be so popular. EMF meters were initially designed to detect mains electricity. The voltage in the wires produces a measurable electromagnetic field: 50 Hz in Europe, UK and Commonwealth; 60 Hz in North America. Nothing particularly paranormal about that. Most of the EMF meters being used in ghost hunting today are still designed to detect mains electricity and other manmade sources of electromagnetic fields. So their utility is doubtful, to say the least.

Many ghost hunters have a vague energy theory relating to the paranormal. TAPS investigators Jason Hawes and Grant Wilson both believe that ghosts need energy to manifest and attribute unusually rapid battery power loss – a common feature of paranormal investigation – to paranormal entities.[40] Ghost hunter Joshua P. Warren argues that apparitions use 'electrostatic charges and EMFs to appear as a plasma' – plasma being defined as a fourth state of matter, such as a flame or lightning flash.[41] On this principle he suggests that an electrostatic generator, such as a Van de Graaff or Wimshurst-Bonetti generator, could be used to 'pump ions into the atmosphere' and create a more conducive environment for apparitional phenomena.[42]

When they find EMF fluctuations, many ghost hunters take this as a sign of paranormal activity. When investigating the USS *North Carolina* battleship, TAPS recorded an EMF 'spike of 2.2' in a shower room where 'a baseline reading in that area would have been 1.0'.[43] However, team members were apparently making their first tour of the ship and no baseline readings had been established. The reported measurement is meaningless.

Even if they do not find EMF fluctuations they tend to

dismiss this as irrelevant. In 2005 TAPS set up an investigation of the reputedly haunted Crescent Hotel, Eureka Springs, Arkansas. According to anecdotal evidence, rooms 212 and 419 were centres of unusual happenings. When team member Dustin Pari tried to enter Room 419 he had to push against an unexpected resistance. He heard a thump and the door opened. Grant Wilson's laptop had been leaning against the back of the door, even though Wilson had placed it on the other side of the room. There was no one in the room at the time this happened. TAPS decided that 'there was genuine activity in the hotel'. When they heard about the incident Jason Hawes and Wilson immediately measured EMF levels in the room, what they called 'an EMF sweep'. However, there were no unusual readings to be had. There was of course some lapse of time between the incident and the 'sweep', which should certainly be taken into account, but this was not reported.[44]

When investigating the haunting of The Stanley Hotel, Colorado, in 2006, TAPS were told that the hotel was built over significantly quartz-rich rock strata. Jason Hawes theorized that 'energy captured by the quartz gets released when conditions are right, allowing spirits to manifest themselves'.[45]

SPR member Anne Arnold Silk had earlier found an association between paranormal phenomena and geological fault lines in the UK and theorized that pressure and movement within the earth at points containing piezo-electric material, such as quartz, created electric and magnetic fields that either generated haunting type effects or stimulated the psychical ability of percipients.[46] Subsequent geological surveys carried out for the Rocky Mountain Paranormal Research Society found no unusual concentrations of quartz underneath The Stanley Hotel.[47]

However, according to research both EMFs and geomagnetic fields (GMFs) do seem to be involved. Persinger and Cameron discovered that the haunted flat in Sudbury lay close to geological faults. They hypothesized that 'tectonogenic forces' were generating electromagnetic fields with a frequency range of 0.01 to 100 Hz that could stimulate the brain's temporal lobe to produce the feeling of strangeness, 'acute fear', 'felt images', sleep disruption and even 'physical changes in matter'.

In the case of the girl and the Holy Spirit, Persinger traced the electromagnetic pulses to an electric alarm clock on the bedside table. When the girl no longer slept with the clock near her head the visions stopped. The average intensity of 50 and 60 Hz power frequencies ranges from between 1 and 50 mG – as we saw in the girl's case it was as high as 40 mG. When Persinger wrote up his results, exposure to about 2 mG was considered safe and long-term exposure to fields above 5 mG was known to be hazardous. Most recent research has brought both exposure levels down.

GMFs comprise a steady-state field of around 500 mG and a fluctuating (time-varying) field of between 0.1 mG and 1 mG with frequencies of between 0.001 Hz and 1 Hz. Even such small ranges have been shown to affect living organisms.[48]

The human brain mostly generates waves with frequencies of between 1 and 30 Hz with a field strength of about 1 to 10 nG. For comparison the strength of the magnet inside the typical refrigerator is about 50 G, a field strength of 160 kG was found to be able to levitate a frog, and at the upper range the field of a super-dense neutron star is measured in giga Gauss.[49] Frequency oscillations in the same range as the human brain, such as those that accompany geomagnetic activity, can stimulate dreamlike imagery. A possible aspect is moving through (physically or temporally) a changing field strength as opposed to the strength of the field itself.[50]

The background levels of most homes in the UK, excluding those near power lines, are between 0.01 and 0.2 µT (0.1 to 2 mG), and few exceed 0.3 µT (3 mG). Fields are strongest around domestic appliances, easily being in the hundreds µT (1000s mG) at a distance of 3 cm, but falling off to background levels at about 1 m distance from the device. One of the biggest culprits is an electric shaver, with a field intensity

Non-ionizing radiation levels at haunted locations[51]

Location	EMF	GMF	+Air ions/ cm^3	−Air ions/ cm^3
Private home, Madison, IN	157 mG	725–847 mG	5,000	17,000
Dragsholm Castle, Denmark	100+ mG	527 mG	–	–
Engsö Castle, Sweden	–	650–752 mG	–	–
Fort Leonard Wood, MO	–	26–561 mG	–	–
McRaven House, Vicksburg, MS	'normal'	690–787 mG	1,900	3,700
Oliver House, Brissbe, CA	–	560–824 mG	18,000	6,400
Private home, Lake Ariel, PA	–	880 mG	36,000	8,000
'Plenty', Port Tobacco, MD	125.7 mG	800–900 mG	102,000	5,000
Average top-range values	127.57 mG	747.25 mG	32,580	8,020

of 165 µT (1650 mG) at a distance of 5 cm. The field around a microwave oven is 1.66 µT (16.6 mG) even 50 cm away.[52]

From the table we can see that in reputedly haunted locations EMF, GMF and positive air ion values are all exceptional. There was little data on EMFs given, but recorded levels ranged from 100 to 157 mG. For GMFs most readings were substantially above the normal background level, except in one case where the inverse was observed. It is also interesting to see an additional correlation with high positive air ion counts, which are also known to adversely affect psychological states. Normal levels of positive air ions are around 500/m^3, and it has been recorded that certain winds such as the Santa Ana of coastal southern California can have levels of up to $5,000/m^3$, and are associated with increased crime rates, suicides and general irritability.[53]

Whereas many TV ghost hunters believe that EMFs somehow trigger and sustain manifestations of spirits of the dead – a traditional spiritualist belief with a technological twist – most scientists studying the phenomena conclude that the action of EMFs (including GMFs) on the human brain may create the range of effects described as paranormal in a straightforward cause and effect model. When Persinger removed the EMF polluting alarm clock, the girl's apparitional encounters ceased. The presence of an EMF was sufficient explanation for the event without recourse to spirits.[54]

However, the electro/geomagnetic theory is not without controversy. In testing Persinger's claims, Wilkinson and Gauld found that there was only 'a small tendency' for poltergeist cases and hauntings to begin on days with a higher than usual level of geomagnetic activity.[55]

Measuring in Tesla and Gauss
Although the Tesla (T) has generally replaced Gauss (G) in the International System of Units (SI) as a unit of measurement for magnetic flux density (magnetic field), much of the research, including Persinger's, uses the older Gauss. To convert: 10^4 G equals 1 T, or 10 mG equals 1 µT. The commonly used range of units is symbolized as follows: 10^3 T are kilotesla (kT); 10^{-3} T are millitesla (mT); 10^{-6} T are microtesla (µT); and 10^{-9} T are nanotesla (nT).

Environmental memory
Popularly known as the 'stone tape theory', this is the postulated ability of certain natural materials to record events and replay them at a future date, like Mother Nature's VCR. Back in the early days of the SPR when video recording was

not even yet science fiction, a certain H. M. Radnor sent in a letter detailing his discussions with the psychic 'Estelle' that a mental impression could be made upon physical surroundings:

> When anyone thinks so continually of a person [...] they imprint their shadow or memory on the surrounding atmosphere. In fact they make a form; and I myself am inclined to think that so-called ghosts, of those who have been murdered, or who have died suddenly, are more often shadows than earthbound spirits; for the reason that they are ever in the thoughts of the murderer, and so he creates as it were, their shadow or image.[56]

Frederic Myers considered it a 'wild conjecture', but thought it worth mentioning nonetheless, that there could be 'a kind of local imprint left by past events, and perceptible at times to persons endowed with some special form of sensitiveness'. Myers would come to call these 'veridical afterimages'.[57] Other researchers, such as Ernesto Bozzano and H. H. Price, would advance their own variations as the 'psychometric' and 'psychic ether' theories of haunting, respectively. Price would refine his theory as that of 'place memories' where the percipient 'remembers' an event experienced by someone else.[58]

The stone tape theory actually comes, not from the annals of the Society for Psychical Research, but from a television play called *The Stone Tape* written by Nigel Kneale and broadcast on BBC Two on 25 December 1972. The plot revolves around a group of scientists discovering that a room in a supposedly haunted house is capable of recording the past. As they carry out further experiments they unleash an ancient evil with murderous consequences, as is the way of things in fiction.

Yet it is the case that vanished things still remain. Devices known as proton magnetometers are used by archaeologists to detect the lines of long-since-demolished walls, foundations and filled-in ditches by measuring minute variations in the Earth's magnetic field in fractions of nano Tesla. It has been suggested that humans have a corresponding ability to detect subtle geomagnetic variations, and although usually applied to dowsing and so on, one could extend such a theory to the experience of hauntings.[59] Others such as Andrew Green postulate some sort of telepathic trace tied to the environment. His ideas are considered under the heading of 'psi' on p. 259.

Deathflash: the necrotic radiation theory
The question of survival of bodily death is often considered to be beyond contemporary scientific methods and conceptual categories. However, recent research into spontaneous radiations from living systems suggests a scientific foundation for the ancient association between light and life, and a biophysical hypothesis of the conscious self that could survive death of the body. All living organisms emit low-intensity light; at the time of death, that radiation is ten to 1,000 times stronger than that emitted under normal conditions. This 'deathflash' is independent of the cause of death, and reflects in intensity and duration the rate of dying. The vision of intense light reported in near-death experiences may be related to this deathflash, which may hold an immense amount of information. The electromagnetic field produced by necrotic radiation, containing energy, internal structure, and information, may permit continuation of consciousness beyond the death of the body.
Janusz Slawinski, 'Electromagnetic Radiation and the Afterlife', *Journal of Near-Death Studies*, 6.2 (Winter 1987), pp. 79–94

Quantum mechanical fluctuations
Italian physicists Pierro Brovetto and Vera Maxia proposed that poltergeists were created by the subject at the epicentre

of the phenomenon 'channelling energy into the quantum mechanical vacuum'. Like many other researchers they found a correlation between the onset of puberty and the manifestation of poltergeists. They theorized that changes in the brain associated with puberty 'involve fluctuations in electron activity' which in rare cases can be powerful enough to cause physical effects outside of the brain. They liken the mechanism to the quantum mechanical fluctuations believed to occur in a vacuum where virtual particle/antiparticle pairs spontaneously appear only to annihilate each other immediately afterwards. By exciting this particle/antiparticle process around it, the poltergeist brain causes an increase in air pressure sufficient to move objects.

The quantum poltergeist

A decrease in entropy (creation of order) in [the] brain of pubescent people throws a greater amount of entropy (disorder) into the brain environment, which, in exceptional cases, originates poltergeist disturbances. In practice, poltergeist is interpreted as a by-product of the entropy increase $(dS/dt)_{Env}$ expected in consequence of the second law. This interpretation is based on two sound achievements of the past century physics, that is, quantum electrodynamics of vacuum and nonequilibrium thermodynamics.

Brovetto and Maxia, 'Some Conjectures About the Mechanism of Poltergeist Phenomenon' (2008)

Asked to comment, Nobel laureate Brian Josephson said 'this looks distinctly flaky to me'. Although *New Scientist* ran the story on April Fool's Day, Brovetto and Maxia did actually publish their research in the academic journal *Neuroquantology*.[60] Whether their theory is adequate or not, quantum mechanics holds considerable promise as a potential model for paranormal phenomena. As Damien Broderick remarked, 'no matter how improbable anything is in the real world, its description lurks there at the margins of the superimposed quantum states of its components'.[61]

The multidimensional multiverse

There is a fifth dimension, beyond that which is known to man. It is a dimension as vast as space and as timeless as infinity. It is the middle ground between light and shadow, between science and superstition, and it lies between the pit of man's fears and the summit of his knowledge. This is the dimension of imagination. It is an area which we call the Twilight Zone.

Rod Serling, *The Twilight Zone* (CBS, 1959–60)

Cult TV show *The Twilight Zone* may have needed five, but it all began with the fourth dimension in the nineteenth century. In 1844 Hermann Grassmann published a work detailing the mathematical existence of another dimension. As one might expect, many Spiritualists and mystics later picked up on the idea to explain the marvels of mediumship, but it was Johann Zöllner, a Professor of Astrophysics at Leipzig, who put the spiritualist theory on a more scientific footing during a series of experiments with the medium Henry Slade.[62] With regard to apparitions, he argued that they existed in a real four-dimensional world, appearing as shadows in our simple three dimensions. The basic premise was still being touted up to the early 1990s when retired communications engineer John Ralphs reiterated the theory that apparitions were fourth-dimensional incursions into three-dimensional space.[63] Since then the number of dimensions postulated by theoretical physics has multiplied alarmingly, up to twenty-six according to string theorists.

Multidimensionality
In Newtonian physics a human organism is extended in a 3-dimensional real space and exists in 1-dimensional time. In the Minkowski interpretation of special relativity the human organism is extended in real 4-dimensional space-time. In Kaluza-Klein and Super string theories a human organism is extended in real 11-dimensional space-time. In the theory of extension (combined with Kaluza-Klein or Super string theories) a human organism is extended in real (11+3)-dimensional space-time, of which one 10-dimensional cross-section is physical space and one 3-dimensional cross-section is phenomenal space (one assumes they share the same time dimension). What could be simpler than that?

John Smythes, letter to the *JSPR*, vol. 61, 842
(January 1996), p. 64

Going one better than multidimensionality is the idea of multiple universes. American physicist Hugh Everett III proposed the Many Worlds Interpretation to explain the appearance of choice at the quantum level. When a particle finds itself heading towards two gaps in the famous double-slit interference experiment it seems to exhibit choice in deciding which hole to go through and this, apparently, divides the universe into two: the universe of the chosen hole and the universe of the unchosen hole. Anthony Peake suggested that this could also account for the survival of the personality after death – the mind continues 'living' in the subjective universe it has created – and, hence by extension, the phenomenon of haunting.[64] M-theory – a development of string theory – has lately taken the idea of a multidimensional universe into the realm of multiple universes with corresponding multiple implications.

Whilst critical of Brovetto and Maxia's quantum explanation of poltergeists, Brian Josephson has proposed that string theory could account for a range of paranormal phenomena.[65] In occultism there has long been the idea of different planes of existence, and hardly less esoterically, but perhaps somewhat more scientifically, Myers proposed a metetherial world of images lying beyond the physical with some suggestion of its being like a fourth dimension.[66] As to how all this might work in practice we should turn to someone with direct experience of the supernatural. Asked what it was like living in a haunted house, Sammy (Samantha) Leslie of Castle Leslie, Co Monaghan, Ireland, said:

> My father used to explain it's like watching television. That, just because you're watching BBC or Channel Four, it doesn't mean that ITN doesn't exist, and that there are different levels, different layers, and you can be tuned into different things at different times. And I think here is maybe one of those places where the veil is just that little bit thinner.[67]

The mind

Normal delusions
'What is a ghost?' asked Felix Octavius Carr Darley in 1865. He went on to tell us:

> In the popular acceptation of the term, it is a visible appearance of a deceased person. It is also called a spirit; but, if visible, it must be matter; consequently not a spirit. [68]

It is an astute point. He concluded from this paradox that the ghost was a figment of the imagination, or as he colourfully put it, one of 'the multifarious phantoms which haunt the sick man's couch in delirium'. He did not, however, satisfactorily answer the question of how the imagination could secretly conspire against consciousness and common sense to produce a vision so real and so alarming that it has borne the name and independent character of 'ghost' all these millennia. Luckily, others have tried.

Misperception

It is a common dismissal to say that an apparition was a 'trick of the light', but sometimes it is. Green and a colleague inadvertently became 'ghosts' through such means. Although the infamous rectory had burnt down by this time, Green was in Borley to hunt ghosts and whilst 'patrolling the area' at a quarter to two in the morning he and his colleague espied a cyclist approaching and stepped off the road to let him past. But he did not pass. He screamed and began pedalling furiously back the way he had come. Green and his colleague looked at each other. Green was wearing a dark jacket and light trousers. His colleague had on dark trousers and a light jacket, with a black balaclava over his head. They realized that in the moonlight they must have looked like 'one legless headless torso next to a bodyless head and an unconnected pair of trousers'. Green drew from this experience a word of caution: 'beware of people dressed in unconventional attire', especially at a quarter to two in the morning.[69]

We see things that are not there all the time. Generally, we recognize them for what they are: after-images. Simply staring at a high-contrast pattern can produce the effect of seeing an inverted pattern of the same when looking away. J. H. Brown published an amusing little volume in 1865 called *Spectropia or Surprising Spectral Illusions Showing Ghosts Everywhere and of Any Colour*. In it were sixteen high-contrast illustrations of angels, devils, witches, skeletons and apparitions in their traditional sheets, with an accompanying explanation of the effects produced and an apology for 'the apparent disregard of taste and fine art'. More recently, Professor Richard Wiseman produced a less exciting two-tone image of a little girl to illustrate the same effect in his book *Paranormality*.

SEAing ghosts: suggestion, expectation and agency
At the University of Wyoming, Professor Edwin Emery Slosson stood in front of his chemistry class. He unpacked a small wooden box and withdrew a bottle of clear liquid wrapped in cotton. As he unwrapped the bottle from the cotton he told the class that he 'wished to see how rapidly an odour would be diffused through the air' and asked that as soon as anyone smelt it they should raise their hand. Turning his head away as if to avoid a strong smell he poured the liquid over the cotton and started his stopwatch. After fifteen seconds the first hand went up. Eventually, three-quarters of the class had their hands in the air. As he subsequently revealed, the bottle had been filled with odourless distilled water.[70]

Slosson reported his experiment in 1899 and since then the same effect or variations of it has been replicated many times. Slosson himself also managed to create illusions of temperature change and even pain. Even earlier, in 1886, members of the Society for Psychical Research concluded that 'there is definite evidence to show that mere expectancy may produce hallucination' – expectancy being used in the same sense as suggestion is today – and rather more clearly stated that 'expectancy may probably be answerable for a good many apparitions seen in rooms believed to be "haunted"'.[71] More than a century later Rense Lange and James Houran postulated the same thing, but also devised some experiments to test it.

In the case of the 'unhaunted house', a married couple living in a house with no previous reputation for being haunted were asked to record any 'unusual occurrences' over the next month. Soon they were noticing strange things, such as their telephone not working properly, someone calling their name, and a voodoo mask moving along a shelf by itself. In total they logged twenty-two inexplicable instances of 'unusual occurrences'.[72] When writing my book on the supernatural, I did the same thing, noting any particular occurrences of what might be more than natural. I found that I soon had a list of things such as the mysterious odour of flowers in the study, notably in the corner of the room where I had a picture of my late grandmother, as well as apparently unusual coincidences and the occasionally strange behaviour of the dog.[73]

Next Lange and Houran took two groups of people to a disused theatre. Again the building had no reputation of being haunted. They told one group that the building was haunted, but not the other, and asked them to report on how they felt after walking round it. The haunted group reported strange things happening here, there and everywhere. The other group experienced nothing out of the ordinary.[74]

In testing the claims of electromagnetism in causing paranormal experiences, a group of researchers led by Pehr Granqvist of Uppsala University discovered that things like sensing a presence or having a mystical experience were related, not to electromagnetism, but to how suggestible the person was.[75] In discussing his own theories, Lambert had also seen the possible link that 'expectancy' caused by perceptible geological disturbances of 'mysterious noises' could 'induce hallucinations'.[76]

Lange and Houran theorized that the suggestion of haunting created fear that in turn stimulated hyper-vigilance in which ordinary sounds are re-interpreted as suspicious, which in turn creates more fear and greater hyper-vigilance in a vicious circle that leads to an increasing tendency to experience more extreme sensations and even hallucinations.[77] As Samuel Johnson said, 'Fear will find every house haunted.'[78]

Expectation of a result was also found to produce that result, whether or not the expectation was justified. In a series of now famous experiments with rats and school pupils, Robert Rosenthal found that by giving people the expectation of better performance than others, animal or human, they themselves seemed to act in ways to produce better performance.[79] It is related to what sociologist Robert Merton called the 'self-fulfilling prophecy'. In a way it can be described as a sort of self-suggestion.[80]

The key to why random strangeness is identified and

collated by the human mind under the heading of 'ghost' was
provided by a cartoon animation of a big triangle, a little triangle and a circle moving in and out of a box. The cartoon was
of course a cunning experiment devised in the mid-1940s by
two psychologists, Fritz Heider and Mary-Ann Simmel, to
explore what people make of meaninglessness and discovered
the attribution of causality.[81] The shapes in the film moved in
and out of the box without purpose, but most viewers developed stories to explain the action, giving personalities and
motives to the geometric forms. Professor of Anthropology,
Stewart Guthrie, called this 'systematic anthropomorphism'
– attributing human characteristics to non-human things.
Rather than a flaw in human cognition, Guthrie argued that it
derived from a hardwired survival strategy to see potentially
threatening agency first and ask questions later.[82] A number
of other scholars have since followed up on this important
theory, including Justin Barrett, who called it the Hyperac-
tive Agency Detection Device (HADD).[83]

Common misperception and normal delusions are greatly
enhanced by suggestion and expectation in the pursuit of
agency. But there is another psychological tick shoring up the
edifice of strangeness: confirmation bias. Where a self-fulfilling prophecy changes behaviour to produce the expected
result, confirmation bias changes information processing in
the collection and interpretation of data to create the desired
result. Both are driven by belief and can be seen as different
sides of expectation. Taken together, these normal psychological functions have disastrous implications for ghost hunting
as a scientifically credible pursuit.

Induced hallucination
Sit in the desert for as long as it takes. Eat nothing. See God,
one of His angels, or Satan. As I showed in my last book on
the supernatural, many of the visionary experiences reported
of Jewish mystics in the biblical period were purposefully
and sometimes accidentally induced hallucinations. Most

frequently fasting and social isolation combined with expectation and a religious framework of interpretation produced the required effects.[84] As regards ghost hunting and encounters with haunting phenomena, a similar mechanism can also be at work. Fatigue, possibly reduced food intake, blood-sugar imbalance and isolation (even several individuals will experience the particular loneliness of a darkened house at night) in combination with the psychological factors addressed above can create the right conditions for hallucinated sounds and forms, and emotional states of being watched or feeling a presence. Everyone who has worked late into the night, particularly on books about ghost hunting, has experienced the sensation of seeing movement out of the corner of the eye. Most ghost hunting reality shows will involve someone seeing a suggestive shadow at some point, which is interpreted as potentially paranormal activity. Here environmental conditions impair physiological and psychological functioning to the point that one sees or hears things that are not there.

Illness, particularly fever, is also known to produce hallucinations, but it is also the case that simple inactivity or inattentiveness is correlated with apparitional experiences. A study conducted in the 1970s found that almost all of the respondents (90 per cent) reported that they were in normal health at the time of experience and the majority of them were physically inactive at the time, either lying down (38 per cent), or sitting (23 per cent).[85]

Fantasy-prone personality
In 1981 the psychologists Sheryl C. Wilson and Theodore X. Barber identified the fantasy-prone personality – the type of person who has intense fantasies often to the point where they cannot tell them apart from reality. Their research showed that 4 per cent of the general population fell into this category. In total they described fourteen indicators of fantasy proneness of which individuals need only describe six or more to be considered fantasy prone. One of their examples

was Helena Blavatsky, founder of the Theosophical Society and fantasist extraordinaire.[86]

Fantasy-prone personality indicators
   1. Being easily hypnotisable;
   2. Having imaginary playmates as a child;
   3. Fantasizing often as a child;
   4. Adopting a fantasy identity;
   5. Experiencing imagined sensations as real;
   6. Having vivid sensory perceptions;
   7. Reliving past experiences;
   8. Claiming psychic powers;
   9. Having out-of-body experiences;
  10. Receiving communications from spirits, or other noncorporeal sources;
  11. Being involved in 'healing';
  12. Having apparitional encounters;
  13. Having hypnogogic hallucinations (waking dreams);
  14. Seeing typical hypnogogic imagery, such as ghosts, monsters, aliens, and so on.

As we can see, having encounters with apparitions is one of the indicators. Professional sceptic Joe Nickell used Wilson and Barber's research to determine that fantasy proneness was high among people reporting paranormal activity at a certain 'haunted' inn, with the highest scorer being the only one to actually witness an apparition.[87]

Further research has found that people who reported having apparitional experiences were not just fantasy prone but also rated higher on the tests for absorption and cognitive perceptual schizotypy.[88] Absorption is the capacity for intense concentration on one thing (including mental images) to the exclusion of everything else. Schizotypy, derived from

Schizotypy core traits[89]

Trait	Indications
Unusual experiences	Magical or religious beliefs, altered sensations and perceptions of the body and the world, hypersensitivity, déjà vu, jamais vu, auditory and pseudo-hallucinations
Cognitive disorganization	Problems concentrating, being attentive and making decisions
Introvertive anhedonia	Schizoid solitariness, lack of feeling, withdrawal from intimacy, emphasis on independence and solitude
Impulsive nonconformity	Disinhibition, impulsiveness, self-harm, recklessness

'schizophrenic genotype', describes a personality type with similar symptoms to those found in schizophrenia and borderline personality disorders. Schizotypy itself is not necessarily seen as a mental illness, but rather lies on a continuum of traits and symptoms that only in their extreme forms result in psychosis. It is a complex state best seen in the range of indications given in the table above.[90]

Considerable research has shown repeated connections between seeing things that should not be there, from ghosts to UFOs, and particular personality traits that could account for these experiences. However, as one researcher noted, 'this need not mean that all apparitions are pure fantasies, since some could still be potentially veridical'.[91] But more than that, including apparitional experiences as an indicator of fantasy proneness and then finding that fantasy proneness correlates with apparitional experiences is logically flawed.

Multiple personality
Elliott O'Donnell tells the story of a certain clergyman of his acquaintance, too scandalous to name names. He delivered

pious sermons from the pulpit on Sunday and was held by his congregation to be a most moral and upstanding man. Nonetheless, he spent several evenings a week gambling in an East End drinking den and joining his fellow reprobates in a chorus of lewd songs. A true Jekyll and Hyde: O'Donnell asked which of the two 'personalities' was the real one. O'Donnell himself confessed that he had 'several distinct personalities [. . .] any one of which might be equally my true, my normal self'. This he supposed, in cases where outright fraud was not apparent, was the true explanation for the professional medium's apparent ability to summon the 'spirits', not spirits of the dead, but multiple personalities of the medium herself. It is an idea that has found some support among psychologists.[92]

A few years ago, Alejandro Parra noted that 'many therapists still regard clients who report apparitions as mentally ill.'[93] They are not always wrong. Given the association between fantasy-prone personality and apparitional experiences, it should also be noted that fantasy proneness is associated with a higher vulnerability to schizophrenia.[94] But the fantasy-prone personality is also a more creative one, in the positive sense.[95]

One of the indications of fantasy proneness is the adoption of a fantasy persona, but for some 1 to 3 per cent of the population this goes far beyond adoption to become the manifestation of several distinct personalities within the same mind.[96] What used to be called multiple personality disorder is now termed dissociative identity disorder (DID), but the essential symptom remains the clinical presentation of two or more personalities. According to research, DID is more common among women than men, has been increasing in prevalence over the last few decades and patients average around fifteen or sixteen personalities. It is a controversial diagnosis, with some criticizing the diagnostic criteria as 'lax and vague' and the treatment as actually increasing patient psychopathology.[97] Even if experiences of things believed to be spirits are the result of a multiple or dissociative personality, it does not rule out the possibility of there being objective and non-pathological experiences of 'spirits'. Whilst dismissing professional mediums, O'Donnell, and possibly his other selves, still thought that amateur mediums could contact the other world.[98]

Psi

Psi is the generally accepted term used by parapsychologists to cover the various postulated manifestations of psychic ability and activity: telepathy, psychokinesis, and so on. Theories using psi can be purely parapsychological, i.e., involving processes of the human mind beyond normal psychology, or involve spiritual aspects.[99] Some have argued that conditions such as fantasy-prone personality and DID may make the subject more psychic and therefore more receptive to spiritual experiences.[100] Other than adding psi to the equation, these views are essentially the same as the traditional spiritualistic interpretation already discussed. Without recourse to the spiritual, Albert Budden proposed a complicated 'electro-staging hypothesis' whereby electromagnetic fields could sensitize individuals to such an extent that they become psychic, but merely hallucinate 'staged' experiences, such as ghosts and alien encounters, with the ability to demonstrate psychokinesis and telepathy in maintaining the staged experience.[101]

TELEPATHIC GHOSTS

After many years ghost hunting, Andrew Green concluded that 'ghosts' were not spirits of the dead after all. Green was convinced of the existence of psychic powers; indeed, he had first-hand experience. He and some colleagues had successfully shattered a glass by the power of their minds, or so he claimed. After that he tended to explain all alleged hauntings as psychic manifestations of the living. Certainly, he documented several cases where the 'apparition' was still alive and well, including one of himself. Green advanced the theory that recurring, unchanging apparitions were the result of mental stress leaving some sort of trace on the environment or existing as a telepathic 'hallucination' that could outlive the originator. These thought forms needed to be 'fed', apparently by being witnessed, or they would fade out over time.[102]

There are certainly examples of apparitions that have deteriorated with the passage of time. The ghost of Alexander Pope was once seen, it is said, about the churchyard of St Mary's in Twickenham, Middlesex, talking and coughing, but by the middle of the twentieth century only the sound, described as that of 'limping footsteps', remained.[103] Again, at Ludlow castle, Shropshire, a ghost, said to be that of 'Marion of the Heath', was once visible, but has now degenerated into a gasping, breathing sound.[104]

Green was not suggesting anything new. As early as 1884, members of the Society for Psychical Research advanced the theory that apparitions, which they called 'veridical hallucinations', were telepathic projections:

> These veridical hallucinations are (many of them, at least) the manifestation on a large scale of the same kind of 'telepathic' impression which is exhibited on a small scale in the Society's experiments on the transference of thoughts, images, pains, tastes, &c.[105]

This was essentially the theory advanced by H. H. Price in the 1930s. He thought that mental images could have independent, objective existence as a 'telepathic charge' and so be able to persist beyond the death of the originating mind as localized effects.[106]

Other researchers have come to similar conclusions, but with different interpretations. Bozzano speculated that the mind could survive the death of the body and without the competition of ideas that characterized its physical existence is able to concentrate more intensely upon a single idea which can then be telepathically received by a living person. Tyrrell held that an apparition was the 'sensory expression of an idea-pattern' involving subconscious telepathic communication. Taking a different approach, Whately Carington accounted for apparitions by supposing that we share a common unconscious mind, which being general was unaffected by individual death, and that the phenomena of haunting arise from this unconsciousness.[107]

Unlike Green, both Bozzano and Tyrrell were still in the realm of the spiritual, arguing that the personality could survive death and communicate with the living with telepathy as the mechanism. But where Green and Price were advocating a psi mechanism for environmental memory or trace, Carington posited what was, in effect, a universal psychic memory that has more in common with the speculative collective unconsciousness of the Swiss psychotherapeutic-mystic Carl Jung.[108]

NOISY MINDS

'Poltergeist', as everyone knows, is German for 'noisy spirit', but *Geist* can also mean 'mind', as well as 'spirit', and there is a theory that, instead of being the product of spirits, poltergeist activity is the product of the mind, a particularly noisy and psychic mind. Known as recurrent spontaneous psychokinesis, or RSPK for short, the theory was developed in the 1950s by William G. Roll. Investigating what he called 'the house of flying objects', a private house in Seaford, Long Island, with Joseph Pratt, they found that poltergeist phenomena centred round the couple's twelve-year-old son. Roll and Pratt recorded sixty-seven incidents during their investigation, including the movement of objects, bottles popping and thumping sounds. After ruling out trickery, memory distortion and physical causes, they found that the incidents occurred around the boy, noticeably falling off in effect as the distance from him increased, suggesting that he was the energy source for the phenomena. They theorized that the boy's unconscious psychokinesis was responsible for the phenomena.[109]

Observation effects in poltergeist cases[110]

Category	Effect	Cases (%)
Type I	Inhibition of phenomena caused by presence of outside observers	6
Type II	Stimulation of phenomena caused by presence of outside observers	22
Type III	Inhibition of object movement caused by direct observation	45

Given this aspect of diminishing effect, RSPK seems to operate in terms of 'psi fields' or 'psi waves'.[111] Roll would later speculate on the relationship between RSPK and Zero Point Energy (ZPE), a 'sea of random electromagnetic fluctuations that fills all of space'. He theorized that the poltergeist agent would not actually produce the energy required for observed physical movement, but instead interact with ZPE to 'loosen the hold of gravity/inertia that ordinarily keeps things in place'.[112]

In contrast, neurophysiologist Paul Burgess has argued from his own experiences that the observable behaviour of poltergeist activity – what he calls 'recurrent spontaneous anomalous physical events' – differs from normal skill acquisition and retention seen in living humans that one would expect if poltergeists were indeed the product of the human mind. He suggests that this may indicate that discarnate agencies are involved, as was thought from the very beginning.[113]

The con
It is an anti-climactic, 'Scooby-Doo' outcome for the ghost hunter, but sometimes people do just make it all up and often for the basest reasons. Possible reasons for fraud include trying to influence a property's value both up and down, trying to be rehoused by the local council, trying to rob the deceived, trying to get more punters through the door of an ailing business, or simply for sheer spite.

Property value

This is a high-risk strategy for the fraudster hoping to influence a property's value by claiming that the house or grounds are haunted. In the 1970s, Green noted that there were some who were willing to pay more for the thrill of owning such a property.[114] However, the chances are that such claims will depress the market value since there are far more people who do not wish to share their living room with spirits of the deceased. Knowing this, proprietors are just as likely to bring lawsuits against those alleging that the property is haunted, than to fabricate stories themselves.[115]

The SPR's Committee on Haunted Houses noted early that it was difficult to gain permission to publish the names of owners or the addresses of their properties because of concern over the possible damage to reputation or property value.[116] As we saw at the beginning, Athenodorus was able to take a large residence on a small sum because of its reputation, or so Pliny said, and the house at the centre of the Morton case was likewise offered for rent at a fraction of its true market value for the same reasons.[117]

One case hit the national headlines in the UK in 1999 that exemplified the negative effect on valuation. The *Telegraph* played up the case, saying, 'for what is believed to be the first time since the Middle Ages, an English court was being asked to decide on the existence of supernatural forces'.[118]

Alleging that their home was haunted, Andrew and Josephine Smith stopped repayments on 250-year-old Lowes Cottage in Upper Mayfield, Staffordshire. The sellers, sisters Susan Melbourne and Sandra Podmore, took them to court to recover the outstanding amount. The Smiths countersued, claiming they had been misled by not being informed of the haunting and sought a reduction in the value of the property. It was said that an estate agent had informed them that they would be legally obliged to disclose the haunting to any prospective buyers, which would see the £44,000 cottage fall to around £25,000 in value. Another estate agent reduced a £70,000 valuation to 'about £20,000'.[119]

Before Judge Peter Stretton presiding at Derby County Court it emerged that mysterious noises, foul smells, oozing slime, cold spots, a 'pig-faced' boy, a woman in nineteenth-century dress and a naked maid were said to manifest in the house. It was claimed that two murders had taken place on the premises. Mrs Smith even claimed that a spirit had attempted to rape her. The judge found against the Smiths and ordered them to repay the amount due plus damages.[120]

There was a similar case concerning an eighteen-room Victorian mansion in Nyack, New York, in 1991. Jeffrey and Patrice Stambovsky had paid a deposit for the house only to discover that it was already inhabited – by ghosts. Unable to live in the property, they took the seller, Helen Ackley, to court to recover their deposit. On this occasion the judge ruled on appeal that the house was haunted and that Mrs Ackley could not have delivered vacant possession on account of the spirits residing there.[121] Finally, in Italy in 2008, Gaetano and Stefania Bastianelli took the sellers of their house in Santo Chiodo road, Spoleto, to court for not disclosing that it was haunted.[122]

In 2005 Lloyds TSB commissioned a report on paranormal beliefs and house purchases. The results revealed that large proportions would not buy a 'haunted house' (45 per cent) or one overlooking a cemetery (50 per cent). Commenting on the survey, Jon Pain, managing director of mortgages at Lloyds TSB, said, 'It is now apparent that purchasers are also swayed by their instincts, superstition and a general aversion to houses they consider unlucky.'[123]

Rehousing and rent reduction

The Smiths had asked Staffordshire Council to rehouse them, at first unsuccessfully, until they were given a new home in Burton-upon-Trent.[124] Green speculated that in several alleged poltergeist cases the motive behind manufactured phenomena was rehousing. Care should be taken, however, before assuming the worst. The Ghost Club investigated a case of haunting at 69 Spenser Grove, Stoke Newington, in the 1960s. The McGees, tenants of the local authority property, had complained to the council, asking for a reduction in rent, after being plagued by strange noises, spontaneous fires and the apparition of a woman in white with black holes for eyes. The £6 a week rent was slashed to 5 shillings, but when the landlord complained, the Rent Committee rejected the McGees' claim. The McGees appealed against the ruling and had it quashed on a point of law. Summing up, Lord Chief Justice Lord Parker said:

> There is no doubt that the tenant and his family, and indeed a number of interested people who went to observe the phenomena, were fully convinced that this was a haunted house, and there were ghosts that manifested themselves from time to time and that there were poltergeists.[125]

John Fraser investigated a case where an unmarried mother had left her council house because of a haunting. He found that her fears were sufficiently genuine for him to forward his report to the local authority to assist in rehousing her.[126] So we see that, even if the haunting is a delusion, it may warrant treatment as if it were true when it adversely affects the well-being of those concerned.

Illegal occupancy
In his career of house breaking in the name of ghost hunting, O'Donnell more than once found the source of the 'haunting' to be a vagrant illegally occupying the property. Memorably, on one occasion when he slipped through an open window into a supposedly haunted house in Brighton, he tripped over a tramp in the darkness. A scuffle ensued and O'Donnell only saved himself by sacrificing a hip flask full of whisky. In another case, an escaped convict turning the lights on and off

in a house believed to be empty was the reason for its becoming known as haunted. While sheltering in an abandoned house can be excused by necessity, other illegal occupants arouse less sympathy.[127]

In 1971 a whole terrace of council houses in London appeared to be falling prey to a creeping haunting. Reports of 'bodies being dragged across the floor', 'whispering' and 'weird scrambling noises and shuffles' moved from first one house then to another until four houses in a row seemed to be infested by the supernatural. When the Council eventually investigated they found that an Asian family had broken through into the attic spaces of their neighbours to provide accommodation for a further fifteen immigrants.[128]

Criminal intent

No. 79 Blythe Road, Hammersmith, London, once known by all as Blythe House, was a 'fine old house with an imposing portico', but by the beginning of the twentieth century fate had thrown up a 'dingy yard' in front of it. It had once been a school, then a reformatory, but had slipped into disuse and acquired the reputation of being haunted. It was said that 'many strange stories were reported of ghosts and apparitions having been seen here'. However, the truth was that all the nocturnal visitations were far from supernatural in origin: a gang of smugglers had made the building their base of operations.[129]

As it turns out, smugglers were often responsible for supposed hauntings. A house in Rottingdean was once so plagued by 'unearthly noises night after night' that the servants gave notice and the house would have been abandoned had not the police apprehended a gang of smugglers who confessed to having manufactured the haunting. They had a secret passage from the beach that passed close by the house and used to roll barrels up it at the dead of night to frighten the occupiers away. Another coastal residence suffered a similar haunting. Nocturnal noises disturbed the kitchen, furniture was found rearranged in the morning, and the cook even saw an apparition. But it was another 'put on' job by smugglers. It was thus remarked that the diligence of the Preventive Service – an armed coastal patrol to combat smuggling – had 'laid many ghosts in Sussex'.[130]

A glowing hearse pulled by glowing headless horses once haunted Devonshire roads. An inventive smuggler had painted the hearse and horses, excepting their heads, with luminous paint. A similar case was reported from Wales at the beginning of the nineteenth century.[131]

A ghost stalking Somerset in the eighteenth century was fond of making off with poultry. A brave individual stood guard one night and knocked the ghost down as it climbed over his wall. It turned out to be one of his neighbours disguised in a shroud. In 1834 terrible groaning sounds coming from the woods between Collingham and Thorp Larch, Yorkshire, were attributed to the ghost of a local blacksmith who had recently died. So terrified was the populace that no one would venture there. Even the turnpike keepers abandoned their posts. The local magistrate ordered an investigation. It was discovered that a gang of poachers employed one of their number in making the sounds with the aid of a speaking-trumpet to clear the locality whilst they got on with their work.[132]

Criminals went to elaborate lengths to use the fear of the supernatural to their advantage. In 1621, Henry Church used the services of London magicians to produce 'delusory shewes and apparitions & voices in goastly and fearfull manner' in an effort to scare his wife into signing her inheritance over to him.[133] Thomas Wilmot, a highwayman and sometime cunning man of the seventeenth century, turned his skill to laying a ghost. Coming upon a grand house in Shropshire, he offered to dispel the spirit of an unhappy barber who had slit his throat rather than live without the love of a certain chambermaid. Leaving the party downstairs engaged with cards and dice, he used a sheet, the 'white off the wall' and blood smeared on his razor to impersonate the ghost of the suicide and descended the stairs to scare off the gamblers and scoop up their winnings.[134] He used the ruse again, adding some trappings of magic, to rob an elderly gentleman and make love to his young wife.[135]

Lodgers with light fingers often blamed the thefts on ghosts, although with less success than Wilmot. Two girls used the defence in the nineteenth century, one of them even brazenly wearing the stolen items in full view of their former owner.[136] More successful were the pickpocket gangs who took advantage of, or actually orchestrated, public ghost hunts. Such hue and cry about a ghost drew a large crowd at St Andrew's Church, Holborn, London, in 1815 and the police were hard pressed to keep the 'light fingered gentry' in check.[137] One William Livins found himself in court, accused of starting the rumours that brought a crowd of ghost hunters to Christchurch graveyard, Blackfriars, London, in 1839 'for the purpose of giving thieves an opportunity of robbing'.[138]

Publicity

Green warned that when dealing with public houses, historic buildings and other properties open to the public as a commercial enterprise one should be aware that the alleged haunting could be nothing more than a publicity stunt.[139] Tony Cornell's investigation of The Ferry Boat Inn, Holywell, in the 1950s quickly snowballed from a low-key investigation into a media circus. Cornell declined to take part in further 'investigations'.

The success of Amityville inevitably spawned copycats. One of them was the possessed wall in a 1950s bungalow in Hackensack, New Jersey. Eric Small lived there with his girlfriend Tara Quinn. Every night they heard voices and banging sounds coming from a wall. Some mysterious force had even pushed them into it. They were terrified and sought help. TAPS turned up with a four-man team. But suspicions began to emerge. Interviewed separately, Small and Quinn gave conflicting versions of the haunting. Investigators also

found books on ghosts hidden under their bed. In the basement wires led up into a locked room above. Later, as the team
sat looking at the wall the noises started up on cue. But they
sounded flat, unconvincing. Jason Hawes and his team asked
about the wires. Small and Quinn became defensive. Then
they asked to be let into the locked back room. Small and
Quinn refused. The tension rose as TAPS insisted. Finally,
the door was unlocked. Inside was a tape recorder and speaker fixed to the back of the 'haunted' wall. Forced to explain,
Small said he had been trying to get his house on the then
popular 1990s TV show *Sightings* and make a fortune cashing
in on the mystery, Amityville style.[140]

Sometimes it is the ghost hunters themselves who may
be guilty of publicity seeking or even outright fraud. Two
of the most important UK investigations – Borley Rectory
and Ballechin House – were marred by suspicions concerning the principal investigators – Harry Price at Borley and
Ada Goodrich-Freer at Ballechin.[141] The conduct of Hawes
and Wilson was called into question by viewers and review-
ers during their investigation of The Myrtles Plantation. One
might even go as far as to consider the whole notion of a reality TV show on ghost hunting to be a massive exercise in publicity seeking.

Maliciousness

At other times, thankfully few and far between, fraudulent
ghosts are manufactured out of what appears to be sheer
maliciousness. A certain 'L. E.' writing to *The Dublin Penny
Journal* in 1835 said that he was aware of a case in Dublin concerning a house believed to be haunted by a screaming ghost.
The house had lain empty for many years on account of it.
Eventually, it was discovered that a neighbour had drilled
through the adjoining wall and was producing the sound
effects himself by howling down a tube inserted between
the two houses.[142] A woman who threw a sheet over herself
and haunted Park Street, Yeovil, in 1866 was out to 'frighten

the children' for no more reason, apparently, than personal enjoyment.[143] Similarly, Anne Page, a servant girl, was convicted of smashing windows in Hanover Street, Newington, as a pretended ghost in 1825.[144] The whole Spring-Heeled Jack caper, begun in late 1837, seems to have been a series of copycat crimes by individuals posing as ghosts, bears and the Devil intended to frighten and in some cases sexually molest members of the public.[145] It is also often suspected that the child, or sometimes young adult, at the centre of poltergeist cases is contriving the whole affair.[146] No one put it better than Reginald Scot, who as early as 1584 remarked 'one knave in a white sheet hath cozened and abused many thousands that way'.[147]

9

SURVIVE

No amount of experience in ghost hunting will ever enable me to overcome that awful, hideous fear that seizes me when I see the last glimmer of daylight fade, and I realise I am about to be brought into contact with the superphysical, and that I must face it – alone.[1]

Ghost hunters have been shot at. They have fallen to their deaths. They have been attacked by unknown assailants. They have been run over by trains. They have heard voices telling them to kill themselves. They have lost their minds. They have been sentenced to death. Fear is only the beginning.

Pioneering ghost hunter Andrew Green felt that fear when he stood three floors up on the roof of 16 Montpelier Road, London W5. The Victorian Gothic tower was seventy feet high, and seventeen-year-old Green was enjoying the wide views across London, when a voice in his mind seemed to say, 'Have a look in the garden. Walk over the parapet, it's only twelve inches on to the lawn. You won't hurt yourself.' At the

last moment his father grabbed the boy and pulled him back
to safety. Twenty suicides and a murder had already taken
place there.[2]

Similar experiences have been reported at Ladram Bay in
Devon, Beachy Head in Sussex, and at the aptly named Devil's
House, an isolated farm in the wild marshlands of Wallasea
Island.[3] While filming at Leap Castle, Ireland, Bob Curran
felt a sudden compulsion to throw himself out of the window
in the 'Bloody Chapel'. He later wondered whether the child
who had supposedly fallen to its death from an upper window
had perhaps instead been compelled by dark forces.[4]

As we saw before, an early case of a 'ghost-detector' was
recounted in the first issue of the *Spiritual Magazine* in January 1860. Events took place twenty years earlier in 1840 at 'the
far-famed house' of Willington Mill, near Newcastle. Joseph
Procter, described as 'a plain unimaginative Quaker', com-
plaining of being troubled by an apparition, attracted the aid
of Edward Drury of Sunderland, 'a valiant and self-confident
man' and 'ghost-detector'. Determined to solve the mystery,
Drury and an accomplice searched the house from cellar to
garret to rule out any 'contrivances being played off upon
them'. Drury then stationed himself in the haunted room,
armed with pistols, whilst his confederate watched the stairs
outside the door. At around midnight, when the candles had
burnt low, 'the well-known female figure issued from the closet
near Drury, walked or glided slowly past him, and approached
his friend on the landing'. The writer notes that this was the
moment to seize the phantom or discharge a pistol at it. Some
say that he did try and grab the ghost, others that Drury's valiant character failed him. By all accounts, he screamed and collapsed on the floor; briefly coming round, 'he went out of one
fit into another till three o'clock in the morning'. His constant
refrain was, 'there she is. Keep her off. For God's sake, keep
her off.' Procter and his friend feared he had lost his mind, but
he recovered after many weeks' recuperation, although never
enough to take up ghost detecting again.[5]

The shooting

A dilapidated house across the road from the cemetery. An overgrown garden, weeds choking what looked like a witch's cauldron. Screams in the night. A disturbed loner living with his mother – a woman who claimed that aliens had once broken into the house and sexually molested her. When the grandmother died they had lived for two days with the body in the house, thinking that she might wake up and be scared. This was 141 Sharon Springs Drive, the 'spooky house' in Worthington, a quiet town of 13,000 residents in Ohio. On 22 August 2006 a group of five teenage girls decided to go on a 'ghost hunt', or what the locals call 'ghosting'.[6]

Described as a 'pretty blonde high-school cheerleader', Rachel Barezinsky, and two friends, crept on to the property, lighting the way with the glow of their mobile phones. 'The house is always dark', one of the girls, Maggie Hester, later told reporters, 'Someone at school said they saw an old-lady witch, but we didn't know for sure that anyone lived there.' Another friend, Una Hrnjak, waiting in a car, leaned on the horn to frighten them and the girls fled. As they drove off they heard 'a "pop, pop, pop" that sounded like a cap gun or firecrackers', according to Tessa Acker. Returning to investigate the noise, Rachel was hit by two bullets in the shoulder and head. 'We were screaming and laughing as we drove away,' said Acker, 'but at the end of the block, Rachel fell into my lap.'[7]

As the .22 calibre hollow-point round penetrated her skull it expanded and fragmented. Entering the parietal region of the brain, it passed through the right temporal lobe and the rear of the right frontal lobe, crossing the midline into the left frontal lobe. When the ambulance brought her into hospital she was in a deep coma, the bullet still lodged in her brain. Doctors gave her a less than 1 per cent chance of survival. A priest was called to give her the Last Rites.[8]

'We were just trying to scare each other,' Acker later said. Amazingly, Rachel lived and went on to make a 90 per cent

recovery with more expected. Loner Allen S. Davis who fired
the rifle was sentenced to nineteen years in prison after plead-
ing guilty to two counts of felonious assault. Commenting
on the 'spooky house' legend, Davis said, 'Wow, a haunted
house, huh?'[9]

The train
The story starts in the summer of 1891. Bostian Bridge spans
Third Creek in North Carolina, USA, carrying trains across
the 100-foot ravine. This time, though, something went
wrong. The train derailed and plunged off the bridge, injur-
ing many and taking somewhere in the region of thirty lives.
Since then people say that every 27 August the disaster repeats
itself. It is one of North Carolina's best-known ghost stories,
with guidebooks claiming that people living in the vicinity
have heard 'the phantom sounds of human screams, crashing
metal, and rupturing of steam pipes'.[10] The 100th anniversary
in 1991 drew a crowd of about 150. For the 119th anniversary
on 27 August 2010, the ghost hunters had the bridge to themselves, or so they thought.[11]

Some years previously, Tina McSwain of Charlotte Area
Paranormal Society had staked out the bridge. 'It was a very
humid night,' she said. 'No wind was moving. And [at] exactly 4 a.m. the candles blew out. A big gust of wind acted like
it came down the track.' She added, 'That's the extent of what
we discovered.' But this time the ghost hunters were in for far
more than they had bargained for.[12]

When the driver of the Norfolk Southern train rounded the
corner he saw a group of about twelve people on the bridge.
He braked, knowing he would not be able to stop in time.
As the wheels screamed across the rails the ghost hunters ran
for their lives back across the bridge. Twenty-nine-year-old
Christopher Kaiser had almost made it when he pushed one
of his colleagues out of the path of the oncoming train. He
saved her life, but the train struck him head-on and sent his
body hurtling into the ravine. Asked to comment, author

and paranormal investigator Jeff Belanger said, 'This person becomes part of the story. This person is now intertwined with that legend forever.'[13]

The fall

Initial police statements described the unidentified twenty-nine-year-old dead woman as a ghost hunter. Her body had been found at 1 Spadina Crescent, an atmospheric ivy-covered Gothic Revival building. Formerly Knox College, it is now part of the University of Toronto and home to the Fine Arts Department. But not to any ghosts, according to tour guide Richard Fiennes-Clinton. There are rumours of a curse on the building and senior arts lecturer David Buller was stabbed to death here in 2001 – a crime that is still unsolved – but it is not clear what drew the woman to this site and her death. Fiennes-Clinton added, 'It's a creepy looking building.'[14]

Later named as Leah Kubrik, a native of Indiana, the victim was apparently out on a first date with a thirty-four-year-old man. They were on the roof of the building when the accident happened. The man had jumped from one roof to another, but as Kubrik attempted to follow, the fence she was balancing on gave way. She fell three storeys onto an inner courtyard below. Police received the emergency call shortly before 2 a.m. Kubrik had no vital signs and was pronounced dead on arrival at St Michael's Hospital. Toronto Police Constable Wendy Drummond told reporters that, 'They were believed to be exploring an old building because it's rumoured to be haunted.' It was also believed that alcohol may have been involved, but the police later withdrew the ghost hunting comment and toxicology reports were not released.[15]

The University of Toronto has some well-known 'haunted' buildings, including Trinity College and the Soldier's Tower, a WWI monument, but none more famous than the legend of the duelling stonemasons, and their ghosts, of University College. ParaResearchers of Ontario commented that 1 Spadina Crescent 'does have a "look"', but noted that they were unaware of any reported hauntings up until the time of the accident. Afterwards, however, they started receiving information about things moving by themselves in the basement and mysterious phenomena connected with the stairwells, the second-floor lights and an office numbered '13'. However, ParaResearchers believed that it was news of the tragic death of Kubrik that was generating the stories as people began 'to knit things together to create a mythos about a place that didn't have a history of ghosts and hauntings to justify an interest and add some spice(?) to a tragic event.'[16]

Hit and run

New York State, 11.30 p.m., 21 June 2003: Rick Rowe, founder and chief investigator of the Paranormal and Ghost Society, was on his way to investigate a reputedly haunted cemetery with nineteen-year-old friend, Rob Carr. It was said that demon dogs roamed Goodleburg Cemetery in Wales, Erie County, after dark. Nicknamed the 'Hill of the Ghouls', the cemetery also had the reputation of being haunted by a 'white lady', the ghost of an illegal abortionist 'Doctor Goodleberg' and the lives he took, and two other male apparitions. It was said that the faint sound of music can sometimes be heard, as well as crying, moaning and screaming. Rumours of Satanic rituals add a final touch of the macabre. 'At night,' said Rob Lockhart of Haunted History Ghost Walks, 'it definitely has the look. It's right out of a horror movie.'[17]

Carr had visited the cemetery before. The previous time, when he had returned to his car he found it covered in children's hand prints. It was night. There were no children around. According to Rowe, 'This cemetery has vibes that something is not right here.'[18]

However, on that fateful night, as the ghost hunters walked down Hunters Creek Road leading to the cemetery, a drunk driver struck Carr. The purple Dodge pick-up accelerated away from the scene without stopping. Carr was killed instantly. Debra Saddleson was later sentenced to seven months' imprisonment for leaving the scene of a fatal accident. Carr's friends returned to Hunters Creek Road. This time to place a memorial cross and wreath.[19]

The murder

A further caution to avoid prison, hospital or the graveyard whilst ghost hunting comes from *The Newgate Calendar*, a choice collection of sensational crimes to titillate low-brow readers in the late eighteenth and early nineteenth centuries. Given the number of people who have fired at, stabbed, bludgeoned and driven over apparitions, this is an apposite warning. The logical end of a hunt, even a ghost hunt, is the kill, and so the case before us is one of murder.[20]

Events took place in the winter of 1803–4 in Hammersmith when it could still be described as 'near London'. A certain churchyard gained the reputation of being haunted. Several incidents and one death from fright were reported.[21]

A wagon crowded with sixteen passengers was rumbling along the highway, eight horses pulling the lumbering hulk, when the driver took fright at the sudden appearance of an apparition. He abandoned his charge and took flight, and 'left the waggon and horses so precipitately, that the whole were greatly endangered'.[22]

Thomas Groom, servant to Mr Burgess, a brewer, had cause to walk past the churchyard late one night. The churchyard and surrounding area had already acquired the reputation of being the haunt of a mad woman.[23] Something, he could not say what, 'caught hold of him by the throat'. He tore himself free and escaped.[24] The newspapers reported that he took to his bed, incapacitated by fright.[25] A nightwatchman, William Girdler, had encountered the ghost by the four-mile marker stone near Beaver Lane, and given chase, but the apparition was fleet of foot and had eluded him.[26]

An expectant mother made her way past the churchyard at about ten o'clock one evening. Imagine her horror when 'she beheld something, as she described, rise from the tomb-stones'. It was 'very tall, and very white'. She tried to run, but the ghost pursued and, catching her, squeezed her in its arms. The woman fainted dead away. She was discovered hours later and carried home. There 'she took to her bed, from which, alas! she never rose'.[27]

The haunting went on for some two months. It was said that 'neither man, woman, nor child could pass that way.'[28] Rumour had it that it was the ghost of a man who had slit his own throat a year past. The whiteness of the ghost was much remarked upon and additional details came to attention such as 'horns and glass eyes'.[29]

The general panic was such that almost anyone out after dark was being apprehended as the ghost. A Chimneysweep, with the most suitable name of Brazier, was walking along Church Lane and suddenly alarmed by what he took to be the apparition hovering before him. Having a stick in his hand he cautiously advanced upon the spectre until within prodding distance. 'Ghost! Or whatever you may be, pray be civil,' he said as he poked it with his stick. Instead of passing through the spiritual substance of this deceased being, his stick met with the very corporeal form of a certain Miss G—, described as 'a young lady of Hammersmith, with her companion.'[30]

Thomas Millwood, a bricklayer, was returning home one evening still wearing his white work clothes when he astonished two ladies and a gentleman passing by. 'There goes the ghost,' said the man. Whereupon Millwood rejoined that 'he was no more a ghost than he was' and, expletive deleted, 'did he want a punch of the head?' In consequence, his wife begged him to wear a great coat in future. For his part, Thomas 'wished the ghost was catched'.[31]

A brewer's clerk thought he saw the spectre one morning at about five o'clock and was 'considerably alarmed'. A drummer of the Chiswick Volunteers and ratcatcher by trade was 'panic-struck' by the news.[32] Mrs Steward of No. 4 Theresa Terrace and her servant saw the ghost standing by the water pump and were 'much alarmed'.

There were yet several hardy souls who attempted to waylay the spirit. In fact, ghost hunting in Hammersmith was then even more popular than it is today. It was said that 'almost all the young men had gone out' in pursuit of it.[33] They were always foiled, however, by the many by-lanes and tracks around Hammersmith, the ghost taking apparent advantage of them to slip his hunters and terrify his victims.

There was one, however, Francis Smith by name, exciseman by profession, who was hardier or luckier than the rest. Armed with a gun, he took up his position on Black Lion Lane and waited for the apparition. Black Lion Lane was then a path between high hedges leading to Hammersmith Terrace, a fine row of Georgian houses dating from 1750 along the waterfront. Smith was also not far from The Black Lion pub at the end of the lane should he require any Dutch courage on his vigil. It was reported that 'Blacklion Lane was very dark at all times . . . and on that evening it was so very obscure, that a person on one side of the road could not distinguish an object on the other.'[34]

Smith was not disappointed. A figure in white appeared out of the gloom before him. He challenged it. It made no answer. He fired.

That night Thomas Millwood was visiting his sister Ann – 'a very genteel young woman'[35] – and their parents on Black Lion Lane. They sat and talked until his mother fell asleep. They heard the watchman cry eleven o'clock and the sister bade him leave. Thomas was again still wearing his work clothes – white linen trousers, white flannel waistcoat and white apron – 'the usual habiliment of his occupation'.[36] Standing at the door after he had gone, Ann heard someone cry out, 'Damn you, who are you, and what are you? Damn you, I'll shoot you.' She heard a gunshot and saw the muzzle flash. She called out 'Thomas?' But heard no reply.[37]

Girdler was doing his rounds when he heard the shot. Cross-examined later, he said of it, 'I did not take any notice of it, because I hear them every quarter of an hour, almost all night.'[38] But soon after a girl came hurrying towards him, a candle in her hand to light the way. She was a maid to the landlady of the White Hart, a Mrs Honor, and called him to the hostelry. There he found Smith, talking about having hurt someone. 'I hope you have not hurt him much,' said Girdler. 'I have, and I fear very bad,' replied Smith.[39]

Ann Millwood woke the household. 'I do think my brother is shot,' she said. Neither her parents nor the lodger would believe her. She called out again from an upstairs window. Still hearing no reply she resolved to investigate for herself. She ran out of the door and down the lane. Ahead she saw her brother lying on the ground. She grasped his hand and said, 'speak to me'. But Thomas was silent. She fled the scene, looking for help.

Smith led Girdler back down Black Lion Lane. On the way they met Smith's neighbour, John Locke, the wine merchant, and George Stowe returning home from The Plough and Harrow. They saw the body lying in the lane. There was, as Locke said, 'no appearance of life'.[40] They carried the body to The Black Lion public house and sent for the high constable.

Mr Flower, a surgeon, later examined the body by order of the Coroner. The face was blackened with powder. He observed a gunshot wound on the left lower jaw. 'Small shot,' he told the court, 'about the size No. 4.' This had broken the jaw and penetrated through to the spinal column. 'It was,' he said, 'what we call necessarily, a mortal wound.'[41]

Smith stood in the dock at the Old Bailey: 'affected by shame and remorse, was now and then so seriously agitated, that he could with difficulty support himself.'[42] His black suit contrasted against the paleness of his face as the twenty-nine-year-old waited for the verdict. The Old Bailey was crowded, even the yard 'was filled with an anxious multitude'.[43] The case was 'the "Town Talk" of that day', not only in Hammersmith, but in the great metropolis itself; as Cruikshank recalled, even the radical philosopher Jeremy Bentham would refer to it a few years later.[44] Smith had pleaded innocent. Twelve witnesses had attested to his good character. 'His life,' one said, 'had been marked by singular acts of humanity and benevolence.' He had 'the sympathy of every spectator'.[45] But it was not enough.

The jury deliberated for three-quarters of an hour to decide his fate. They returned a verdict of manslaughter. The presiding judge, the Lord Chief Baron, Sir Archibald Macdonald, would not allow it, there were no circumstances that could allow manslaughter. The accused was either guilty or not guilty of murder. 'The prerogative of showing mercy,' he told them, 'lay in the Crown.'[46] The jury reconsidered: guilty. Sentence was passed: death, 'his body given to the surgeons to be dissected'. Smith 'sank into a state of stupefaction exceeding despair'. He had to be carried from the court.[47]

The Lord Chief Baron immediately reported the case to the king, George III. Before seven o'clock a 'respite during pleasure' was granted and before the month was out he was pardoned on condition of one year's imprisonment.[48] But the case raised a legal problem that was not settled for another 180 years: could mistaken belief be a justifiable defence for one's actions? The situation was not settled until 1984.

Gladstone Williams was coming home from work when he saw a man dragging a black youth down the street and repeatedly hitting him. Williams thought the youth was being attacked and punched his attacker in the face. In fact, the youth was being arrested for mugging and Williams was subsequently found guilty of assault occasioning actual bodily harm. On appeal, the conviction was overruled on the basis that Williams believed, however mistakenly, that he was defending another person.[49] The decision was later written into law. Finally, the legal ghost of Francis Smith's case was laid to rest, but not the ghost itself.

Had Millwood been the ghost, taking advantage of his work clothes to put the wind up the neighbourhood, or was it a tragic case of mistaken identity? Mr Moody of the Six Bells had already uncovered the 'mad woman' as in fact a butcher's boy who had taken to dressing up in the maid's clothes and loitering about the churchyard and elsewhere to frighten people, especially the maid it seems. After being discovered and 'reprimanded' by Moody, he gave up the prank, but soon after a figure all in white – the ghost – started to haunt the locality. When Girdler gave chase to the ghost he told the court how it had thrown off a white sheet or tablecloth, he could not say which, in order to better make its escape. But the ghost was not the butcher's boy.[50]

Shortly after Smith's imprisonment, John Graham, of Dorvell's Row and cobbler by profession, came forward and confessed. He said that he had worn a white sheet to frighten his apprentice with a taste of his own medicine. The apprentice was fond of scaring his master's children with ghost stories, even going so far as to make scratching noises on the walls of the house. Described as a person of otherwise 'excellent character' – he sang in the Trinity Chapel choir – Graham nonetheless seems to have enjoyed the turmoil he occasioned. When he met Girdler following his close escape he enquired of the watchman, 'Were not you very much frightened the other night?' 'No,' replied Girdler, 'he was not, but whoever the ghost was, he will go to hell, die when he will.'[51]

The story has entered the annals as the 'Hammersmith Ghost' and there is a plaque on The Black Lion pub commemorating the incident. It is even said that the ghost of the murdered man lingers there. Computers have been reported to turn on by themselves. Floorboards creak overhead as though someone is walking through the upstairs rooms, but, of course, no one is there. People have complained of hearing their names whispered by an unearthly voice. According to local legend, the ghost returns on the night of 3 January every fifty years. To mark the 200th anniversary the Ghost Club staked out the pub in 2004. Landlord Kevin Sheehy said:

> We do have some strange goings-on in the pub. The chef lives upstairs and has been woken up half a dozen times by someone speaking his name – but there was no-one there.[52]

The pitfall

In our scientific, technical age it is natural that the scene of the ghost should move from the mythical, legendary and religious to the scientific. The ghost is no longer to be sought with sheep's blood (Homer), or grimoire (Levi), but with circuit board and LED in the hurried sweep of the EMF meter. However, when it comes to protecting oneself in the investigation of the paranormal, the methods might seem positively medieval. I was surprised to find both the Bible and a Wiccan spell book in the list of items carried by ghost hunters. In Louisiana people do things differently, where items carried for protection include red brick dust against ghosts, garlic against vampires, hot peppers against the 'grunch', and salt against zombies, according to Haunts of Owensboro ghost tour operator David Wolfe II. Ghost hunting necromancer Lisa Lee Harp Waugh always ends her work with a banishing ritual.[53]

To avoid the majority of pitfalls, however, a dose of common sense is all that is required. The Society for Psychical Research sets out several sensible guidelines for today's investigators:[54]

1. Do not go by yourself.
2. Keep your relations with the experients/witnesses as relaxed and friendly as possible.
3. Keep an open mind.
4. Be tactful, or even reticent, in expressing your views.
5. Do not play the amateur psychiatrist.
6. Respect the confidentiality of the case.
7. Take particular care where children are involved.
8. Avoid publicity.
9. Learn from one's mistakes.

From the record of disastrous ghost hunting we could add several more suggestions: make sure you ascertain whether a building is inhabited or not, especially by disturbed individuals with guns, and get the owner's permission to avoid committing criminal trespass; do not stand on the rail tracks waiting for a ghost train – it may be you that becomes the ghost; do not drink and jump from tall buildings; take care when walking badly lit or unlit streets in the pursuit of the supernatural; and on no account open fire on ghosts.

Elliott O'Donnell made a career out of ignoring almost every one of the SPR's sensible guidelines. He usually went alone. He always expected trouble of the supernatural kind and was convinced that ghosts were the spirits of the dead, or demonic entities terrorizing mankind for fun. He made his views on this well known and published all the most scandalous details he could, although often concealing identities and locations. He courted publicity and if he made mistakes, such as ignoring the SPR's advice, he just went out and did it all again.

As regards the 'don'ts' derived from today's ghost hunting catastrophes, he would have fallen foul of almost every one. He broke into buildings without making sure they were uninhabited – and once got into a fight with a tramp on account of this. He enjoyed a tipple on the job, although rarely undertook any dangerous acrobatics. Luckily, he lived in an age when the rare motor car was more likely to sustain serious damage from running into him than vice versa. His recklessness was only tempered by frequently enjoying the hospitality of his friends and pursuing ghosts after a good meal in salubrious surroundings, often whilst actually sleeping on the job.

There was a price to pay, however. Throughout his life O'Donnell felt he was being stalked by one of his neutrarians and had the unshakable conviction that it meant him harm. Ghost hunting, he concluded, 'is bad both for body and mind, and even in the case of the strongest people, sooner or later it is sure to tell.'[55]

Other ghost hunters have also brought themselves into the way of harm, some of them deliberately. *Ghost Adventures'* Zak Bagans has a secret dungeon under his house, pumps a lot of iron and is licensed to carry a concealed weapon. For some this might make him scarier than the stories he tells. It is reassuring to read, then, that he has never worshipped the Devil nor drunk blood. He does, however, have an unhealthy relationship with one too many demons, including a succubus from the Ancient Ram Inn, even to the point of undergoing an exorcism.[56]

Bagans's confrontational style also gets bystanders into trouble. During his investigation of the Goldfield Hotel, Nevada, the caretaker Virginia Ridgeway claimed she was attacked by two 'dark shadow figures' and physically lifted off the floor and slammed against a wall. Another member of his team was pelted with stones. He also says that four of his past girlfriends have been attacked by spirits following his investigations.[57]

For their part, TAPS members have been frozen, burnt, smashed in the face and hit by flying drums in the course of their work.[58] It is no surprise that just over half of all the ghost hunters I interviewed said that on at least one occasion they had been truly frightened during an investigation. Clearly, ghost hunting is not for the faint-hearted.

Words of warning
I have known people who required psychiatric help after facing an incident and what started out as 'a bit of a laugh' escalated into a very real fear of all things paranormal. Two people I know remain somewhat disturbed several years later and would never go near haunted premises again. Of course, these people were probably not of the right mindset to undertake research in the first instance; but nevertheless, it shows that this can be a rather disturbing pastime for the unprepared.

Bill Marshall, Ghost Club member (GHS, 2012)

POSTSCRIPT

Ghost hunting implies that ghosts exist and can be caught. The jury is still out on whether they do 'exist', and even if they do it is unlikely that they could be 'caught' in any physical sense. More important, perhaps, is the way in which one goes about ghost hunting. We can do no better than remember the words attributed to Chilon of Sparta, one of the Seven Sages of Greece: '*De mortuis nil nisi bonum dicendum est*' ('Nothing must be said about the dead except the good'). Whatever we believe apparitions, poltergeists and the sundry phenomena that comprise a haunting to be, we should enter this realm with heads bowed because, even if ghosts are not the spirits of the dead, we still trespass upon their memory. The apparitions that people see, shadows and misty shapes aside, are not the sheet-wearing spooks of our childhood (and many a Victorian prank), but the similitude of people who once lived and breathed as we do now. This pale tribe calls us all into its ranks, hopefully later rather than sooner, but call it does and listen we must. So tread lightly, for these bones underfoot are our bones, those disembodied whispers on the wind are our voices. We will all know what ghosts are as the light dies on that last day.

ENDNOTES

Preface

1. Private conversations, name withheld, 30 September 2011 and 11 May 2012.
2. Stacey Graham, *The Girl's Ghost Hunting Guide* (Naperville: Sourcebooks, 2012); James May, *Man Lab: The Book of Usefulness* (London: Hachette, 2011).
3. Daniel Defoe, *The Novels and Miscellaneous Works of Daniel De Foe, Vol. XIII: The History and Reality of Apparitions* (Oxford: D.A. Talboys, 1840), p. 1.

1. Prepare

1. Pliny the Younger, 'LXXXIII. To Sura', in Charles W. Eliot (ed.), *Letters*, tr. William Melmoth (New York: P. F. Collier & Son, 1909–14).
2. Surveys in order cited: Consumer Analysis Group (2001); Gallup (2001); Ipsos–Mori (2007); Gallup (2005); Society for Psychical Research (1894); Roper (1992).
3. William Purcell Witcutt, 'Notes on Warwickshire Folklore', *Folklore*, vol. 55, 2 (1944), p. 72.
4. Andrew Green, *Ghost Hunting: A Practical Guide* (St Albans: Mayflower, 1976 [1973]), p. 11. His figures add up to 115 per

cent – 50 per cent poltergeists, 25 per cent old cases, 40 per cent new cases – so these can only be taken as a guideline at best.

5. Homer, *The Odyssey*, 11.13–97, and Lucian, *Philopseudes*, 15, in Daniel Ogden (ed.), *Magic, Witchcraft, and Ghosts in the Greek and Roman Worlds* (Oxford: Oxford University Press, 2002), pp. 180–1, 255.

6. Plautus, *Mostellaria*, 446–531; Lucian, *Philopseudes*, 30–1; in Ogden, *Magic*, pp. 154–7.

7. R. C. Finucane, *Ghosts: Appearances of the Dead and Cultural Transformation* (Amherst: Prometheus Books, 1996), p. 2.

8. James Boswell, *The Life of Samuel Johnson* (London: John Sharpe, 1830), p. 396.

9. Andrew Lang, *Cock Lane and Common-Sense* (London: Longmans, 1894); 'Ingoldsby Legends' later collected and published in book form as Richard Harris Barham, *The Ingoldsby Legends; or, Mirth and Marvels*, vol. 3 (London: Bentley, Wilson & Fley, 1847 [1840]), p. 163; O'Hara Family [Michael Banim], *The Ghost Hunter and his Family*, The Library of Romance, vol. 1, Leitch Ritche (ed.) (London: Smith, Elder and Co., 1833). The earliest occurrence of the term is in a misspelling of Robert Greene, *Ghost-haunting Conie-catchers* (London: Jackson and North, 1602) in *A Catalogue of the Libraries of [. . .] Henry, Lord Viscount Colerane* [etc.], vol. 2 (London: T. Osborne and J. Shipton, 1754), p. 441.

10. Harry Price, *Poltergeist Over England* (London: Country Life, 1945), p. 75; Joseph Glanvill, *Saducismus Triumphatus; or Full and Plain Evidence Concerning Witches and Apparitions* (London: J. Collins and S. Lownds, 1681).

11. Quoted in Herbert Thurston, *Ghosts and Poltergeists*, J. H. Crehan (ed.) (London: Burns Oates, 1953), p. 56.

12. 'A Great Wonder in Heaven, Shewing the Late Apparitions and Prodigious Noyses of War and Battels Seen on Edge-Hill' (London: Thomas Jackson, c. 1643). The pamphlet is dated 23 January 1642 (Old Style) and refers to events taking place at Christmas, presumably 1642. The phenomenon continued for a week, was absent for a week and then returned for another week, and at some point after that the king's officers arrived, taking us well into January 1643 (New Style). George William Brown (ed.), *Dictionary of Canadian Biography*, vol. 1

(Toronto: University of Toronto Press, 1966); Peter Underwood, *The A–Z of British Ghosts* (London: Chancellor Press, 1992), p. 62.

13. Glanvill, *Saducismus*. The edition I consulted was the third of 1700, part 2, p. 49 ff.

14. Glanvill, Saducismus, p. 55. Additional letters pertaining to the case are reprinted in Alan Gauld and A. D. Cornell, *Poltergeists* (London: Routledge & Kegan Paul, 1979), pp. 43–62.

15. Charles G. Harper, *Haunted Houses* (London: Chapman and Hall, 1907), pp. 9–10.

16. Edward Moor, *Bealings Bells* (Woodbridge: John Loder, 1841); William Howitt, 'Modern Sadducism', *Spiritual Magazine*, vol. 1, 1, 1860, pp. 15–16.

17. Margaret Maria Gordon, *The Home Life of Sir David Brewster* (Edinburgh: David Douglas, 1881), p. 143.

18. Rueben Briggs Davenport, *The Death-Blow to Spiritualism* (G. W. Dillingham Co., 1888), p. 51.

19. *Report on Spiritualism of the Committee of the London Dialectical Society* (London: Longmans, Green, Reader and Dyer, 1871), p. 13.

20. The articles from the *Quarterly Journal of Science*, 1870–1, are reproduced in William Crookes, *Researches in the Phenomena of Spiritualism* (London: J. Burns, 1874).

21. Louis Blanc, *Letters on England*, vol. II (London: Sampson Low, Son and Marston, 1867), p. 25.

22. Blanc, *Letters*, p. 25.

23. J. J. Smith (ed.), *The Cambridge Portfolio*, vol. II (London: John W. Parker, 1840), p. 521.

24. Charles Babbage, *Passages from the Life of a Philosopher* (London: Longman, Green, Longman, Roberts & Green, 1864), pp. 34–5.

25. Denison (ed.), *Church and State Review*, vol. V (1864), p. 182.

26. Often also referred to as the 'Ghost Society', as by Eric Russell, *Ghosts* (London: B.T. Batsford, 1970), p. 71.

27. *North British Review* (November 1860–May 1861), vol. XXXIV, p. 112.

28. Reproduced as Appendix A in Robert Dale Owen, *Footfalls on the Boundary of Another World* (London: Trübner & Co., 1860), pp. 377–80.

29. Owen, *Footfalls*, pp. xv, 14; William Howitt, *The History of the Supernatural* (London: Longman, Green, Longman, Roberts & Green, 1863), p. 433.

30. Echoes of the Week', *The Illustrated London News*, 5 September 1863.

31. 'A Haunted House!' *Punch*, vol. XLVL, 5 March 1864, p. 99.

32. *The Lancet*, vol. 2 (3 October 1863), p. 403. There was a further reference in *Once A Week*, vol. 11 (1 October 1864), p. 400.

33. George Cruikshank, *A Discovery Concerning Ghosts, With a Rap at the 'Spirit-Rappers'* (London: Frederick Arnold, 1863).

34. Peter Underwood, *The Ghost Club: A History* (Limbury: Limbury Press, 2010), p. 8.

35. Sir Charles William Chadwick Oman, *Memories of Victorian Oxford and of Some Early Years* (London: Taylor and Francis, 1943), p. 82; Schiller, 'Some Logical Aspects of Psychical Research', in Carl Murchison (ed.), *The Case for and Against Psychical Belief* (Oxford: Oxford University Press, 1927), p. 216; M. R. James, *Collected Ghost Stories*, Darryl Jones (ed.) (Oxford: Oxford University Press, 2011), pp. xix, 31 and note p. 428. 'The Mezzotint' was first published in *Ghost Stories of an Antiquary* (London: Edward Arnold, 1904).

36. From the catalogue entry for British Library, Named Manuscripts Collections and Archives, 52258–73.

37. Shane McCorristine (ed.), *Spiritualism, Mesmerism and the Occult, 1800–1920*, vol. 3 (London: Pickering and Chatto, 2012), pp. 19–22, 390–1.

38. Blanc, *Letters*, p. 26.

39. Russell, *Ghosts*, p. 72.

40. William Barrett et al., 'First Report of the Committee on Haunted Houses', *PSPR* (1882), p. 114.

41. Taylor Innes, 'Where are the Letters. *The Nineteenth Century* (August 1887); Edmund Gurney, 'Letters on Phantasms: A Reply', *The Nineteenth Century* (October 1887). Both of these are collected in James Knowles (ed.), *The Nineteenth Century*, vol. XXII, July–December 1887 (London: Kegan, Paul, Trench & Co., 1887), pp. 174–94 and pp. 522–33 respectively.

42. Gordon Stein (ed.), *The Encyclopedia of the Paranormal* (Amherst: Prometheus Books, 1996), p. 709; Henry Sidgwick et al., 'Report on the Census of Hallucinations', *PSPR*, 10 (1894), p.

394; Fraser Nicol, 'The Founders of the SPR', *PSPR*, 55 (March 1972), pp. 353–5.

43. See *PSPR*, 1 (1882–3).

44. Stein, *Encyclopedia*, pp. 582, 708; 'First Report on Thought-Reading', *PSPR*, 1 Stein, *Encyclopedia*, (1882), p. 13, and (1883), pp. 322, 326; Nicol, 'Founders', p. 350.

45. P. T. Barnum, *The Humbugs of the World* (New York: Carleton, 1866), pp. 255–6.

46. 'The Vienna Disturbances', *JSPR* (March 1884), p. 27.

47. 'Fighting Ghost: Midnight Struggle with a Spectre', *Evening News* (26 January 1904).

48. 'Ghost Scare in Blyth', *Blyth News and Ashington Post* (14 March 1904).

49. 'Spectral Visitor at Kirkstall', *Daily Mirror* (9 September 1904).

50. 'Ambushing a Ghost', *Daily Chronicle* (19 November 1908).

51. His Carnacki short stories first appeared in *The Idler* (1910) and *The New Magazine* (1912), before being published as a collection *Carnacki the Ghost Finder* (London: Eveleigh Nash, 1913).

52. Owen Davies, *The Haunted: A Cultural History of Ghosts* (Basingstoke: Palgrave Macmillan, 2006), p. 95.

53. Elliott O'Donnell, *Twenty Years' Experience as a Ghost Hunter* (London: Heath Cranton, 1916): against science, pp. 154; O'Donnell's mediumship, p. 119, other mediums, p. 120, see also pp. 153–4. Reference to the 'Psychical Research Society' in *Bona-Fide Adventures with Ghosts* (Bristol: Baker and Son, 1908), p. 1; and on the title page of *Some Haunted Houses* he is described as an 'Associate of the Psychical Research Society'.

54. John Fraser, *Ghost Hunting: A Survivor's Guide* (Stroud: The History Press, 2010), p. 24.

55. Friedrich Nietzsche, *Jenseits von Gut und Böse* (Leipzig: C. G. Naumann, 1886), Aphorism 146.

56. V. C. Wall, 'Ghost Visits to a Rectory', *Daily Mirror* (10 June 1929).

57. V. C. Wall, 'Weird Night in Haunted House', *Daily Mirror* (14 June 1929). The journalist wrote 'Lucy Kaye', but Price's biographers have disagreed: Paul Tabori, *Harry Price: Ghost-Hunter* (London: Sphere Books, 1974 [1950]) gives 'Lucie Kaye', Richard Morris, *Harry Price: The Psychic Detective*

(Stroud: Sutton, 2006) 'Lucy Kay'. According to Morris, p. 111, it was Price himself who made this change in 1929.

58. Harry Price to David Fraser-Harris, 15 October 1931, Harry Price Collection, University of London.

59. Tabori, *Price*, pp. 246, 251–2.

60. Morris, *Price*, pp. 126–8, 195.

61. Eric J. Dingwall et al., 'The Haunting of Borley Rectory', *PSPR*, vol. 51, p. 186 (January 1956).

62. The *Observer* and *Gloucester Echo* quoted on www.peterunderwood.co.uk, accessed 8 December 2012, and the *Lincolnshire Echo* quoted on the back cover of Peter Underwood, *The Ghost Hunters* (London: Robert Hale, 1985).

63. John Stoker, 'Memoirs of a Ghost-Hunting Man', *Paranormal*, March 2010, p. 55. See Peter Underwood, *No Common Task: The Autobiography of a Ghost-Hunter* (London: Harrap, 1983).

64. Green quoted in Alan Murdie, 'Foreword', in Bowen Pearse, *Ghost-Hunter's Casebook: The Investigations of Andrew Green Revisited* (Stroud: Tempus, 2007), p. 8. Pearse, pp. 10, 18. Alan Murdie recommended Green's book to me at the beginning of my research for this book.

65. Pearse, *Casebook*, pp. 14–15.

66. Fraser, *Ghost Hunting*, p. 40; Val Hope, 'ASSAP History', and other pages, www.assap.ac.uk, accessed 9 December 2012.

67. John Newland, *One Step Beyond* (ABC, 1959–61).

68. Mike Hale, 'Consigning Reality to Ghosts', *The New York Times* (10 December 2009).

69. Will Storr, *Will Storr vs. the Supernatural* (London: Ebury Press, 2006), p. 68.

70. Ghost Hunting Survey (GHS), fielded September and November 2012. Out of 402 questionnaires sent, 53 were returned, yielding a response rate of 13.18 per cent.

2. Equip

1. 'The Ghost of Raynham Hall: An Astonishing Photograph', *Country Life*, 26 December 1936, p. 673.

2. Elliott O'Donnell, *Some Haunted Houses* (London: Eveleigh Nash, 1908), p. 22.

3. Green, *Ghost Hunting*, p. 54.

4. Tom Perrott, 'Credo', *GCN* (Summer 2003), http://www.ghostclub.org.uk/summer2003.htm, accessed 24 July 2012.

5. Ross McGuiness, 'Ghost Stories: It's Horror Potter and the Deathly Hellos for Daniel Radcliffe', *Metro* (13 February 2012).

6. www.amazon.com and specialist websites – www.ghoststop.com, www.theghosthunterstore.com, www.ghosthuntersequipment.com, www.canadianghosthuntsupplies.ca – surveyed 18–20 May 2012.

7. Personal communication, 13 June 2012.

8. www.ghoststop.com, accessed 17 May 2012; Shawn Porter, personal communication, 17 May 2012.

9. Green, *Ghost Hunting*, pp. 65–6.

10. Russell, *Ghosts*, p. 139; Underwood, *A–Z*, p. 115.

11. 'The Phantom of Lincoln's Inn', *Daily Mail* (13 May 1901).

12. Jason Hawes and Grant Wilson, *Ghost Hunting* (New York: Pocket Books, 2007), p. 238.

13. Hawes and Wilson, *Ghost Hunting*, pp. 123, 194.

14. K. Lerner et al., *The Gale Encyclopedia of Science*, 4th ed., 6 vols (Farmington Hills, MI: Thomson Gale, 2008), p. 1578.

15. Tom Ruffles, 'The Brown Lady of Raynham Hall', *Nth Position* (January 2009), http://www.nthposition.com/the-brownladyofraynham.php, accessed 9 August 2012. Jones's statement is dated 18 November 1936.

16. Quoted in Fodor, 'A Letter from England' [dated January 1937], *Journal of the American Society for Psychical Research*, vol. 31, 1937, p. 57.

17. Alan Murdie, 'The Brown Lady of Raynham Hall', *Fortean Times* (September 2006).

18. Barnum, *Humbugs*, p. 257.

19. 'Spiritualism in Court', *New York Daily Tribune* (22 April 1869), p. 2; 'Spiritual Photography', *Harper's Weekly* (8 May 1869); Frank Podmore, *Modern Spiritualism: A History and Criticism*, vol. 2 (London: Methuen, 1902), p. 117; see Louis Kaplan, *The Strange Case of William Mumler, Spirit Photographer* (Minnesota: Minnesota University Press, 2008).

20. 'M. A. Oxon' [William Stainton Moses], 'Researches in Spiritualism', *Human Nature* (May 1875), p. 202.

21. 'Spirit Photography: Sceptic's Talk to the Ghost Club', *The Times* (7 June 1936), p. 14.

22. Podmore, *Modern Spiritualism*, p. 121.
23. Rosemary Ellen Guiley, *The Encyclopedia of Ghosts and Spirits* (New York: Facts on File, 1992), p. 358.
24. Russell, *Ghosts*, pp. 96–9.
25. Guiley, *Encyclopedia*, p. 186.
26. Jason Karl, *An Illustrated History of the Haunted World* (London: New Holland, 2007), p. 80.
27. Letter from Fodor to Lady Townshend, 13 January 1937, quoted in Ruffles, 'Brown Lady'.
28. Fodor, 'Research Officer's Report', 11 January 1937, p. 2, quoted in Ruffles, 'Brown Lady'. Ruffles was the first to point out the presence of Mrs Shira.
29. Quoted in Murdie, 'Brown Lady'.
30. Quoted in Rick Darby, 'U.S. Television Looks at "Real Ghosthunters"', *Paranormal Review*, 14 (April 2000), p. 4.
31. Lerner, *Science*, pp. 2295–7.
32. W. J. Crawford, *The Reality of Psychic Phenomena* (London: Watkins, 1916); W. Whately-Smith, 'The Reality of Psychic Phenomena', *PSPR*, vol. 30 (1918–19), p. 324.
33. George Bagshawe Harrison, *The Day Before Yesterday: Being a Journal of the Year 1936* (London: Cobden-Sanderson, 1938), p. 65; Davies, *Haunted*, p. 95.
34. Gauld and Cornell, *Poltergeists*, p. 228.
35. Hilary Evans, *Seeing Ghosts* (London: John Murray, 2002), p. 93.
36. Harry Price, 'A Model Laboratory', *British Journal of Psychical Research*, vol. 1, 1, May–June 1926, pp. 11–19.
37. Joshua P. Warren, *How to Hunt Ghosts* (New York: Fireside, 2003), pp. 171–2; Hawes and Wilson, *Ghost Hunting*, p. 156.
38. James Tacchi, personal communication, 11 May 2012.
39. Lerner, *Science*, p. 1580.
40. James Tacchi, personal communication, 11 May 2012.
41. Warren, *How to*, p. 204.
42. Townsend, 'Humidity, Lighting and Ghosts', www.assap.ac.uk, 2006, accessed 11 December 2012.
43. Quoted in Tony Cornell, *Investigating the Paranormal* (New York: Helix, 2002), p. 235.
44. Quoted in H. P. Blavatsky, *Isis Unveiled*, vol. 2 (1877), p. 594, from the *Library Table* (19 July 1877); Fairfield discusses

his experiments in greater depth in *Ten Years with Spiritual Mediums* (New York: D. Appleton and Company, 1875), pp. 149–52.

45. Cornell, *Investigating*, pp. 225–42.

46. Cornell, *Investigating*, p. 387.

47. Michael Persinger as editor: *ELF and VLF Electromagnetic Field Effects* (New York: Plenum Press, 1974); and *The Paranormal*, 2 parts (New York: M.S.S. Information, 1974).

48. Green, *Ghost Hunting*, p. 56.

49. Peter Underwood, *The Ghost Hunter's Guide* (Poole: Blandford, 1986), pp. 35–7.

50. Underwood, *Guide*, p. 27.

51. www.kiimeter.com, accessed 11 December 2012.

52. 'Edinburgh Vaults', *Most Haunted*, Series 3, Episode 3, 21 October 2003.

53. 'Waikumete Cemetery', *Ghost Hunt*, Series 1, Episode 8, 2005–6.

54. Troy Taylor, *The Ghost Hunter's Guidebook* (Alton: Whitechapel, 2001), pp. 111–12.

55. Steve Parsons and A. Winsper, 'O. H. Farm, Cheshire 2003–2004', http://www.parascience.org.uk/investigations/ohfarm/ohfarm.htm, accessed 12 October 2012.

56. Warren, *How to*, pp. 52–4; Jonathan Dillon, 'The Coal Clough House Hotel: Place of Uninvited Guests', *The Psi Researcher*, 12 (Winter/Spring 1994).

57. Radiation Alert Monitor 4 being sold on www.amazon.com, 20 May 2012.

58. http://www.allhandsfire.com/personal-radiation-detector-and-dosimeter, accessed 20 May 2012.

59. Product information and pricing from www.amazon.com, 20 May 2012.

60. http://www.emwatch.com/emf-meter-emf-detector.htm, accessed 21 May 2012.

61. Oliver J. Lodge, 'Effect of Light on Long Ether Waves and Other Processes', *JSPR*, vol. 19 (February–March 1919), pp. 33–4.

62. Rick Darby, 'U.S. Television Looks at "Real Ghosthunters"', *Paranormal Review*, 14 (April 2000), p. 4.

63. Hawes and Wilson, *Ghost Hunting*, p. 233.

64. Lerner, *Science*, p. 4019.

65. Lerner, *Science*, p. 4504.

66. 'Are Apparitions Obective, and Do Animals See Them?', *JSPR*, vol. 4 (June 1889), p. 95.

67. 'General Meeting', *JSPR*, vol. 7 (March 1896), p. 248.

68. 'Phonographic Record of Ghosts', *Light*, 7 August 1915; W. J. Crawford, *The Reality of Psychic Phenomena* (London: Watkins, 1916); reviewed in *JSPR*, vol. 18 (February–March 1917), pp. 29–31; quotations from excerpts in W. Whately-Smith, 'The Reality of Psychic Phenomena', *PSPR*, vol. 30 (1918–19), p. 314.

69. Hawes and Wilson, *Ghost Hunting*, pp. 19, 62, 68, 76, 87, 130, 152, 177. Note that 'EVP' is already in the plural and so should not be pluralized with a final 's'.

70. David Ellis, 'Listening to the "Raudive Voices"', *JSPR*, vol. 48 (1975), pp. 31–42; James Alcock, 'Electronic Voice Phenomena: Voices of the Dead?', *Skeptical Inquirer*, 21 December 2004. See also Anabela Cardoso, 'David Ellis and his *The Mediumship of the Tape Recorder*', *JSPR*, vol. 70, 1, no. 882 (January 2006), p. 57.

71. Arthur S. Berger, Gerd H. Hövelmann and Walter von Lucadou, 'Spirit Extras on Video Tape?', *JSPR*, 58 (1992), pp. 153ff.

72. W. H. Wilmer, 'Effects of Carbon Monoxide upon the Eye', *American Journal of Ophthalmology*, series 3, vol. 4, no. 2 (February 1921), pp. 473–90.

73. Hawes and Wilson, *Ghost Hunting*, pp. 180–1.

74. Underwood, *Guide*, pp. 27, 37. Green, *Ghost Hunting*, pp. 56–7, had already discussed the demonstration of a custom device by an unnamed member of the SPR in the early 1970s.

75. Cornell, *Investigating*, p. 379, referring to the Mark II version.

76. Zak Bagans and Kelly Crigger, *Dark World* (Las Vegas: Victory Belt, 2011), p. 107.

77. Professional Measurement website http://www.pro-measure.com/mel_meters_s/97.htm, accessed 15 May 2012.

78. 'Connecticut Dad Builds Gadgets for Ghost Hunters to Honor Late Daughter', www.foxnews.com (25 April 2012); Lee Taylor, 'Gary Galka Creates Ghost Hunting Devices to Speak to his Dead Daughter', www.news.com.au (27 April 2012).

79. http://www.amazon.com/the-ghost-meter-pro-sensor/dp/B004RBM6I2/, accessed 18 May 2012. Customer comments

by Randy Gilbert, 28 August 2011, Heide Hart, 26 July 2011, and 'rakmup', 9 November 2011. Manufacturer feedback by 'mgauss', 27 November 2011, edited 29 December 2011.

80. 'New Gadget from Japan Hailed as Ghost Detector', *Irish Examiner* (4 January 2005).

81. http://www.strapya-world.com/products/56988.html, accessed 18 July 2012.

82. http://itunes.apple.com, accessed 18 July 2012.

83. http://www.ccparanormal.com/equipment.htm, accessed 3 September 2012; http://southwesternohionightstalkers.blogspot.de/2009/07/southwest-ohio-paranormal-society-swops.html, accessed 3 September 2012.

84. 'Mulberry House Joint Investigation with R.I.P. Wales', http://www.ghostinvestigationteam.com/Mulberry-House-27-11-10.html, accessed 3 September 2012.

85. Green, *Ghost Hunting*, p. 30–1.

86. Underwood, *A–Z*, p. 67; Russell, *Ghosts*, p. 150.

87. Arthur Palliser, Jr, 'Are Apparitions Obective, and Do Animals See Them?', *JSPR*, vol. 4 (June 1889), pp. 94–5.

88. Underwood, *A–Z*, pp. 24, 64.

89. Green, *Ghost Hunting*, pp. 102–3.

90. Tamar Love Grande, 'Ghost Hunting Dog on TV: Meet Maddie', www.petsadvisor.com, 28 March 2011, accessed 23 July 2012.

91. Hawes and Wilson, *Ghost Hunting*, pp. 197, 202.

92. Quoted in Russell, *Ghosts*, pp. 76–7.

93. Peter Underwood, *No Common Task: The Autobiography of a Ghost-Hunter* (London: Harrap, 1983), p. 61.

94. Green, *Ghost Hunting*, p. 56; Underwood, *Guide*, pp. 26–7.

95. Green, *Ghost Hunting*, p. 55.

96. Underwood, *Guide*, p. 24.

97. Paul Keene, Gemma Bradley-Stevenson and Bryan Saunders, *The Ghost Hunter Chronicles* (London: New Holland, 2006), unpaginated digital edition.

98. Yvette Fielding and Ciarán O'Keefe, *Ghost Hunters* (London: Hodder & Stoughton, 2006), p. 198; Keene et al., *Chronicles*, unpaginated digital edition.

99. Hawes and Wilson, *Ghost Hunting*, pp. 133, 163–4.

100. Warren, *How to*, p. 173.

101. Warren, *How to*, p. 173.
102. Underwood, *Task*, p. 71.
103. Richard Harris Barham, *The Ingoldsby Legends; or, Mirth and Marvels*, vol. 3 (London: Bentley, Wilson & Fley, 1847), p. 163.
104. O'Donnell, *Twenty Years'*, p. 201.
105. Green, *Ghost Hunting*, p. 20. Zak Bagans takes a more combative approach to ghost hunting and has claimed to have been attacked on several occasions.
106. Oliver J. Lodge, 'On the Difficulty of Making Crucial Experiments [. . .]', *PSPR*, vol. 10 (1894), p. 23.
107. Cornell, *Investigating*, pp. 380–1.
108. Karl, *Illustrated*, pp. 148–9.
109. Underwood, *Guide*, p. 27.
110. Hawes and Wilson, *Ghost Hunting*, p. 137.
111. Troy Taylor, *Confessions of a Ghost Hunter* (Decatur: Whitechapel, 2007), p. 34.
112. James Tacchi, personal communication, 11 May 2012.
113. McGuiness, 'Horror Potter'.

3. Investigate

1. Harrison, *The Day Before*, p. 65; Davies, *Haunted*, p. 95.
2. Green, *Ghost Hunting*, p. 61. ·
3. Based on GHS 2012.
4. Underwood, *Guide*, p. 40.
5. http://www.ghostpi.com/whataretheteams.htm, accessed 9 September 2012. Fraser, *Ghost Hunting*, pp. 126–9, outlines broadly similar roles.
6. http://www.ghostclub.org.uk, accessed 9 September 2012.
7. Hornell Hart, 'Six Theories About Apparitions', *PSPR*, vol. 50, pt 185 (May 1956), p. 157.
8. Gillespy, *A Disquisition upon the Criminal Laws* (Northampton, 1793), p. 34.
9. Henry C. Black, *A Law Dictionary*, 2nd ed. (Union, NJ: The Lawbook Exchange, 1995), pp. 232–3.
10. Adapted from John Bouvier, *A Law Dictionary*, 6th ed. (Philadelphia: Childs & Peterson, 1856).
11. Black, *Dictionary*, p. 296.
12. Plutarch, *Life of Dion*, tr. John Dryden (New York: Modern Library Editions, 1950), p. 1156.

13. Underwood, *Task*, p. 75.
14. Green, *Ghost Hunting*, p. 17.
15. Green, *Ghost Hunting*, p. 27–8. Derren Brown and Andy Nyman, *An Evening of Wonders* [television broadcast] (London: Channel 4, 13 January 2009).
16. Green, *Ghost Hunting*, pp. 28–9.
17. Green, *Ghost Hunting*, p. 105.
18. Cornell, *Investigating*, p. 78.
19. Ian Wilson, *In Search of Ghosts* (London: Headline, 1995), p. 1.
20. 'USAF Guide to Aviation Safety Investigation', Air Force Pamphlet 91–211 (23 July 2001), http://www.e-publishing.af.mil/shared/media/epubs/AFPAM91-211.pdf, accessed 29 October 2012.
21. Cornell, *Investigating*, p. 170.
22. Green, *Ghost Hunting*, p. 105.
23. Loyd Auerbach, *Ghost Hunting* (Berkeley: Ronin, 2004), p. 79.
24. Underwood, *Guide*, p. 40.
25. Auerbach, *Ghost Hunting*, p. 81; Taylor, *Guidebook*, p. 175.
26. See for example an account of the lighting required by the medium Eusapia Palladino in Massimo Polidoro and Gian Marco Rinaldi, 'Eusapia's Sapient Foot', *JSPR*, vol. 62, 850 (January 1998), pp. 245–6.
27. P. G. Maxwell-Stewart, *Ghosts* (Stroud: Tempus, 2006), p. 68.
28. Quoted in Russell, *Ghosts*, p. 139.
29. 'Dr Butts' Ghost', *Occult Review* (March 1905).
30. Leo Ruickbie, *A Brief Guide to the Supernatural* (London: Robinson, 2012), pp. 98–100.
31. Michael Hallows in 'Waikumete Cemetery', *Ghost Hunt*, Series 1, Episode 8, 2005–6.
32. 'The Ghost of "Leathery Colt"', *Halifax Courier* (12 July 1915).
33. Warren, *How to*, p. 125.
34. Underwood, *Task*, p. 209.
35. Ryan D. Buell, 'What is Dead Time', 1 April 2011, http://paranormalresearchsociety.org/blog/what-is-dead-time/, accessed 13 August 2012.
36. For example, see http://answers.yahoo.com/question/index?qid=20080207102824AAmoriZ, accessed 13 August 2012. The time is interpolated from Mark 15:25.

37. At the time of writing the official website www.chicagofilm-critics.org had been hacked, but numerous other sources on the internet give the complete list for 2006.

38. Scott Derrickson (dir.), *The Exorcism of Emily Rose* (Lakeshore Entertainment, 2005). The film is loosely based on the case of Anneliese Michel.

39. Hawes and Wilson, *Ghost Hunting*, p. 113.

40. Cornell, *Investigating*, pp. 168–9, 170, 172, 174.

41. Hawes and Wilson, *Ghost Hunting*, pp. 18, 255–6.

42. Hawes and Wilson, *Ghost Hunting*, p. 249–50.

43. http://www.theparanormalsociety.org/library/3am-dead-time, accessed 13 August 2012. See www.333amparanormal.com/.

44. All of these views are found in forum postings at http://www.paranormalsoup.com/forums/index.php?showtopic=33202, accessed 13 August 2012.

45. Quoted in Wilson, *In Search*, p. 339.

46. Letter to David Cohen, a member of the SPR, in the 1960s: see Underwood, *Ghost Hunters*, p. 16.

47. Taylor, *Confessions*, p. 114.

48. Hawes and Wilson, *Ghost Hunting*, pp. 107, 223.

49. http://www.sentinelpi.co.uk/pastinvestigations.htm, accessed 12 October 2012.

50. Maurice Townsend, 'Analysing Paranormal Vigil Data', ASSAP (2008 and 2012), www.assap.ac.uk/newsite/htmlfiles/analysing vigil data.html, accessed 12 October 2012.

51. Townsend, 'Analysing Paranormal Vigil Data', http://www.assap.ac.uk/newsite/htmlfiles/analysing vigil data.html, accessed 15 December 2012.

52. Hawes and Wilson, *Ghost Hunting*, p. 208.

53. Barrett et al., 'First Report [. . .] Haunted Houses', p. 114.

54. http://www.parascience.org.uk/articles/MHCL1.htm, accessed 25 November 2012.

55. Barrett et al., 'First Report [. . .] Haunted Houses', pp. 114–15.

56. Quoted in Wilson, *In Search*, p. 325.

57. Green, *Ghost Hunting*, pp. 23, 28; a point also made by Underwood, *Task*, p. 167.

58. Hawes and Wilson, *Ghost Hunting*, pp. 233–4.

4. Identify

1. O'Donnell, *Twenty Years'*, p. 47.
2. Homer, *Odyssey*, 10.488, Plato, *Phaedo*, 81c–d, in Ogden, *Magic*, pp. 147, 179.
3. Underwood, *A–Z*, p. 160.
4. Hawes and Wilson, *Ghost Hunting*, p. 173.
5. Paul Sieveking and Jen Ogilvie, *It Happened To Me!*, vol. 1 (London: Dennis, 2008), pp. 125, 129–30; Paul Sieveking, *It Happened To Me!*, vol. 2 (London: Dennis, 2009), p. 111.
6. Apuleius, *Metamorphoses*, 30, in Ogden, *Magic*, p. 152.
7. Underwood, *A–Z*, p. 124.
8. Underwood, *A–Z*, pp. 165, 166, 188.
9. Russell, *Ghosts*, p. 139.
10. Quoted in Peter A. McCue, 'Recurrent Spontaneous Phenomena and UFO Sightings: A Case Report', *Paranormal Review*, 28 (October 2003), p. 8.
11. G.N.M. Tyrrell, *Apparitions* (London: Duckworth, 1943), p. 59.
12. Underwood, *A–Z*, p. 169.
13. Leo Ruickbie, 'Evidence for the Undead: The Role of Medical Investigation in the 18th Century Vampire Epidemic', in Barbara Brodman and James E. Doan (eds), *The Universal Vampire*, vol. 1 (Lanham: Rowman and Littlefield/Fairleigh Dickinson, 2013).
14. Underwood, *A–Z*, p. 134.
15. For an apparition with the sound of footsteps see Piddington, 'Review', p. 280.
16. Russell, *Ghosts*, pp. 138–9; Underwood, *A–Z*, pp. 114, 126–7.
17. Piddington, 'Review', p. 281.
18. Derek Green, 'The Curse of the Black Lady of Broomhill', *GCJ*, 3 (2012), p. 17.
19. 'Hotel Bedroom Ghost', *Vale of White Horse Gazette* (18 August 1933).
20. 'The Ghost of Oscar Wilde', *News Chronicle* (3 February 1934).
21. Underwood, *A–Z*, p. 117.
22. Guy Lyon Playfair, 'Mediawatch', *Paranormal Review*, 17 (January 2001), p. 16.
23. Hawes and Wilson, *Ghost Hunting*, p. 179.
24. Underwood, *A–Z*, p. 160.

25. Underwood, *A–Z*, p. 14.
26. Bengt af Klintberg, *Råttan i pizzan* (Stockholm: Nordstedts Förlag, 1992).
27. R. S. Kirby (ed.), *Kirby's Wonderful and Eccentric Museum* (London: Barnard and Sultzer, 1805), vol. 3, p. 70. The Cock Lane Ghost was later determined to be largely 'cock and bull'.
28. 'Phantom Ship Off Cape Town', *Manchester Guardian* (19 October 1925).
29. Underwood, *A–Z*, pp. 77, 166.
30. Lerner, *Science*, p. 1006.
31. Barnum, *Humbugs*, p. 253.
32. Edmund Gurney, Frederic Myers and Frank Podmore, *Phantasms of the Living*, vol. 2 (London: Trubner and Co., 1886), pp. 16–18.
33. Felix Octavius Carr Darley, *Ghost Stories* (Philadelphia: Carey & Hart, 1846), p. 6.
34. Barnum, *Humbugs*, p. 113.
35. Cyril Scott (ed.), *The Boy Who Saw True* (London: C.W. Daniel, 1953).
36. Gurney et al., *Phantasms*, vol. 2, p. 296.
37. Guiley, *Encyclopedia*, pp. 310–11; Underwood, *A–Z*, pp. 112–13, 221; 'Frankenstein's Castle', *Ghost Hunters International*, SyFy, Season 1, Episode 7, 20 February 2008.
38. Charlotte Latham, 'Some West Sussex Superstitions Lingering in 1868', *The Folklore Record*, vol. 1 (1878), p. 20.
39. Underwood, *A–Z*, pp. 109, 130, 132, 136.
40. Francis Balfour, 'A Phantom Army', *The Times* (2 August 1926), pp. 19–20.
41. Underwood, *A–Z*, p. 149.
42. 'Slaughter in the Mountains', *The Scotsman* (14 October 1941), p. 36; O'Donnell, *Twenty Years*, p. 142.
43. 'Ghostly Visitation in Suffolk Rectory', *Daily Mirror* (10 June 1929), p. 23.
44. Underwood, *A–Z*, p. 165.
45. Russell, *Ghosts*, pp. 37–41.
46. Guiley, *Encyclopedia*, pp. 338–9; Underwood, *A–Z*, pp. 164–5.
47. George Sinclair, *Satan's Invisible World Discovered* (Edinburgh: Thomas George Stevenson, 1871 [1685]), p. 243.
48. Sinclair, *Satan's*, p. 244.

49. Underwood, *A–Z*, p. 160.
50. Russell, *Ghosts*, p. 11; Underwood, *A–Z*, pp. 92, 121.
51. Underwood, *A–Z*, pp. 44, 117.
52. Guiley, *Encyclopedia*, pp. 303.
53. Sieveking, *It Happened*, vol. 2, p. 160; Underwood, *A–Z*, pp. 91, 165.
54. 'Fighting Ghost: Midnight Struggle with a Spectre', *Evening News* (26 January 1904).
55. O'Donnell, *Twenty Years'*, pp. 86, 102–3, 158.
56. Dennis Wheatley, *Gunmen, Gallants and Ghosts* (London: Arrow, 1975), pp. 242–3.
57. Underwood, *A–Z*, p. 150.
58. Wheatley, *Gunmen*, p. 243.
59. Underwood, *A–Z*, pp. 147–8. Charles G. Harper, *Haunted Houses* (London: Chapman and Hall, 1907), pp. 9–10; Alan Murdie, 'Ghost, Bear or Devil?' *GCJ*, 4 (2012), pp. 27–30.
60. Warren, *How to*, p. 88.
61. Nicola J. Holt, 'Developing Perspectives on Anomalous Experiences', *Paranormal Review* (October 2005), p. 23.
62. See Barbara Allen Woods, 'The Devil in Dog Form', *Western Folklore*, vol. 13, 4 (October 1954), pp. 229–35.
63. 'Secret of Peel Castle', *Westminster Gazette* (5 June 1929).
64. Sieveking, *It Happened*, vol. 2, pp. 101–2.
65. Sieveking and Ogilvie, *It Happened*, vol. 1, pp. 95–6.
66. Underwood, *A–Z*, p. 83.
67. 'Photographing a Ghost Dog', *Daily Mirror* (13 May 1937).
68. Sieveking, *It Happened*, vol. 2, pp. 109–110.
69. Cornell, *Investigating*, pp. 127–9.
70. Sieveking and Ogilvie, *It Happened*, vol. 1, pp. 93–5.
71. Sinclair, *Satan's*, pp. 242–7.
72. The story comes from Henry Wim in the 1840s, in James Obelkevich, *Religion and Rural Society: South Lindsey, 1825–75* (Oxford: Clarendon Press, 1976), p. 282.
73. Underwood, *A–Z*, pp. 15–16, 239–40; *Daily Mail* (13 May 1901).
74. There is a lively debate as to whether horses are indeed livestock. Because of their largely entertainment role today many see them as 'companion animals'; however, according to the American Association of Equine Practitioners, horses

are traditionally and legally classed as livestock in the USA: 'Definition of Horses as Livestock', www.thehorse.com (5 October 2001), accessed 20 July 2012. In the UK horses are legally defined as livestock in the Animals Act 1971.

75. Underwood, *A–Z*, pp. 16, 162–3.

76. 'Unusual Haunting in Kent', *Daily Mail* (28 May 1906).

77. Edwin Sidney Hartland (ed.), *English Fairy and Other Folk Tales* (London: The Walter Scott Publishing Co., *c.* 1906), pp. 217–18.

78. Samuel Bamford, *Early Days* (London: Simpkin, Marshall & Co., 1849), p. 30.

79. Ella Mary Leather, *The Folk-Lore of Herefordshire* (Hereford: Jakeman & Carver, 1912), p. 35.

80. Percy Manning, 'Stray Notes on Oxfordshire Folklore', *Folklore*, vol. 14, 2 (June 1903), p. 65.

81. Henry Penfold, 'Superstitions Connected with Illness, Burial, and Death in East Cumberland', *Transactions of the Cumberland and Westmorland Antiquarian and Archaeological Society*, vol. VII (1907), p. 59.

82. Manning, 'Stray Notes', p. 65.

83. Elliott O'Donnell, *Animal Ghosts* (London: William Rider & Son, 1913), digital edition.

84. Martin Coventry, *Haunted Places of Scotland*, p. 11.

85. *Sad and Wonderful Newes from the Faulcon at the Bank Side* (London: George Horton, 1661), p. 3.

86. Latham, 'West Sussex Superstitions', p. 20; O'Donnell, *Animal Ghosts*.

87. Underwood, *A–Z*, pp. 70–1.

88. *Strange and Wonderful News from Lincolnshire; or, A Dreadful Account of a Most Inhumane and Bloody Murther* (London: n.p., 1679), p. 4.

89. Underwood, *A–Z*, pp. 240–1.

90. O'Donnell, *Twenty Years'*, pp. 149–51.

91. 'Ghost of an Elephant at Luna Park', *Brooklyn Eagle* (18 September 1903).

92. Nick Redfern, 'The World's Most Haunted Places', http://www.ehow.co.uk/slideshow_12245114_worlds-haunted-places.html#pg=2, accessed 10 October 2012.

93. O'Donnell, *Twenty Years'*, pp. 138, 141, 142, 146.

94. Fraser, *Ghost Hunting*, p. 147.

95. Field trip, guesthouse (name withheld), Lake District, UK, *c*. 1999.

96. Underwood, *A–Z*, pp. 178–9.

97. Underwood, *A–Z*, pp. 175–6; Dennis Bardens, *Ghosts and Hauntings* (London: Zeus Press, 1965), p. 226, gives the location as West Yorkshire; Cornell, *Investigating*, pp. 189–207.

98. Bardens, *Ghosts*, pp. 228–31.

99. Russell, *Ghosts*, p. 45.

100. Green, *Ghost Hunting*, p. 34: all three dated from 1972.

101. Hawes and Wilson, *Ghost Hunting*, p. 210.

102. Elliott O'Donnell, *Byways of Ghost-Land* (London: William Rider and Son, 1911), pp. 34–7; Rachel [no surname], 'Somewhat Alarmed', *Paranormal*, 50, August 2010, p. 77; Underwood, *A–Z*, p. 146.

103. Hawes and Wilson, *Ghost Hunting*, p. 169.

104. Hawes and Wilson, *Ghost Hunting*, p. 160; Joanna Walters, 'America's Most Haunted', *Guardian*, 25 October 2003.

105. Greg Morgan, 'The Mystery of Knighton Gorges', *GCN* (Summer 2003), http://www.ghostclub.org.uk/summer2003. htm, accessed 10 July 2012.

106. 'A Poltergeist Case', *JSPR*, 12 (May 1906), pp. 260–6.

107. 'Phantom Cyclist?', *Daily Mirror* (24 December 1903).

108. 'The Ghost of "Leathery Colt"', *Halifax Courier* (12 July 1915).

109. See Leo Ruickbie, *Witchcraft Out of the Shadows* (London: Robert Hale, 2004), pp. 51–4.

110. Yeats quoted in Enright, *Supernatural*, p. 251.

111. John and Anne Spencer, *The Ghost Handbook* (London: Macmillan, 1998), pp. 187–8.

112. 'Phantom Ship Off Cape Town', *Manchester Guardian* (19 October 1925).

113. Nigel Blundell and Roger Boar, *The World's Greatest Ghosts* (London: Octopus, 1983), pp. 92–3.

114. Blundell and Boar, *Greatest*, pp. 121–3.

115. '"Ghost Train" in Sweden', *Morning Post* (3 October 1933).

116. Spencer, *Handbook*, pp. 188–190.

117. 'Ghost Bus of Kensington', *Morning Post* (16 June 1934); Spencer, *Handbook*, p. 190.

118. Richard Holland, comment to 'Abergele Ghost Ship', www.bbc.co.uk, 12 May 2008, accessed 20 July 2012.
119. Green, *Ghost Hunting*, pp. 102–3.
120. O'Donnell, *Twenty Years'*, pp. 82–5.
121. G. W. Lambert, 'Phantom Scenery', *JSPR*, 42 (1963), pp. 1–6; M. H. Coleman, 'Phantom Scenery', *JSPR*, 63 (1998–9), pp. 47–8.
122. Blundell and Boar, *Greatest*, p. 116.
123. Underwood, *A–Z*, pp. 185.
124. 'The Farm of Spooks', *Warwickshire Advertiser* (14 April 1923).
125. Penfold, 'Superstitions', pp. 60–1.
126. Davies, *Haunted*, p. 38.
127. Hawes and Wilson, *Ghost Hunting*, pp. 157, 204–6, 223, 240–59.
128. Derek Green, 'Official Investigation Report into Alleged Hauntings Culcreuch Castle Hotel – Fintry, Scotland', 31 January 2005, http://www.ghostclub.org.uk/culcreuch.htm, accessed 13 June 2012.
129. 'CASPER's Spooky Investigations at Old Coaching Inn Run by Corps', *Shepton Mallet Journal*, 25 August 2011.
130. Auerbach, *Ghost Hunting*, p. 104.
131. Hawes and Wilson, *Ghost Hunting*, pp. 23, 123, 191, 194, 197.
132. Peter A. McCue, 'Recurrent Spontaneous Phenomena and UFO Sightings: A Case Report', *Paranormal Review*, 28 (October 2003), pp. 9–10.
133. O'Donnell, *Twenty Years'*, p. 165.
134. Sidney Glanville, 'The Strange Happenings at Borley Rectory', *Fate* (October 1951), pp. 97, 99.
135. Harry Price, *The End of Borley Rectory* (London: Harrap & Co., 1946), pp. 64, 195.
136. Sieveking and Ogilvie, *It Happened*, vol. 1, pp. 12–14.
137. 'Hotel Bedroom Ghost', *Vale of White Horse Gazette* (18 August 1933).
138. Sieveking and Ogilvie, *It Happened*, vol. 1, p. 14.
139. Wheatley, *Gunmen, Gallants and Ghosts* (London: Arrow, 1975), p. 244, italics in the original.
140. Underwood, *A–Z*, pp. 91, 126, 208.
141. L. E., 'A Ghost Story', *The Dublin Penny Journal*, vol. 4, 168 (19 September 1835), pp. 90–1.

142. Derek Green, 'Investigation at Alloa Tower', 8 November 2008, http://www.ghostclub.org.uk/alloa_nov08.htm, accessed 6 July 2012.

143. O'Donnell, *Twenty Years'*, p. 198.

144. See Ruickbie, *Supernatural*, pp. 230–2.

145. Barrie Colvin, 'The Acoustic Properties of Unexplained Rapping Sounds', *JSPR*, vol. 73, 899 (2010), pp. 65–93.

146. Quoted in Russell, *Ghosts*, p. 152.

147. Gurney et al., *Phantasms*, vol. 2, pp. 12–16.

148. Underwood, *A–Z*, p. 160.

149. 'Hotel Bedroom Ghost', *Vale of White Horse Gazette* (18 August 1933).

150. Underwood, *A–Z*, p. 14.

151. See also Melvyn J. Willin, 'Paranormal Manifestations of Music', *JSPR*, vol. 64, 859 (April 2000).

152. Underwood, *A–Z*, pp. 71, 79–80, 119; 'Ghostly Submerged Bell Heard', *Brecon and Radnor Express* (19 December 1935).

153. Underwood, *A–Z*, p. 16.

154. Celia Green and Charles McCreery, *Apparitions* (London: Hamish Hamilton, 1975), p. 80; Erlendur Haraldsson cited in Wilson, *In Search*, p. 155.

155. Peter Underwood, *Nights in Haunted Houses* (London: Headline, 1994), p. 15.

156. Underwood, *A–Z*, p. 137.

157. John Shaw, 'Marquess Buys Family Manor – And its Ghost', *Sunday Telegraph* (9 June 1985).

158. Wilson, *In Search*, p. 156.

159. Hawes and Wilson, *Ghost Hunting*, pp. 43, 154–5.

160. 'Haunting Aroma', *GCJ* (Autumn 1998).

161. Green, *Ghost Hunting*, p. 78.

162. Hawes and Wilson, *Ghost Hunting*, pp. 19, 57.

163. Hawes and Wilson, *Ghost Hunting*, pp. 24, 44.

164. Jeff Belanger, *The World's Most Haunted Places* (New York: Rosen Publishing Group, 2009), p. 18.

165. Hawes and Wilson, *Ghost Hunting*, pp. 144, 146.

166. Hawes and Wilson, *Ghost Hunting*, p. 156; 'Frankenstein's Castle', *Ghost Hunters International*, SyFy, Season 1, Episode 7, 20 February 2008.

167. Underwood, *A–Z*, p. 15.

168. Sir Simon Marsden, *The Haunted Realm* (London: Little, Brown and Company, 1998), p. 106.
169. Underwood, *A–Z*, p. 179.
170. 'Goosed by a Ghost!' www.bbc.co.uk, 28 May 2008, accessed 20 July 2012.
171. Hawes and Wilson, *Ghost Hunting*, pp. 50–3.
172. Quoted in Russell, *Ghosts*, pp. 147–8.
173. 'Couple Refuse to Pay for "Haunted" House', *Telegraph* (16 January 1999).
174. O'Donnell, *Twenty Years'*, p. 199; Sieveking and Ogilvie, *It Happened*, vol. 1, pp. 102.
175. Sieveking and Ogilvie, *It Happened*, vol. 1, pp. 16–18.
176. Underwood, *A–Z*, pp. 127–8.
177. Underwood, *A–Z*, pp. 140–1.
178. O'Donnell, *Byways*, p. 37: and *Twenty Years'*, pp. 27–30.
179. Wilson, *In Search*, p. 155; Anna Eliza Bray, *Traditions, Legends, Superstitions and Sketches of Devonshire*, vol. II (London: John Murray, 1838), p. 298; Leather, *Folklore*, p. 33; Chris Barber, *Ghosts of Wales* (Cardiff: John Jones, 1919), p. 7.
180. O'Donnell, *Twenty Years'*, p. 200.
181. Underwood, *A–Z*, p. 142.
182. Quoted in Enfield, *Supernatural*, p. 262.
183. Underwood, *A–Z*, p. 180.
184. Underwood, *A–Z*, pp. 143–4.
185. Underwood, *A–Z*, p. 133.
186. Davies, *Haunted*, pp. 4–6.
187. Underwood, *A–Z*, pp. 145.
188. Penfold, 'Superstitions', p. 59.
189. Gurney et al., *Phantasms*; see also Sidgwick et al., 'Census'.
190. Green, *Ghost Hunting* pp. 34–6.
191. Underwood, *Ghost Hunters*, pp. 41–2; Pearse, *Casebook*, pp. 15–16; Underwood, *Task*, pp. 83–4.

5. Locate (1): What?

1. Mrs [Elizabeth F.] Ellett, 'Traditions and Superstitions', *The American Review* (January 1846), p. 106.
2. To gauge reputation this ranking is based on a meta-analysis of eight online top ten or top five lists plus the Strongbow

Hallowe'en marketing campaign to find the most haunted pub in 2004. Points were calculated by scoring in relation to the position on each list, from 10 points for position 1 to 1 point for position 10. Top five lists were treated as the top five of a list of ten for scoring purposes. A total of twenty-eight locations was generated. Sources: http://uk.askmen.com/top_10/dating/top-10-most-haunted-pubs-in-britain.html, http://www.spooky stuff.co.uk/britainstoptenhauntedpubs.html, http://him.uk.msn.com/time-off/the-most-haunted-pubs-in-britain, http://www.boredpage.com/index.php/travelandleisure/78-top-ten-most-haunted-pubs-in-england, http://blog.thistle.com/top-5-most-haunted-pubs-in-britain/,http://www.countryfile.com/countryside/britains-best-haunted-pubs,http://www.ukwand erer.com/travel-interests/top-5-most-haunted-pubs-in-britain/, http://www.dorsetghostinvestigators.com/#/most-haunted-pubs/4556697378, all accessed 20 September 2012.

3. 'Ghostly Hangman's Pub Wins Most Haunted Award', *Morning Advertiser* (4 November 2004).

4. Cornell, *Investigating*, p. 73.

5. Underwood, *A–Z*, p. 137; http://liquidassetsnj.ning.com/, accessed 12 September 2012.

6. Meta-analysis of eleven online lists using the scoring system explained above, giving a total of thirty castles worldwide. Sources: http://weburbanist.com/2009/10/28/10-of-the-most-chilling-haunted-castles-in-the-world/, http://www.gadling.com/2012/06/04/the-worlds-10-scariest-haunted-castles/,http://www.hotelclub.com/blog/5-haunted-castles-worth-explor ing/, http://www.eventective.com/blog/castles/2008/03/25/worlds-most-haunted-castles/, http://urbantitan.com/10-creep iest-castles/, http://www.vacationhomes.net/blog/2011/12/28/top-10-creepiest-castles-in-the-world/, http://intercultural comm.wikispaces.com/Top+Ten+Haunted+Castles+worldw ide, http://medievalcastles.stormthecastle.com/essays/haunted -castles.htm, http://kids.aol.com/2012/06/04/the-worlds-most most-haunted-castles/, http://www.thatsfit.com/videos-partn er/worlds-5-most-haunted-castles-517457809-148, http://www.zimbio.com/Bram+Stoker%27s+Dracula/articles/31DlYyUSxHO/Top+10+Most+Horrifying+Castles+World+Amazing, all accessed 8 October 2012.

7. 'Highland Road in Spookiest Top 10', *BBC News* (31 October 2006); Martin Wainwright, 'Roman Soldiers March on M6, Britain's Most Haunted Road', *Guardian* (31 October 2006); Sarah Darnell, 'Ghosts in the News', *GCJ* (Winter, 2007).

8. 'Top Ten Haunted Universities', *Telegraph*, no date, http://www.telegraph.co.uk, accessed 8 October 2012.

9. http://listverse.com/2010/12/01/top-10-haunted-us-college-campuses/, http://www.llewellyn.com/blog/2012/10/america%E2%80%99s-top-five-haunted-universities/,http://www.squidoo.com/haunted-universities, http://www.ranker.com/list/sf-universe_s-10-haunted-colleges-of-us/web-infoguy, http://kittythedreamer.hubpages.com/hub/top-ten-haunted-schools-in-america,http://www.huffingtonpost.com/2010/10/29/13-haunted-campuses_n_775428.html#s165436&title=keene_state_college, all accessed 8 October 2012.

10. Cheri Revai, *Haunted New York* (Mechanicsburg: Stackpole Books, 2005), p. 33.

11. http://sghc.wordpress.com/2009/09/14/the-graveyard-shift-series-old-muslim-cemetery-pusara-abadi/, accessed 11 September 2012; 'Burial, Cremation & Ash Storage', http://www.nea.gov.sg/passesaway/burial.htm, accessed 11 September 2012.

12. Taylor, *Guidebook*, p. 94.

13. Meta-analysis of seven online lists and one book using the scoring system explained above. Due to the paucity of top-ten haunted cemetery lists some listings of general haunted locations were used. Duplicate listings of the same source were discarded. This gave a total of twenty-two cemeteries worldwide with a bias towards the USA. Sources: http://paranormal.lovetoknow.com/Slideshow:10_Most_Haunted_Cemeteries; 'The Top Ten Most Haunted Cemetery [sic] and Graveyards in the United States of America', http://www.hauntedamericatours.com/hauntedcemeteries/toptenhauntedcemeteries/; 'The Most Haunted Cemeteries in the World',http://nightlyhorro,blogspot.de/2011/07/most-haunted-cemeteries-in-world.html; '10 Most haunted Haunted Places on Earth', http://www.environmentalgraffiti.com/news-seven-most-haunted-spots-earth;http://blog.indianluxurytrains.com/2011/09/top-ten-most-

haunted-places-in-world.html; http://www.smashinglists.com
/10-most-haunted-places-in-the-world/; all accessed 21 September 2012; and *The Ultimate Book of Top Ten Lists*, pp.
684–8.

6. Locate (2): Where?

1. Camille Flammarion, *Haunted Houses* (London: T. Fisher
   Unwin, 1924), p. 127.
2. Marsden, *Haunted Realm*, pp. 5, 8.
3. Redfern, 'Most Haunted'.
4. Holly Kirkwood, 'Top 10 Haunted Country Houses', *Country Life* (31 October 2007); Nick McDermott, 'Britain's 10
   Most Haunted Historic Homes Unveiled by National Trust',
   Daily Mail (28 October 2007).
5. 'Top 10 Most Haunted Places', http://www.visitbritain.com/
   en/Top-10-most-haunted-places/, accessed 21 September
   2012.
6. 'Ten Spooky Places to Scare Yourself', *Guardian* (30 October
   2009).
7. Paul Tabori and Peter Underwood, *The Ghosts of Borley*
   (Newton Abbot: David and Charles, 1973), pp. 11–12.
8. The individuals, groups and programmes included in the
   research were, in alphabetical order: Derwent Paranormal Investigators; ESSIVE; *Ghost Adventures*; Ghost Club;
   Ghost Finders Scotland; *Ghostwatch Live*; Andrew Green
   (Pearse, *Casebook*): *Ghost Hunters*; *Ghost Hunters International*; Marsden, *Haunted Realm*; *Most Haunted*; *Most
   Haunted Live!*; *Northern Ireland's Greatest Haunts*; Para-
   Investigations; Para.Science; www.paranormalinvestigators.
   co.uk; Paranormal Research UK; Real or Otherside Paranormal Research; Scottish Paranormal; Scottish Paranormal
   Investigators; Spirit Team UK; Underwood, *Nights*; Richard
   Wiseman et al., 'An Investigation into Alleged Hauntings',
   British Journal of Psychology, 94 (2003), pp. 195–211.
9. Underwood, *Nights*, p. 192.
10. Charles Dickens, *All the Year Round*, vol. 14 (14 October
    1865), p. 276.
11. Edward Walford, *Old and New London*, vol. 2 (London:

Cassell, Petter & Galpin, 1878), p. 60; field trip, 20 April 2012.

12. 'Tower of London Ghosts Hunted', *BBC News* (25 October 2001), http://news.bbc.co.uk/2/hi/uk_news/england/1619622.stm, accessed 23 October 2012; Andy Matthews, personal communication, 23 October 2012.

13. Andy Matthews, personal communication, 23 October 2012.

14. 'The Very Haunted Tower of London', http://www.montreal-paranormal.com/p-uk-london-toweroflondon.php, accessed 23 October 2012.

15. Abbott, *Ghosts of the Tower of London* (Nelson: Hendon Publishing, 2008), pp. 15, 18, 24–5.

16. *Mayfair* (10 May 1879), reproduced by W.E. Howlett in *Notes and Queries* (2 August 1879), pp. 87–8.

17. F. B. Doveton, *Sketches in Prose and Verse* (London: Sampson Low, Marston, Searle and Rivington, 1886), p. 422.

18. H. A. B., *Notes and Queries*, series 4, vol. 10 (9 November 1872), p. 373, and Lyttelton (16 November 1872), p. 399.

19. *Notes and Queries*, series 4, vol. 11 (25 January 1873), p. 85.

20. Dorothy Nevill, *The Reminiscences of Lady Dorothy Nevill* (London: Edward Arnold, 1906), pp. 261–4.

21. *Notes and Queries*, series 6, vol. 2 (25 December 1880), p. 515.

22. Frederick George Lee, *Glimpses in the Twilight* (Edinburgh: Blackwood, 1885), p. 55.

23. Harper, *Haunted*, p. 109.

24. Elliott O'Donnell, *Ghosts, Helpful and Harmful* (London: Rider, 1924), p. 175. He retold the story many times and with some variations.

25. Price, *Poltergeist*, pp. 195–202.

26. Blundell and Boar, *Greatest*, pp. 73–4.

27. Clarry, *Notes and Queries*, series 6, vol. 2 (25 December 1880), p. 515, and confirmed by C.C.M., p. 516.

28. *Antiquarian Book Review Monthly*, vol. 15, 164 (1988), p. 35.

29. 'Haunted Bookshop', *UCLA Librarian*, vol. 23, 1 (January 1970), p. 18.

30. Bardens, *Ghosts*, p. 160; http://www.hampshireghostclub.net/modules/newbb/viewtopic.php?viewmode=thread&topic_id=1846&forum=1&post_id=23688, accessed 25 October 2012.

31. Christoph Driessen, 'Geisterjagd in Edinburgh', *Rheinische Post*, 8 October 2011, p. M11; Neil Wilson, *Lonely Planet Edinburgh Encounter* (London: Lonely Planet, 2011).

32. Gordon Rutter, *Ghosts Caught on Film*, 3 (David & Charles, 2011), pp. 10–11. See, for example, www.listverse.com, *The Ultimate Book of Top Ten Lists* (Ulysses Press, 2009), p. 48, or Trevor MacDonald, *Britain's Favourite View* (London: Cassell, 2007), p. 94.

33. 'Ghostbusters Probe Edinburgh Castle', *BBC News* (4 April 2001), http://news.bbc.co.uk/2/hi/uk_news/scotland/1260728.stm, accessed 19 October 2012.

34. Alan Murdie, *Haunted Edinburgh* (Stroud: The History Press, 2011), p. 71.

35. James Grant, *Memorials of the Castle of Edinburgh* (Edinburgh: William Blackwood and Sons, 1850), pp. 152–3.

36. Martin Coventry, *Haunted Places of Scotland* (Musselburgh: Goblinshead, 2000), p. 81.

37. 'Castle of Screams', *The Scotsman* (19 June 2002); Robert Law, *Memorials* (Edinburgh: Archibald Constable & Co., 1818), p. xci.

38. Derek Green, 'Edinburgh: The Haunted Capital', *GCJ* (Winter, 2007).

39. Jan-Andrew Henderson, *The Town Below the Ground* (Edinburgh: Mainstream, 1999), pp. 35–49.

40. *Encyclopaedia Perthensis*, vol. 8 (Edinburgh: John Brown, 1816), p. 16. Modern sources often refer to only nineteen arches.

41. 'Edinburgh Vaults', *Most Haunted*, Series 3, Episode 3, 21 October 2003.

42. http://www.ghostfinders.co.uk/edinburghvaults.html, accessed 29 August 2012.

43. http://www.australianparanormalinvestigators.com/investigations_niddryst.htm, accessed 31 August 2012.

44. http://www.ghostfinders.co.uk/edinburgh_vaults_evp.html, accessed 29 August 2012.

45. http://www.australianparanormalinvestigators.com/blairst.pdf, accessed 31 August 2012.

46. 'Edinburgh Vaults', *Most Haunted*, Series 3, Episode 3, 21 October 2003.

47. 'Haunted Ulster', http://www.bbc.co.uk/northernireland/autumn/haunted/ballygally.shtml, accessed 22 October 2012; Belanger, *World's*, pp. 15–20; Lionel Fanthorpe and Patricia Fanthorpe, *The World's Most Mysterious Castles* (Toronto: Dundurn, 2005), pp. 208–9.

48. Al Tyas, 'An Evening at Leap Castle', http://www.dchauntings.com/id24.html, no date, accessed 22 August 2012.

49. http://www.simonmarsden.co.uk/books-phantomsoftheisles-sample.htm, accessed 22 August 2012.

50. 'Correspondence', *Occult Review*, vol. 9 (January 1909), pp. 44–7.

51. Derek Acorah, *The Psychic Adventures of Derek Acorah* (Llewellyn, 2008), pp. 136–7.

52. Bob Curran, *The World's Creepiest Castles* (New Page, 2012), digital edition.

53. Camille DeAngelis, *Moon Ireland* (Avalon Travel, 2007), p. 252.

54. Curran, *World's Creepiest*.

55. 'Les Catacombes de Paris', http://www.catacombes-de-paris.fr/english.htm, accessed 1 November 2012; guard quoted in Belanger, *World's*, p. 75.

56. 'The Catacombs, November 25, 2008', http://tuscaloosaparanormal.com/index.php?option=com_content&view=article&id=93&Itemid=58, accessed 1 November 2012.

57. Duncan Light, 'Taking Dracula on Holiday', in Laurajane Smith, Emma Waterton and Steve Watson (eds), *The Cultural Moment in Tourism* (Abingdon: Routledge, 2012), p. 71.

58. Lucy Mallows, *Transylvania* (Chalfont St Peter: Bradt, 2013), p. 118; 'British Ghost Hunt at Bran Castle', http://www.youtube.com/watch?v=wJZSFWA4pnE, accessed 1 November 2012.

59. Quoted in Sondra London and Nicolas Claux, *True Vampires* (Port Townsend: Feral House, 2003), p. 21.

60. Keith Hopkins, *The Colosseum* (London: Profile, 2011), p. 51.

61. 'Rome Catacombs to Reveal Secrets', *Agenzia Nazionale Stampa Associata* (10 February 2009).

62. http://www.syfy.com/ghosthuntersinternational/episodes/season/2/episode/222/unfaithful_spirit_germany, accessed 2 November 2012.

63. Jeff Belanger (ed.), *Encyclopedia of Haunted Places* (Franklin Lakes: New Page Books, 2005), p. 317.
64. Michael Dengg, *Lungauer Volkssagen* (Salzburg: Josef Brettenthaler, 1957), p. 104.
65. http://www.syfy.com/ghosthuntersinternational/episodes/season/s02/episode/e204/witches_castle, accessed 2 November 2012.
66. Strudwick, 'The Whaley House'; Kathy Flanigan, 'Whaley Chronology', http://whaleyhouse.org/chrono.htm; Martin Jones Westlin, 'Weeping and Waling at SD's Certified Haunted House', www.sdnews.com, 26 October 2006, http://www.sdnews.com/view/full_story/300332/article-weeping-and-wailing-at-SD-s-certified-haunted-house-, accessed 30 October 2012.
67. Matt Schulz, comment, 14 October 2010, to 'An Officially Certified Haunted House?', open salon, 11 October 2010, http://open.salon.com/blog/piercing_the_veil/2010/10/11/an_officially_certified_haunted_house, accessed 30 October 2012.
68. Barbara Sillery, *The Haunting of Louisiana* (Gretna: Pelican, 2001), p. 17.
69. Hawes and Wilson, *Ghost Hunting*, p. 137.
70. Hawes and Wilson, *Ghost Hunting*, p. 146.
71. Abstracted from Joe Nickell, *Adventures in Paranormal Investigation* (Lexington: University of Kentucky Press, 2007), pp. 1–9; and Hawes and Wilson, *Ghost Hunting*, pp. 139–43.
72. James Hibberd, 'In Search of Ghosts', *TV Week* (22 August 2005), p. 19, http://www.tvweek.com/news/2005/08/in_search_of_todays_ghost_stor.php, accessed 29 October 2012; Joe Nickell, 'Scientific Investigation vs. Ghost Hunters', *Skeptical Inquirer*, vol. 20, 3 (September 2010); and 'Haunted Plantation', *Skeptical Inquirer*, vol. 27, 5 (September/October 2003), pp. 12–15.
73. Hawes and Wilson, *Ghost Hunting*, pp. 142–6.
74. Troy Taylor said he found reference to Winter's murder in the *Point Coupee Democrat* newspaper for January 1871, see 'The Legends, Lores and Lies of The Myrtles Plantation', http://www.prairieghosts.com/myrtles.html, accessed 30 October 2012. The US Library of Congress holds details of a *Pointe*

Coupee Democrat published between 1858 and 1862, http://
chroniclingamerica.loc.gov/lccn/sn86053686/, accessed 30
October 2012. Marian Patricia Colquette, 'Graceful Death:
The Use of Victorian Elements in Grace Episcopal Churchyard, St Francisville, Louisiana, and St Helena's Episcopal
Churchyard, Beaufort, South Carolina', MA Thesis, Louisiana State University, 2003, p. 159, refers to William Winter
'shot at his own door'.

75. Nickell, *Adventures*, pp. 3, 8–9; Nickell, 'Scientific Investigation'; Hibberd, 'In Search'.

76. Robert Hall, 'The Myrtles Plantation Investigation', http://
www.paranormalinvestigators.com/myrtles/myrtles_report.
htm, accessed 27 October 2012.

77. http://natchezparanormal.com/casefilesevidence/themyrtle-
splantation.html, accessed 26 October 2012.

78. David Marshall, 'The Convocation of Souls at the Historic
Whaley House', *Save Our Heritage Organisation Magazine*,
vol. 32, 2 (June 2001).

79. "Ghostly Legends of the Whaley House', http://whaleyhouse.
org/ghostly.htm, accessed 30 October 2012; Johnny Dwyer,
'The Most Haunted House in America', *Life Magazine* (21
October 2005); Belanger, *World's*, pp. 231–3.

80. The *San Diego Herald*, quoted in 'The Whaley Family', The
Whaley House Museum, http://whaleyhouse.org/whaley-
family.htm, accessed 30 October 2012.

81. Quoted in Dean Glass, 'The Ghosts at the Whaley House get
all the Publicity', *Save Our Heritage Organisation Magazine*,
vol. 36, 4 (2005).

82. June A. Strudwick, 'The Whaley House', *Journal of San Diego
History*, vol. 6, 2 (April 1960).

83. 'Inquisition by Coroner's Jury, State of California, County of
San Diego, In the Matter of the Inquisition upon the Body
of Violet E. Whaley Deceased', 19 August 1885, reproduced
at http://whaleyhouse.org/coroner.htm, accessed 31 October
2012.

84. 'The Whaley Family'.

85. Quoted in Belanger, *Encyclopedia*, p. 232.

86. Belanger, *World's*, p. 231. The story is told by Holzer in his
Ghosts of the Golden West and *Ghosts. Celebrity Ghost Sto-*

ries, Season 3, Episode 1, original broadcast date 18 June 2011, A&E Television Networks.

87. Marshall, 'Convocation'; 'San Diego Whaley House Museum', http://www.sandiegoghosthunters.com/whaley/whaley-house-museum.html, accessed 30 October 2012.

88. Quoted in Belanger, *World's*, p. 99.

89. Joe Nickell, *Real-Life X-Files* (Lexington: University of Kentucky Press, 2001), pp. 114–15.

90. The White House Museum, http://www.whitehousemuseum. org, accessed 31 October 2012.

91. See, for example, Judith Joyce, *The Weiser Field Guide to the Paranormal* (San Francisco: Weiser, 2010), p. 132, although I could find no reputable sources for this story. Churchill is often transposed to the Lincoln Bedroom, but the White House Museum places him in the Queen's Bedroom.

92. Sara Nelson, 'Fright House: Jenna Bush on the Ghostly Music Playing in the Presidential Home Already "Haunted" by Abraham Lincoln', *Daily Mail* (5 November 2009); Sheridan Alexander, 'The Demon Cat and Other Ghosts of the US Capitol', www.examiner.com (1 October 2009), http://www. examiner.com/article/the-demon-cat-and-other-ghosts-of-the-us-capitol-washington-dc-ghost-stories-and-haunted-places, accessed 31 October 2012; Lee Davidson, 'No-Show "Demon Cat" Gives Election to Bush', *Deseret News* (2 November 1988).

93. Joan Page, 'President Reagan's White House Ghost Story', 30 October 2009, http://open.salon.com/blog/ joanpgage/2009/10/30/president_reagans_white_house_ ghost_story, accessed 1 November 2012. Page was at the Reagans' dinner party and heard the stories from Reagan himself.

94. Nelson, 'Fright House'.

95. Nelson, 'Fright House'.

96. 'Ghost Stories Haunt The White House', *Reuters* (1 November 2003).

97. Nelson, 'Fright House'.

98. Case# M3002, http://www.coldspot.org/mackenziehouse. html, accessed 19 October 2012.

99. John Robert Colombo and Jillian Hulm Gilliland, *Ghost Sto-*

ries of Canada (Toronto: Dundurn Press, 2000), pp. 102–3; Andrew McFarlane, 'The Ghosts that Live in Toronto', *Toronto Telegram* (28 June 1960); http://www.pararesearchers. org/index.php?/20080806570/Ghosts-Hauntings/Mackenzie-House.html, accessed 31 May 2012; according to Chris Raible 'Ghosts at Mackenzie House' (Toronto: Toronto Historical Board, 1998), the inventory is now lost.

100. 'Top 10 Ghostly Encounters', http://www.southafrica.net/ za/en/top10/entry/top-10-ghostly-encounters, accessed 5 September 2012; Richard George, Denise Slabbert and Kim Widman, *Offbeat South Africa* (Cape Town: Struik, 2006), p. 17.

101. Arthur Goldstuck, *The Ghost that Closed the Town Down* (Johannesburg: Penguin, 2006), p. 5.

102. Poll results: 'Do you believe in ghosts?' Yes: 49.15% (1,985 votes); No: 25.5% (1,030 votes); 'if I see one I will': 25.35% (1,024 votes); from http://www.adelaidenow.com.au/news/ south-australia/supermarket-ghosts-has-a-sweet-tooth/ story-e6frea83-1226303715526, accessed 27 August 2012.

103. Reginald Ryan, 'Monte Cristo Ghosts', http://www.mon-tecristo.com.au/hauntings.html, accessed 27 August 2012; Rowena Gilbert, 'Monte Cristo: Australia's Most Haunted. Investigation Report', http://www.castleofspirits.com/mon-tecristo/montecristo5.html, accessed 2 November 2012.

104. 'Monte Cristo Ghost Tours', www.montecristo.com.au/ mctour.html, accessed 27 August 2012.

105. http://www.environment.sa.gov.au/adelaidegaol/, accessed 27 August 2012.

106. Jeff Fausch and Alison Oborn, '[Gladstone Gaol] The Investigation', http://paranormalfieldinvestigators.com/glad-stone_gaol_investigation.html, 2006, accessed 27 August 2012.

107. Tom Bowden, 'Supermarket Ghost Story Prompts Tales of Adelaide Sightings', *The Advertiser* (21 March 2012).

108. http://www.adelaidehauntedhorizons.com.au/, accessed 27 August 2012.

109. 'St John's Reformatory Kapunda', http://paranormalfieldin-vestigators.com/st_johns_history.html, accessed 27 August 2012.

110. www.ghost-tours.com.au, accessed 28 August 2012.

111. Melinda Siegmeier, 'Criterion Hotel Calls on Psychic to Oust Ghost', *The Bulletin* (14 January 2009).

112. Fiona Breen, 'Ghost Hunters Haunt Old Mental Asylum', *ABC News* (22 February 2011).

113. Lyndal Redman, 'Security camera Footage Shows Supermarket has a Penchant for Sweets', *The Advertiser* (20 March 2012).

114. Jon Bassett, 'Ghost Hunters Busted at "Haunted" Hospital', *PerthNow* (27 August 2012).

115. 'Historic Dunedin Castle Rich in Myth', *One News* (14 July 2005); Hamish McNeilly, 'Ghost Pushed Us, Larnach Castle Tourist Claims', *Otago Daily Times* (23 May 2012).

116. Kirsty Johnston, 'New Zealand's Spookiest Stories', www.stuff.co.nz (29 October 2010), accessed 24 August 2012.

117. 'Fortune Theatre, Dunedin', *Ghost Hunt*, Episode 4, TV2 (2005–6).

118. 'Ghost Hunters in for the Chill', *New Zealand Herald* (6 November 2011); Julie Miller and Grant Osborn, *Unexplained New Zealand* (Auckland: Reed, 2007); http://www.spookers.co.nz/hauntedhouse.php, accessed 25 August 2012; Beth Watson, personal communication, 3 September 2012.

119. 'Top 10 Haunted Holidays', http://www.news.com.au/travel/galleries/gallery-e6frflw0-1226279306659?page=1, accessed 18 October 2012.

120. 'The Top 10 Most Haunted Places in India', http://zeenews.india.com/slideshow/top-10-most-haunted-places-in-india_39.html, accessed 18 October 2012.

121. Gaurav Tiwari, 'Bhangarh: Myth Busted', http://paranexus.org/index.php?action=blog&bact=memberart&member=229&blogid=6&article=108&where=Member_Article, accessed 18 October 2012. I contacted GRIP in 2012 for further clarification, but received no reply.

122. Lyle Brennan, 'The Suicide Forest of Japan', *Daily Mail* (9 April 2012); Rob Gilhooly, 'Inside Japan's "Suicide Forest"', *The Japan Times* (26 June 2011); 'Japan's Harvest of Death', *Independent* (24 October 2000).

123. Joe Teh, 'Being a Guest Paranormal Investigator with Singapore Haunted Team', www.techielobang.com, http://techielobang.com/blog/2011/10/31/being-a-guest-paranor-

mal-investigator-with-singapore-haunted-team/, accessed 18 October 2012.

124. 'The Haunted Changi', http://www.spi.com.sg/haunted/haunted_changi/changi_pt.htm, accessed 19 October 2012.

125. 'A Compassionate Night at Changi/Our Final Analysis', http://www.spi.com.sg/spi_files/index.htm, accessed 19 October 2012.

7. Contact

1. As late as 2010 allegations surfaced on the internet concerning Fuller's nefarious career, revealing that at least one attempt on his life had been made earlier: EddieJ, 'Re: whos the evilest person you have ever met?', www.therevcounter.com, 19 June 2010. See also Skullfudge [Clive], 'Off for a weird evening tonight', www.p1woc.co.uk, 21 October 2011.

2. 'Couple's Murderer Jailed in "Ouija Board" Retrial', *Independent* (17 December 1994); 'Our Daughter's Killer Wrecked Our Lives Too', *The Argus* (26 March 2004).

3. Nick Cohen and Ann Steele, 'Murder Bride's Father Sues Over 999 "Bungle"', *Independent* (10 April 1994).

4. 'Couple's Killer gets Two Life Sentences: Security Video and Tape of Phone Call Trapped Insurance Man', *Independent* (24 March 1994); 'Murder Appeal Thrown Out by Judges', *The Argus* (8 December 2004).

5. 'Couple's Killer'.

6. Jenny Randles and Peter Hough, Psychic Detectives: *The Mysterious Use of Paranormal Phenomena in Solving True Crimes* (Enderby: Silverdale, 2002), p. 203.

7. R. vs Young [1995] QB 324. 'Ray' is a pseudonym.

8. '"Ouija Board" Appeal Dismissed', *BBC News* (7 December 2004).

9. R. vs Young [1995] QB 324.

10. Lewis Spence, *An Encyclopedia of Occultism* (New York: Cosimo, 2006 [1920]), pp. 324–5. Spence attributed the information on Pythagoras to an unreferenced French source. Modern sources, such as www.encyclopedia.com, continue to repeat this.

11. Letters Patent No. 446, 054, United States Patent Office, filed 28 May 1890, issued 10 February 1891.

12. US Trademark No. 18, 919, registered 3 February 1891.

13. Letters Patent No. 462, 819, United States Patent Office, filed 18 February 1891, issued 10 November 1891.

14. Epes Sargent, *Planchette; or, The Despair of Science* (Boston: Roberts Brothers, 1869), p. 1; 'Le Spiritisme et les Spiritwa', *Revues des Deux Mondes*, vol. XLVII (1863), p. 392.

15. Nellie Irene Walters, *The Secret of the Successful Use of the Ouija Board* (No place: no publisher, 1919), p. 5.

16. Herbert Asbury, 'Is the Ouija-Board Controlled Subconsciously', *Popular Science*, vol. 98, 2 (February 1921), p. 85.

17. Hereward Carrington, *The Psychical Phenomena of Spiritualism: Fradulent and Genuine* (New York: Dodd, Mead & Co., 1920), p. 141. The procedure is detailed in Nevil Monroe Hopkins, *Twentieth Century Magic* (Philadelphia: David McKay, 1898), pp. 63–6.

18. *JSPR*, vol. 16 (January 1913), p. 3; *JSPR*, vol. 18 (May–June 1917), p. 59.

19. 'Meetings of the American Branch', *JSPR* (March 1892), p. 218; *JSPR*, vol. 7 (February 1895), pp. 30–1; Robert Hare, *Experimental Investigation of the Spirit Manifestations* (New York: Partidge & Brittan, 1856).

20. M. R. Barrington, 'Mediumship', in Ivor Grattan-Guinness (ed.), *Psychical Research: A Guide to its Principles and Practices* (Wellingborough: The Aquarian Press, 1982), p. 73. See W. F. Prince, *The Case of Patience Worth* (Boston: Boston Society for Psychic Research, 1927).

21. Ada Goodrich-Freer and John, Marquess of Bute (eds), *The Alleged Haunting of B— House* (London: George Redway, 1899), pp. 98, 100.

22. Goodrich-Freer and Bute, *B— House*, p. 101.

23. Goodrich-Freer and Bute, *B— House*, pp. 104–5; Frank Podmore, *PSPR*, vol. 15 (1900–1), p. 100.

24. Cornell, *Investigating*, pp. 65–78.

25. Cornell, *Investigating*, pp. 69–70.

26. Cornell, *Investigating*, p. 71.

27. Alan Murdie, 'Investigation: The Ferry Boat Inn, Holywell', *GCN* (Spring 2003), http://www.ghostclub.org.uk/spring2003.htm, accessed 23 July 2012.

28. Cornell, *Investigating*, pp. 167–75.

29. Cornell, *Investigating*, p. 167.
30. Cornell, *Investigating*, pp. 168–9, 170, 172, 174.
31. Gerald Brittle, *The Demonologist: The Extraordinary Career of Ed and Lorraine Warren* (No place: iUniverse, 2002), p. 102.
32. Hawes and Wilson, *Ghost Hunting*, p. 52.
33. Sue Clough, 'Broadmoor for Ouija Killer', *Telegraph* (20 December 1999); 'Ouija Killer Sent to Broadmoor', *Independent* (20 December 1996).
34. David J. Krajicek, 'The Ouija Board Murder: Tricking Tribal Healer Nancy Bowen to Kill', *New York Daily News* (21 March 2010).
35. 'Wife is Convicted in "Ouija" Murder', *St Petersburg Times* (10 June 1934); Turley vs State, Arizona Supreme Court, 29 June 1936.
36. 'Woman Acquitted of Ouija Board Killing', www.seattlepi.com (18 September 2001).
37. 3 out of 57 (5.3%) publicly available investigations for the years 1999 to 2010 at http://www.ghostclub.org.uk/gc_invest_main.htm; Green, *Ghost Hunting*, p. 159; Warren, *How to*, pp. 197–9; Fraser, *Ghost Hunting*, pp. 110–11; Fielding and O'Keeffe, *Ghost Hunting*, p. 189; Auerbach, *Ghost Hunting*, pp. 104–5; Bagans and Crigger, *Dark World*, p. 147; 'Monte Cristo Ghost Tours', http://www.montecristo.com.au/mctour.html, accessed 27 August 2012.
38. Fielding and O'Keeffe, *Ghost Hunting*, p. 335.
39. Claude Dechales, *Cursus seu mundus mathematicus*, vol. II (Lyons: 1674), p. 190.
40. Green, *Ghost Hunting*, p. 79.
41. The only description I could find of this device was in Harry Bell, *Glasgow's Secret Geometry* (No place: Leyline Publications, 1993), p. 25.
42. George P. Hansen, 'Dowsing: A Review of the Experimental Research', *JSPR*, vol. 51, 792 (October 1982), p. 356.
43. William Barrett, 'On the So-Called Diving Rod, or Virgula Divina', *PSPR*, vol. 13 (1897–8), p. 58; William Barrett and Theodore Besterman, *The Divining-Rod: An Experimental and Psychological Investigation* (London: Methuen & Co., 1926), p. 2; Hansen, 'Dowsing', pp. 343–4.
44. Barrett, 'Diving Rod', p. 246.

45. T.C. Lethbridge, *Ghost and Divining Rod* (London: Routledge and Kegan Paul, 1963) and *The Power of the Pendulum* (London: Routledge and Kegan Paul, 1976).

46. Hansen, 'Dowsing', pp. 356–8.

47. Alan Murdie, 'Ghostwatch', unpublished MS (July 2011), pp. 3–4.

48. http://www.ghostclub.org.uk/rye.htm, accessed 5 July 2012.

49. Murdie, 'Ghostwatch', p. 3 citing *Reynold's News* (4 June 1950).

50. Race Rock Lighthouse, Fishers Island, and Adam Zubrowski cases in Hawes and Wilson, *Ghost Hunting*, pp. 93, 95, 129.

51. Hawes and Wilson, *Ghost Hunting*, p. 129.

52. 18 out of 57 (31.6%) publicly available investigations for the years 1999 to 2010 at http://www.ghostclub.org.uk/gc_invest_main.htm.

53. Warren, *How to*, pp. 269–71.

54. Fielding and O'Keeffe, *Ghost Hunters*, p. 210.

55. Alan Murdie, 'Ghost-Hunters and the Delights of Dowsing', *Fortean Times*, 279 (January 2012).

56. 15 out of 57 (26.3%) publicly available investigations for the years 1999 to 2010 at http://www.ghostclub.org.uk/gc_invest_main.htm.

57. Derek Green, 'Investigation at Alloa Tower', 8 November 2008, http://www.ghostclub.org.uk/alloa_nov08.htm, accessed 6 July 2012.

58. Barrett, 'Diving Rod', p. 3.

59. Barrett, 'Diving Rod', p. 253.

60. Barrett, 'On the Detection of Hidden Objects by Dowsers', *JSPR*, 15 (1910), pp. 183–93; Barrett and Besterman, *Divining-Rod*.

61. Barrett and Besterman, *Divining-Rod*, p. 258.

62. Hansen, 'Dowsing', pp. 352, 354.

63. Evon Z. Vogt and Ray Hyman, *Water Witching U.S.A.*, 2nd ed. (Chicago: Chicago University Press, 1979).

64. Field trip, Ratskeller, Im Zwengel 1, Stromberg, Rheinland-Pfalz, Germany, 2007.

65. 55 out of 57 (96.5%) publicly available investigations for the years 1999 to 2010 at http://www.ghostclub.org.uk/gc_invest_main.htm.

66. Kathy Gearing, 'First Investigation at The Old Swan, Ched-

dington', 31 August 2002, http://www.ghostclub.org.uk/cheddington.htm, accessed 9 July 2012.

67. See for example, A. T. T. Peterson, *Essays from the Unseen, Delivered Through the Mouth of W. L., a Sensitive* (London: 1885). The term traces an earlier connection with research into Mesmerism, as in Karl, Baron von Reichenbach, *Wer ist Sensitiv, Wer Nicht? Oder Kurze Anleitung, sensitive Menschen mit Leichtikeit zu finden* (Vienna, 1856).

68. O'Donnell, *Twenty Years'*, p. 160.

69. 'The Ghost of Charles Dickens', *Daily Star* (10 July 1930).

70. Podmore, *Modern Spiritualism*, pp. 120–1.

71. Matt Roper, 'Spooky Truth: TV's Most Haunted Con Exposed TV', *Mirror* (28 October 2005).

72. 'Bodmin Gaol', *Most Haunted*, Series 6, Episode 1, 22 March 2005.

73. 'Prideaux Place', *Most Haunted*, Series 6, Episode 4, 12 April 2005.

74. 'Craigievar Castle', *Most Haunted*, Series 6, Episode 14, 28 June 2005.

75. 'The Asylum', *Most Haunted Live!*, 2–4 September 2005.

76. Interviewed on *Justin Lee Collins: Good Times*, Channel 5, 10 May 2010.

77. 'Can this Man Talk to the Dead?', *Sun* (10 March 2011); Aaron Tinney, 'TV Psychic's Sick "Maddie's Dead" Claims', *Sun* (15 May 2012).

78. 1 Samuel 28, King James Version (1611).

79. William Bliss Ashley, *Modern Necromancy: A Sermon Preached at St. Paul's Church, Syracuse, on Septuagesima Sunday Evening, A.D. 1855* (Syracuse: William T. Hamilton, 1855); Edward Cridge, *"Spiritualism", or, Modern Necromancy* (Victoria, B.C.: David W. Higgins, 1870); 'Dr. Wilkinson's Branding of Spiritualism as the "Modern Necromancy" Causes Storm', *Lewiston Saturday Journal* (30 August 1919), p. 1.

80. 1 Samuel 28:3.

81. Johannes von Tepl, *Der Ackermann und der Tod*, tr. Felix Genzmer (Philipp Reclam, 1984 [1401]); Johannes Hartlieb, *Das Buch der Verbotenen Künste*, tr. Falk Eisermann and Eckhard Graf (Eugen Diedrichs Verlag, 1998 [1456]), p. 69, my translation. See Ruickbie, *Supernatural*, pp. 199–201.

82. Henry Cornelius Agrippa, *Henry Cornelius Agrippa, His Fourth Book of Occult Philosophy*, tr. Robert Turner (London: John Harrison, 1655), p. 70.

83. Agrippa, *Fourth Book*, pp. 70–1.

84. Cornelius Agrippa, *Three Books of Occult Philosophy*, tr. John French (London: Gregory Moule, 1651), pp. 128, 134.

85. John Weever, *Ancient Funeral Monuments of Great-Britain, Ireland and the Islands Adjacent* (London: W. Tooke for J. Wilkie, 1767 [1631]), pp. xlv–xlvi.

86. Eliphas Levi, *Transcendental Magic: Its Doctrine and Ritual*, trans. A. E. Waite (London: William Rider & Son, 1923) p. 118.

87. Hawes and Wilson, *Ghost Hunting*, p. 205; 'Two Houses', Season 2, Episode 7, 7 September 2005.

88. www.ghosthuntersofamerica.com, accessed 15 December 2012. The group is variously referred to on the website as 'The American Ghost Hunters Society', 'The Ghost Hunters of America', 'The American Ghost Hunters and Paranormal Research Society' and 'The Ghost Hunters of America Paranormal Investigation'.

89. Levi, *Transcendental*, pp. 119–20.

8. Explain

1. Robert O. Becker, *The Body Electric: Electromagnetism and the Foundation of Life* (New York: William Morrow, 1985), pp. 264–5.

2. Hart, 'Six Theories', p. 159.

3. Ernest Bozzano, *Les Phénomènes de Hantise* (Paris: Alcan, 1929); Sidgwick quoted in Stein, *Encyclopedia*, p. 306.

4. Hart, 'Six Theories', p. 159.

5. Frederic W. H. Myers, *Human Personality and Its Survival of Bodily Death*, vol. 2 (London: Longmans, Green and Co., 1903), p. 4.

6. Brittle, *Demonologist*, p. 156.

7. O'Donnell, *Twenty Years'*, p. 190.

8. Hawes and Wilson, *Ghost Hunting*, p. 88.

9. Hawes and Grant, *Ghost Hunting*, pp. 215–19.

10. O'Donnell, *Twenty Years'*, p. 86.

11. Green, *Ghost Hunting*, p. 74.

12. G. W. Lambert, Review of Tabori and Underwood, *Ghosts of*

Borley, in *JSPR*, vol. 47 (March 1974), p. 332; and Tabori and Underwood, *Borley*, pp. 160–5.

13. A. T. J. Dollar, 'Catalogue of Scottish Earthquakes 1916–49', in *Transactions of the Geological Society of Glasgow*, vol. 21, 2 (1951), pp. 283–361.

14. G. W. Lambert, 'Scottish Haunts and Poltergeists II', *JSPR*, vol. 42, 718 (March 1964), p. 226.

15. E. J. Dingwall and Trevor H. Hall, *Four Modern Ghosts* (London: Duckworth, 1958), p. 20.

16. G. W. Lambert, 'Poltergeists: A Physical Theory', *JSPR*, vol. 38, 684 (June 1955), pp. 49–71; G. W. Lambert, 'Scottish Haunts and Poltergeists: A Regional Study', *JSPR*, vol. 40, 701, pp. 108–20. For criticism see A. D. Cornell and Alan Gauld, 'The Geophysical Theory of Poltergeists', *JSPR*, vol. 41 (September 1961), pp. 129–47.

17. G. W. Lambert, Reply to Cornell and Gauld, 'The Geophysical Theory of Poltergeists', *JSPR*, vol. 41 (September 1961), p. 152.

18. Adapted from Lambert, Reply to Cornell and Gauld, p. 149.

19. Green, *Ghost Hunting*, p. 79.

20. Barrett et al., 'First Report [. . .] Haunted Houses', p. 108.

21. James Clark, 'Hunting for Ghosts with John Fraser', The Morton Report (4 October 2011), http://www.themortonreport.com/discoveries/paranormal/hunting-ghosts-with-john-fraser/, accessed 21 November 2011.

22. 'Cottage Buyers' Haunting Defence', *Guardian* (16 January 1999).

23. 'Judge Exorcises Haunted Home', *Guardian* (19 January 1999).

24. MAPIT, 'A Cottage Mystery', http://www.mapit.kk5.org/#/a-cottage-mystery/4545260358, accessed 22 June 2012. MAPIT now stands for Manchester's Association of Paranormal Investigation and Training.

25. Wilmer, 'Effects of Carbon Monoxid [sic]', pp. 73–86. For a different interpretation see Walter F. Prince, *Carbon Monoxid or Carbon Monoxid Plus?* (Boston: Boston Society for Psychic Research, 1926).

26. Hawes and Wilson, *Ghost Hunting*, pp. 189–92.

27. Hawes and Wilson, *Ghost Hunting*, p. 187.

28. Peter Haining (ed.), *The Mammoth Book of True Hauntings* (London: Constable & Robinson, 2008), p. xv.

29. Based on the report of 'Mrs H.' given in Wilmer, 'Effects', pp. 77–86.

30. Green, *Ghost Hunting*, p. 80.

31. Gauld and Cornell, *Poltergeists*, pp. 249–51.

32. Mark E. Reed, GHS 2012.

33. Peter Eastham, 'Ticking Off a Poltergeist', *JSPR*, vol. 55, 811 (April 1988), pp. 80–3, but see D. Scott Rogo and the reply in *JSPR*, vol. 49, 778 (December 1978), pp. 980–1, for a different interpretation.

34. Vic Tandy and Tony R. Lawrence, 'The Ghost in the Machine', *JSPR*, vol. 62, 851 (April 1998), pp. 360–4.

35. Jason J. Braithwaite and Maurice Townsend, 'Good Vibrations: The Case for a Specific Effect of Infrasound', *JSPR*, vol. 70.4, 885 (October 2006), p. 218.

36. Independent Advisory Group on Non-Ionising Radiation, 'Health Effects of Exposure to Ultrasound and Infrasound', *Documents of the Health Protection Agency* (February 2010); 'Infrasound: Brief Review of Toxicological Literature', National Toxicology Program, Department of Health and Human Services (November 2001), p. 9. For the latest research see Steve T. Parsons, 'Infrasound and the Paranormal', *JSPR*, vol. 72.3, 908 (July 2012), pp. 150–73.

37. Michael Persinger and R. A. Cameron, 'Are Earth Faults at Fault in Some Poltergeist-like Episodes?', *Journal of the American Society for Psychical Research*, 80 (1986), p. 56 [49–73].

38. Michael Persinger and S. A. Koren, 'Experiences of Spiritual Visitation and Impregnation: Potential Induction by Frequency-Modulated Transients from an Adjacent Clock', *Perceptual and Motor Skills*, 57 (2001), pp. 868–70.

39. Y. H. Q. Chen and S. Hammin, 'An Investigation on the Physiological and Psychological Effects of Infrasound on Persons', *Journal of Low-Frequency Noise Vibration and Active Control*, vol. 23, 1 (2004), pp. 71–6; V. Gavreau, 'Infrasound', *Science Journal*, vol. 4 (1968), pp. 33–7; Colin H. Hansen (ed.), *The Effects of Low-Frequency Noise and Vibration on People* (Brentwood: Multi-Science Publishing, 2007); N. I. Karpova et al., 'Early Response of the Organism to Low-Frequency Acoustic Oscillations', *Noise and Vibration Bulletin*, vol. 11

(1970), pp. 100–3; I.M. Lidstrom et al., 'The Effects of Infrasound on Humans', *Investigation Report* (Umeå, Sweden: University of Umeå, 1978), vol. 33, pp. 1–42; G. C. Mohr et al., 'Effects of Low Frequency and Infrasonic Noise on Man', *Aerospace Medicine*, vol. 36 (September 1965), pp. 817–24; Henrik Møller, 'Physiological and Psychological Effects of Infrasound on Humans', *Journal of Low Frequency Noise Vibrations*, vol. 3, 1 (1984), pp. 1–17; R. W. B. Stephens, 'Infrasonics', *Ultrasonics* (January 1969), pp. 30–5.

40. Hawes and Wilson, *Ghost Hunting*, pp. 194, 197.

41. Warren, *How to*, pp. 54, 88.

42. Warren, *How to*, p. 61.

43. Hawes and Wilson, *Ghost Hunting*, p. 175.

44. Hawes and Wilson, *Ghost Hunting*, pp. 211–12.

45. Hawes and Wilson, *Ghost Hunting*, p. 258.

46. Arthur Ellison, 'Fields and Consciousness', *The Psi Researcher* (January 1992), p. 19.

47. 'Investigations of the Stanley Hotel', Rocky Mountain Paranormal Research Society, http://www.rockymountainparanormal.com/smallstanley.pdf, accessed 27 July 2012.

48. S. Subrahmanyam et al., 'Effect of Magnetic Micropulsations on Biological Systems – A Bioenvironmental Study', *International Journal of Biometeorology*, 29 (1985), pp. 293–305.

49. 'Frog Defies Gravity', *New Scientist*, issue 2,077 (12 April 1997).

50. Michael Persinger, 'Increased Geomagnetic Activity and the Occurrence of Bereavement Hallucinations: Evidence for Melatonin-Mediated Microseizuring in the Temporal Lobe?', *Neuroscience Letters*, 88 (1988), pp. 271–4; William Roll and Michael Persinger, 'Investigations of Poltergeists and Haunts: A Review and Interpretation', in James Houran and Rense Lange (eds), *Hauntings and Poltergeists: Multidisciplinary Perspectives* (Jefferson: McFarland, 2001), pp. 156, 162.

51. Abstracted from Roll and Persinger, 'Investigations', pp. 153–60. Not all values were routinely reported. Where ranges for air ion values were given, only the higher of the two values is indicated.

52. Advisory Group on Non-Ionising Radiation, 'ELF Electromagnetic Fields and the Risk of Cancer', *Documents of the*

NRPB [National Radiological Protection Board], vol. 12, 1 (2001), pp. 17–18.

53. Roll and Persinger, 'Investigations', p. 154.

54. For further discussion see Jason J. Braithwaite, 'Putting Magnetism in its Place: A Critical Examination of the Weak-Intensity Magnetic Field Account for Anomalous Haunt-Type Experiences', *JSPR*, vol. 72.1, 890 (January 2008), pp. 34–50.

55. H. P. Wilkinson and Alan Gauld, 'Geomagnetism and Anomalous Experiences, 1868–1980', *PSPR*, vol. 57 (1993), pp. 275–310.

56. H. M. Radnor, 16 January 1893, in F. W. H. Myers, 'The Subliminal Consiousness', *PSPR*, vol. 9 (1893–4), p. 79.

57. Myers, *Human Personality*, vol. 2, pp. 56, 360. He also reproduced the Radnor letter, p. 453.

58. E. Bozzano, *Dei Fenomeni d'Infestazione* (Rome: Luce e Ombra, 1919); H. H. Price, 'Haunting and "Psychic Ether" Hypothesis', *PSPR*, 45 (1939), pp. 307–43; H. H. Price, 'Some Philosophical Questions about Telepathy and Clairvoyance', *Philosophy*, 15 (1940), pp. 363–74.

59. Francis Hitching, *Pendulum: The Psi Connection* (London: Fontana/Collins, 1977).

60. ' "They're Here": The Mechanism of Poltergeist Activity', *New Scientist* (1 April 2008); P. Brovetto and V. Maxia, 'Some Conjectures About the Mechanism of Poltergeist Phenomenon', *Neuroquantology*, vol. 6, 2 (2008).

61. Damien Broderick, *Outside the Gates of Science* (New York: Thunder's Mouth Press, 2007), p. 190.

62. Johann Karl Friedrich Zöllner, *Transcendental Physics: An Account of Experimental Investigations from the Scientific Treatises of Johann Carl Friedrich Zöllner*, tr. Charles Carleton Massey (London: W. H. Harrison, 1880). Slade was later exposed as a fraud.

63. John D. Ralphs, *Exploring the Fourth Dimension: Secrets of the Paranormal* (Slough: W. Foulsham & Co., 1992). For criticism see the review by J. L. Randall, *JSPR*, vol. 62, 848 (July 1997), pp. 72–4.

64. See Anthony Peake, *Is There Life After Death?* (Slough: W. Foulsham & Co., 2006).

65. Brian D. Josephson, 'String Theory, Universal Mind and the

Paranormal', *Proceedings of the Second European Samueli Symposium* (December 2003). See also B. J. Carr, *Universe or Multiverse?* (Cambridge: Cambridge University Press, 2007).
66. Myers, *Human Personality*, vol. 1, p. xix.
67. 'Castle Leslie', *Most Haunted*, Season 5, Episode 5, 21 September 2004.
68. Darley, *Ghost Stories*, p. 5.
69. Green, *Ghost Hunting*, p. 75.
70. E. E. Slosson, 'A Lecture Experiment in Hallucinations', *Psychological Review*, vol. 6, 4 (July 1899), pp. 407–40.
71. Gurney et al., *Phantasms*, vol. 1, pp. xxxii, 513.
72. James Houran and Rense Lange, 'Diary of Events in a Thoroughly Unhaunted House', *Perceptual and Motor Skills*, 83 (1996), pp. 499–502.
73. Ruickbie, *Supernatural*, p. 26. See also 'the poltergeist that wasn't' in Robert A. Baker and Joe Nickell, *Missing Pieces: How to Investigate Ghosts, UFOs, Psychics and Other Mysteries* (Buffalo, NY: Prometheus Books, 1992), pp. 135–9.
74. Rense Lange and James Houran, 'Context-Induced Paranormal Experiences: Support for Houran and Lange's Model of Haunting Phenomena', *Perceptual and Motor Skills*, 84 (1997), pp. 1455–8.
75. P. Granqvist et al., 'Sensed Presence and Mystical Experiences are Predicted by Suggestibility, Not by the Application of Transcranial Weak Complex Magnetic Fields', *Neuroscience Letters*, 379 (2005), pp. 1–6.
76. Lambert, Reply to Cornell and Gauld, p. 153.
77. Rense Lange and James Houran, 'The Role of Fear in Delusions of the Paranormal', *Journal of Nervous and Mental Disease*, 187 (1999), pp. 159–66. See also Rense Lange, James Houran, Timothy M. Harte and Ronald A. Havens, 'Contextual Mediation of Perceptions in Hauntings and Poltergeist-Like Experiences', *Perceptual and Motor Skills*, vol. 82 (1996), pp. 755–62; and Rense Lange and James Houran, 'Ambiguous Stimuli Brought to Life: The Psychological Dynamics of Hauntings and Poltergeists' in James Houran and Rense Lange (eds), *Hauntings and Poltergeists* (Jefferson: McFarland, 2001), pp. 280–306.
78. Samuel Johnson, *The Idler*, no. 11 (24 June 1758), in Arthur

Murphy (ed.), *The Works of Samuel Johnson*, vol. 7 (London: H. Baldwin, 1801), p. 44.

79. R. Rosenthal and K. Fode, 'The Effect of Experimenter Bias on the Performance of the Albino Rat', *Behavioral Science*, 8 (1963), pp. 183–9; R. Rosenthal and L. Jacobson, *Pygmalion in the Classroom: Teacher Expectations and Pupils' Intellectual Development* (New York: Holt, Rinehart and Winston, 1968).

80. Robert K. Merton, *Social Theory and Social Structure* (New York: Free Press, 1968), p. 477.

81. Fritz Heider and Mary-Ann Simmel, 'An Experimental Study of Apparent Behaviour', *American Journal of Psychology*, 57 (1944), pp. 243–59.

82. Stewart Guthrie, *Faces in the Clouds: A New Theory of Religion* (Oxford: Oxford University Press, 1995). He was developing these ideas even earlier, as in 'A Cognitive Theory of Religion', *Current Anthropology*, vol. 21, 2 (1980), pp. 181–203.

83. Justin Barrett and A.H. Johnson, 'Reseach Note: The Role of Control in Attributing Intentional Agency to Inanimate Objects', *Journal of Cognition & Culture*, vol. 3, 3 (2003), pp. 208–17; and Justin Barrett, *Why Would Anyone Believe in God?* (AltaMira Press, 2004). Also sometimes referred to as the 'Hypersensitive Agency Detection Device'. See also Ilkka Pyysiäinen, *Supernatural Agents: Why We Believe in Souls, Gods and Buddhas* (Oxford: Oxford University Press, 2009).

84. Ruickbie, *Supernatural*, pp. 79–80.

85. Green and McCreery, *Apparitions*, pp. 123–4.

88. Sheryl C. Wilson and Theodore X. Barber, 'The Fantasy-Prone Personality: Implications for Understanding Imagery, Hypnosis, and Parapsychological Phenomena', in Anees A. Sheikh (ed.), *Imagery: Current Theory, Research and Application* (Chichester: John Wiley and Sons, 1983), pp. 340–90. For more on Blavatsky, see Leo Ruickbie, '"So Terrible a Force": Spirit Communication in the Hermetic Order of the Golden Dawn and its Relationship to Spiritualism', in Christopher M. Moreman (ed.), *The Spiritualist Movement: Speaking with the Dead in America and Around the World*, 2 vols (Santa Barbara: ABC-CLIO, 2013).

87. Nickell, 'Phantoms, Frauds or Fantasies?', in Houran and Lange, *Hauntings and Poltergeists*, p. 215.

88. S. Myers and H. Austrin, 'Distal Eidetic Technology', *Journal of Mental Imagery*, 9 (1985), pp. 57–66; J.R. Council and K. Huff, 'Hypnosis, Fantasy Activity, and Reports of Paranormal Experiences in High, Medium and Low Fantasizers', *British Journal of Experimental and Clinical Hypnosis*, 7 (1990), pp. 9–13; Alejandro Parra, ' "Seeing and Feeling Ghosts": Absorption, Fantasy Proneness and Healthy Schizotypy as Predictors of Crisis Apparition Experiences', *Proceedings of Presented Papers, The Parapsychological Association 50th Annual Convention* (2007), pp. 84–94.

89. Based on Holt, Simmonds-Moore and Moore, 'Benign Schizotypy', pp. 82–96.

90. Nicola Holt and Christine Simmonds-Moore, 'Trait, State and Psi: An Exploration of the Interaction Between Individual Preference and Psi Performance in the Ganzfeld and Waking ESP Control', *JSPR*, vol. 71 (2007), pp. 197–215; Nicola Holt, C. Simmonds-Moore and S. Moore, 'Benign Schizotypy: Investigating Differences Between Clusters of Schizotype on Paranormal Belief, Creativity, Intelligence and Mental Health', *Proceedings of Presented Papers: The Parapsychological Association 51st Annual Convention* (2008), pp. 82–96. Some traits appear to be contradictory, for example absorption and cognitive disorganization described in schizotypy.

91. Parra, ' "Seeing" ', p. 90.

92. O'Donnell, *Twenty Years*, quotations from p. 155; on family séances, p. 157. The example of the clergyman seems a little too good to be true. See I. Hacking, *Rewriting the Soul: Multiple Personality and the Sciences of Memory* (Princeton: Princeton University Press, 1995).

93. Parra, ' "Seeing" ', p. 84.

94. R. D. Merritt and T. G. Waldo, 'MMPI Code Types and the Fantasy Prone Personality', *Assessment*, vol. 7, 1 (March 2000), pp. 87–95.

95. S. J. Lynn and J. W. Rhue, 'The Fantasy-Prone Person: Hypnosis, Imagination, and Creativity', *Journal of Personality and Social Psychology*, vol. 51, 2 (August 1986), pp. 404–8.

96. International Society for the Study of Trauma and Dissociation, 'Guidelines for Treating Dissociative Identity Disorder

in Adults, Third Revision', *Journal of Trauma & Dissociation*, vol. 12, 2 (2011), p. 117.

97. Steven Jay Lynn et al., 'Dissociative Disorders', in Michael Hersen and Deborah C. Beidel (eds), *Adult Psychopathology and Diagnosis* (Hoboken, NJ: John Wiley & Sons, 2012), p. 505; August Piper and Harold Merskey, 'The Persistence of Folly: Critical Examination of Dissociative Identity Disorder, Part II: The Defence and Decline of Multiple Personality or Dissociative Identity Disorder', *Canadian Journal of Psychiatry*, vol. 49, 10 (October 2004), pp. 678–83.

98. O'Donnell, *Twenty Years*', p. 157.

99. Peter McCue, 'Theories of Haunting: A Critical Overview', *JSPR*, vol. 661, 866 (January 2002), pp. 1–21.

100. Parra, ' "Seeing" ', p. 90.

101. Albert Budden, *Psychic Close Encounters* (London: Blandford, 1999). His *Electric UFOs: Fireballs, Electromagnetics and Abnormal States* (London: Blandford, 1998) presented a more naturalistic interpretation.

102. Green, *Ghost Hunting*, pp. 33, 35, 47.

103. Underwood, *A–Z*, pp. 236–7.

104. Underwood, *A–Z*, p. 157.

105. 'General Meeting', *JSPR* (April 1884), p. 38, on the Third Report of the Literary Committee comprising a 'Theory of Apparitions'.

106. H. H. Price, 'Haunting and "Psychic Ether" Hypothesis', *PSPR*, 45 (1939), pp. 307–43.

107. Bozzano, *Fenomeni*; Tyrrell, *Apparitions*; W. Carington, *Telepathy* (London: Methuen, 1945).

108. Carl Jung, 'The Concept of the Collective Unconscious', *Collected Works of C. G. Jung*, vol. 9, part 1, 2nd ed. (Princeton: Princeton University Press, 1968), pp. 42–53.

109. Roll and Persinger, 'Investigations', p. 138. They note that in 64 per cent of cases there were no noticeable observer effects, so I assume this data refers to the remaining 36 per cent of cases, although the figures given do not add up to 100 per cent.

110. J. G. Pratt and William G. Roll, 'The Seaford Disturbances', *Journal of Parapsychology*, vol. 2 (1958), pp. 79–124.

111. William G. Roll, 'The Psi Field', *Proceedings of the Parapsychological Association*, 1 (1964), pp. 32–65; William Joines, 'A

Wave Theory of Psi Energy', *Research in Parapsychology, 1974* (1975), pp. 147–9.

112. William G. Roll, 'Poltergeists, Electromagnetism and Consciousness', *Journal of Scientific Exploration*, vol. 17, 1 (2003), pp. 75–86.

113. Paul R. Burgess, 'Recurrent Spontaneous Anomalous Physical Events Suggestive of Poltergeist Activity: Evidence for Discarnate Agency? Clinical, Evolutionary and Learning Perspectives', *JSPR*, vol. 76, 1, 906 (January 2012), pp. 1–16.

114. Green, *Ghost Hunting*, p. 62.

115. An early case was Barrett vs Associated Newspapers, see 'Defamation – Printing Report of Ghost Haunting Premises', *The Virginia Law Register*, vol. 13, 9 (January 1908), p. 738.

116. Russell, *Ghosts*, p. 77.

117. Russell, *Ghosts*, p. 137.

118. 'Couple Refuse to Pay for "Haunted" House', *Telegraph* (16 January 1999). Barrister and president of the Ghost Club, Alan Murdie, noted that the 'first time' claim was incorrect in 'Lowes Cottage, Derbyshire, and Other Strange Court Cases', *GCN* (Winter 1998/1999).

119. 'Judge Exorcises Haunted Home', *Guardian* (19 January 1999).

120. 'Couple Refuse to Pay'; 'Judge Ghostbusts Tale of Haunted House', *Telegraph* (19 January 1999); 'Cottage Buyers' Haunting Defence', *Guardian* (16 January 1999); 'Judge Exorcises Haunted Home'.

121. 'Judge Declares House is Haunted', *Associated Press* (20 July 1991).

122. 'Devil's in the Detail of "Haunted" House Sale', *Telegraph* (30 August 2008).

123 D. Siddall, 'Spooked Home Owners Haunt to Know Better', *News & Star* (19 May 2005); Sinclair McKay, 'Anyone There . . . ?' *Telegraph* (28 October 2006). The survey size was 2,000 people.

124. 'Couple Refuse to Pay'; 'Judge Exorcises Haunted Home'.

125. Quoted in Murdie, 'Lowes Cottage'. See Hackney London Borough Council ex P. McGee (1969) reported in the *Rating and Valuation Reporter* (22 May 1969), p. 343.

126. Fraser, *Ghost Hunting*, p. 124.

127. O'Donnell, *Twenty Years*, pp. 188–91; Gauld and Cornell, *Poltergeists*, p. 251.

128. Green, *Ghost Hunting*, pp. 77–8.

129. G. E. Mitton and J. C. Geikie, *The Fascination of London: Hammersmith, Fulham and Putney* (London: Adam & Charles Black, 1903), p. 23. Blythe House was also the name of an earlier ghost story by Rosa Hill in 1864, which may have contributed something to the aura of the building. It should not be confused with the other 'Blythe House' at 23 Blythe Road, which was built between 1899 and 1903.

130. Latham, 'West Sussex Superstitions', pp. 21–2.

131. Eric Maple, *The Realm of Ghosts* (London: Robert Hale, 1964), p. 127; *Morning Chronicle* (21 January 1804).

132. James Lackington, *Memoirs* (London: n.p., 1793), p. 39; *The Times* (12 February 1834 and 1 March 1834).

133. Quoted in Davies, *Haunted*, p. 180.

134. 'The Life, Trial, and Execution of Thomas Wilmot', *The Annals of Crime and New Newgate Calendar*, 24 (1833), pp. 189–90.

135. Davies, *Haunted*, p. 180.

136. Davies, *Haunted*, pp. 180–1.

137. *The Times* (26 August 1815).

138. *The Times* (27 November 1839).

139. Green, *Ghost Hunting*, p. 62.

140. Hawes and Wilson, *Ghost Hunting*, pp. 30–2. For criticism of the Amityville case see Theodore Schick and Lewis Vaughan, *How To Think About Weird Things: Critical Thinking for a New Age* (Palo Alto: Mayfield, 1998), pp. 269–70, or Stephen and Roxanne Kaplan, *The Amityville Horror Conspiracy* (Laceyville: Belfry Books, 1995).

141. See, for example, Dingwall, Goldney and Hall, *The Haunting of Borley Rectory* (London: Duckworth, 1955); T. H. Hall, 'The Strange Story of Ada Goodrich Freer', in J. L. Campbell and T. H. Hall, *Strange Things* (London: Routledge and Kegan Paul, 1968).

142. L. E., 'A Ghost Story', *The Dublin Penny Journal*, vol. 4, 168 (19 September 1835), pp. 90–1.

143. *Somerset County Herald* (28 August 1886).

144. *The Times* (13 December 1825).

145. Mike Dash, 'Spring-Heeled Jack: To Victorian Bugaboo from Suburban Ghost', *Fortean Studies*, vol. 3 (1996), pp. 7–125.

147. An early explanation of this sort can be found in F. S. Hughes, 'Report on the "Shropshire Disturbances"', *JSPR* (March 1884), pp. 19–26.

148. Reginald Scot, *The Discoverie of Witchcraft* (London: Richard Cotes, 1651 [1584]), p. 113.

9. Survive

1. O'Donnell, *Twenty Years*', p. 198.

2. Andrew Green, *Our Haunted Kingdom* (London: Wolfe, 1973).

3. Andrew Green, 'Credo', *GCN* (Spring 2003), http://www.ghostclub.org.uk/spring2003.htm, accessed 23 July 2012; Maple, *Realm*, pp. 198–9.

4. Bob Curran, *The World's Creepiest Places* (Open Road Media, 2012), digital edition.

5. William Howitt, 'Modern Sadducism', *Spiritual Magazine*, vol. 1, 1, 1860, pp. 15–16; W.T. Stead, *Real Ghost Stories* (London: Grant Richards, 1897), pp. 261, 264–5.

6. Theodore Decker et al., 'Prank Gone Awry Stuns Worthington', *The Columbus Dispatch* (24 August 2006); Pamela Willis, 'We Were Just Trying to Scare Each Other', *The Worthington News* (30 August 2006); Julie Carr Smyth, ' "Spooky House" Case Splits Ohio Suburb', *USA Today* (21 August 2007).

7. Willis, 'Scare Each Other'.

8. 'Rachel's Miracle', http://www.rachelsmiracle.com/, accessed 15 May 2012.

9. Willis, 'Scare Each Other'; Decker, 'Prank'.

10. Daniel W. Barefoot, *Piedmont Phantoms* (Winston-Salem: John F. Blair Publishing, 2002), p. 75.

11. Steve Lyttle, 'Train Hits, Kills Man Waiting for Ghosts', *Charlotte Observer* (28 August 2010).

12. Jeff Atkinson, 'Legend of Bostian's Bridge', www.wbtv.com (28 August 2010).

13. Atkinson, 'Legend of Bostian's Bridge'.

14. 'Ghost-Hunting Woman Dies at U of Toronto', *United Press International* (10 September 2009); Iain Marlow, 'Ghost Hunt on Gothic Rooftop Turns Tragic', *Toronto Star* (11 September 2009); Betina Alonso, 'Death at 1 Spadina Crescent', *The Strand*

(16 September 2009); Megan Ogilvie, 'Art Teacher's Unsolved Murder Still Haunts Family', *Toronto Star* (17 January 2011).

15. 'Ghost-Hunting Woman'; Alonso, 'Death'; 'Woman Killed in U of T Fall was on 1st date', *CBC News* (14 September 2009).

16. Martin L. Friedland, *The University of Toronto: A History* (Toronto: University of Toronto Press, 2002), p. 62; Joe Howell, 'School Spirits: Tales of the Supernatural Abound at U of T', *UofT Magazine*, Autumn 2008; http://www.pararesearchers. org/index.php?/20090923678/ghosts-hauntings/one-spadina-crescent.html, accessed 4 June 2012, unusual orthography in the original.

17. http://www.paranormalghostsociety.org/hisnormalistrack-ingparanormal.htm and http://www.paranormalghostsociety. org/goodleburg2.htm, accessed 4 June 2012; 'Holland Woman Surrenders in Fatal Wales Hit-Run', *Buffalo News*, 23 June 2003. Lockhart quoted by Michelle Kearns, 'The Ghostly menace of Goodleberg Cemetery', *Buffalo News*, 27 October 2007. Site information from http://www. thecabinet.com/darkdestinations/location.php?sub_id=dark_ destinations&letter=g&location_id=goodleberg_cemetery_ wales_new_york, accessed 4 June 2012; Maureen Wood and Ron Kolek, *A Ghost a Day: 365 True Tales of the Spectral, Supernatural and Just Plain Scary* (Avon: Adams Media, 2010), p. 233.

18. http://www.paranormalghostsociety.org/goodleburg.htm, accessed 4 June 2012.

19. http://www.paranormalghostsociety.org/hisnormalistracking-paranormal.htm and http://www.paranormalghostsociety.org/ goodleburg2.htm, accessed 4 June 2012.

20. 'Francis Smith, Condemned to Death for the Murder of a Supposed Ghost', *The Newgate Calendar*, vol. 3 (1825), pp. 361–7. The original case can be found in *The Proceedings of the Old Bailey*, Second Session, No. 139 (11 January 1804), pp. 101–4.

21. 'Francis Smith', p. 361. It is not clear which churchyard this was as the present St Peter's standing at the end of Black Lion Lane (an identified focus of activity) was built in 1829 and Hammer-smith Cemetery, lying some distance away, was opened in 1863.

22. 'Francis Smith', p. 362.

23. R. S. Kirby, *Kirby's Wonderful and Scientific Museum: Or Magazine of Remarkable Characters*, vol. II (London: Barnard and Sultzer, 1804), p. 76.
24. 'Francis Smith', p. 364.
25. Kirby, *Kirby's*, p. 77, although Kirby denies this.
26. 'Francis Smith', p. 363, gives the name as Girdle, but the *Proceedings* (p. 101) are to be preferred as more accurate.
27. 'Francis Smith', p. 362.
28. 'Francis Smith', p. 362.
29. 'Francis Smith', p. 364.
30. Kirby, *Kirby's*, pp. 76–7.
31. *Proceedings*, p. 104. Kirby, *Kirby's*, p. 66, described Millwood as a plasterer.
32. Kirby, *Kirby's*, pp. 77–8.
33. *Proceedings*, p. 101.
34. 'Francis Smith', p. 363. Kirby, *Kirby's*, p. 66, speculates that as Smith lodged near the White Hart he had already imbibed, and this is generally repeated as fact in later sources, as by Davies, *The Haunted*, p. 21, for example. The role of alcohol was not brought up in the trial.
35. Kirby, *Kirby's*, p. 69.
36. 'Francis Smith', p. 362.
37. *Proceedings*, p. 103. 'Francis Smith', p. 364, gives a slightly different version of the words reported.
38. *Proceedings*, p. 101.
39. *Proceedings*, p. 102.
40. *Proceedings*, p. 101.
41. *Proceedings*, p. 103.
42. 'Francis Smith', p. 366.
43. 'Francis Smith', p. 366.
44. Cruikshank, *Discovery Concerning Ghosts*, p. 37; Stephen Conway (ed.), *The Collected Works of Jeremy Bentham: The Correspondence of Jeremy Bentham*, vol. 9 (Oxford: Oxford University Press, 1989), p. 103.
45. 'Francis Smith', p. 366.
46. *Proceedings*, p. 104.
47. 'Francis Smith', p. 366.
48. 'Francis Smith', pp. 366–7.

49. Citations: Regina vs Williams (Gladstone) [1987] 3 All ER 411; (1984) 78 Cr App R 276.

50. Kirby, *Kirby's*, p. 77; *Proceedings*, p. 102.

51. Kirby, *Kirby's*, pp. 78–9.

52. 'The Case of the Murdered Ghost', *BBC News* (3 January 2004).

53. Quoted in Louis Jennet, 'What is in your Personal Paranormal Survival Kit?', http://www.hauntedamericatours.com/ghost-hunting/paranormalsurvivalkit.php, accessed 15 December 2012; '20 Questions with Lisa Lee Harp Waugh', http://www.hauntedamericatours.com/20questions/lisaleeharpwaugh.htm, accessed 15 December 2012.

54. Adapted from 'Notes for Investigators', www.spr.ac.uk, 2009, http://www.spr.ac.uk/main/page/notes-investigators-paranormal, accessed 16 December 2010.

55. Quoted in Underwood, *Ghost Hunters*, p. 47.

56. Bagans and Crigger, *Dark World*, pp. 145–1, 160.

57. Bagans and Crigger, *Dark World*, pp. 160, 166–7.

58. Hawes and Wilson, *Ghost Hunting*, pp. 124–5.

FURTHER READING

The book itself is fully referenced throughout to allow anyone to follow up on certain aspects of the research, or check my data. In addition, as part of my ghost hunting survey I asked a group of respondents what books they would recommend to anyone interested in becoming involved in ghost hunting. It is worth highlighting that the most frequently mentioned were *Paranormality*, *Will Storr vs The Supernatural* and *The Ghost Hunter Chronicles*. For a broader view of the subject, I would, of course, recommend my own *A Brief Guide to the Supernatural* (London: Robinson, 2012). Here is the full list in alphabetical order:

Auerbach, Loyd, *ESP, Hauntings and Poltergeists*. Boston; MA: Warner Books, 1986.

Auerbach, Loyd, *Ghost Hunting: How to Investigate the Paranormal*. Berkeley, CA: Ronin, 2004.

Carroll, Robert Todd, *The Skeptic's Dictionary: A Collection of Strange Beliefs, Amusing Deceptions and Dangerous Delusions*. Hoboken, NJ: Wiley, 2003.

Fraser, John, *Ghost Hunting: A Survivor's Guide*. Stroud: The History Press, 2010.

Gauch Jr, Hugh G., *Scientific Method in Brief*. Cambridge: Cambridge University Press, 2012.

Giancoli, Douglas C., *Physics: Principles with Applications*, 2nd ed. London: Prentice-Hall, 1985.

Hawes, Jason, Grant Wilson and Michael Jan Friedman, *Ghost Hunting: True Stories of Unexplained Phenomena from The Atlantic Paranormal Society*. New York: Pocket Books, 2007.

Hawes, Jason, Grant Wilson and Michael Jan Friedman, *Seeking Spirits: The Lost Cases of The Atlantic Paranormal Society*. New York: Pocket Books, 2009.

Holzer, Hans, *Ghosts: True Encounters with the World Beyond*. New York: Black Dog & Leventhal, 1997.

Hope, Valerie, and Maurice Townsend (eds), *The Paranormal Investigator's Handbook*. London: Collins & Brown, 1999.

Johnson, Keith, *Paranormal Realities*. N.p.: Summer Wind Press, 2009.

Jones, Richard, *Haunted Britain and Ireland*. London: New Holland, 2001.

Kachuba, John, *Ghosthunters: On the Trail of Mediums, Dowsers, Spirit Seekers and Other Investigators of America's Paranormal World*. Franklin Lakes, NJ: Career Press/New Page Books, 2007.

Karl, Jason, *Jason Karl's Great Ghost Hunt*. London: New Holland, 2004.

Keene, Paul, Gemma Bradley-Stevenson and Bryan Saunders, *The Ghost Hunter Chronicles*. London: New Holland, 2006.

Nickell, Joe, *The Science of Ghosts: Searching for Spirits of the Dead*. Buffalo, NY: Prometheus Books, 2012.

Nickell, Joe, and Robert A. Baker, *Missing Pieces: How to Investigate Ghosts, UFOs, Psychics and Other Mysteries*. Buffalo, NY: Prometheus Books, 1992.

O'Keeffe, Ciarán, and Billy Roberts, *The Great Paranormal Clash*. Clacton on Sea: Apex Publishing, 2008.

Playfair, Guy Lyon, *This House is Haunted: The Investigation of the Enfield Poltergeist*. London: Souvenir Press, 1980.

Radford, Benjamin, *Scientific Paranormal Investigation: How to Solve Unexplained Mysteries*. Boston, MA: Rhombus, 2010.

Rich, Jason, *The Everything Ghost Book*. Avon, MA: Adams Media, 2001.

Roll, William G., *The Poltergeist*. New York: Nelson Doubleday, 1972.

Rountree, David, *Paranormal Technology: Understanding the Science of Ghost Hunting*. Bloomington, IN: iUniverse, 2010.

Solomon, Grant, and Jane Solomon, *The Scole Experiment: Scientific Evidence for Life After Death*. Malaga, WA: Campion Books, 2006.

Southall, Richard, *How to be a Ghost Hunter*. St Paul: Llewellyn, 2002.

Storry, Will, *Will Storr vs The Supernatural: One Man's Search for the Truth About Ghosts*. London: Ebury Press, 2006.

Taylor, Troy, *Ghost Hunter's Guidebook: The Essential Guide to Investigating Ghosts and Hauntings*. Alton, IL: Whitechapel Press, 2001.

Telesha, Craig, *Strange Frequencies: A Practical Guide to Paranormal Technology*. Alton, IL: Whitechapel Press, 2008.

Underwood, Peter, *The Ghost Hunter's Guide*. Poole: Blandford, 1986.

Warren, Ed, and Lorraine Warren, *Ghost Hunters: True Stories From the World's Most Famous Demonologists*. New York: St Martin's Press, 1989.

Warren, Joshua P., *How to Hunt Ghosts: A Practical Guide*. New York: Fireside, 2003.

Wiseman, Richard, *Paranormality: Why We See What Isn't There*. London: Macmillan, 2011.

Zaffis, John, *Shadows Of The Dark*. Bloomington, IN: iUniverse, 2004.

For anyone who wishes to delve deeper into the subject, I would recommend the following:

Cornell, Tony, *Investigating the Paranormal*. New York: Helix Press, 2002. The summation of a lifetime's work as a psychical researcher.

Davies, Owen, *The Haunted: A Social History of Ghosts*. Houndmills: Palgrave Macmillan, 2007. A valuable historical analysis of hauntings, focusing chiefly on the eighteenth and nineteenth centuries.

Finucane, R. C., *Ghosts: Appearances of the Dead and Cultural Transformation*. Amherst, NY: Prometheus, 1996. The classic history of apparitions and their changing social representations.

Gauld, Alan and A. D. Cornell, *Poltergeists*. London: Routledge & Kegan Paul, 1979. The definitive book on poltergeist phenomena.

Haining, Peter, *The Mammoth Book of True Hauntings*. London: Robinson, 2008. Contains a wealth of sourced documents from newspaper reports to eyewitness accounts, as well as a useful summarization of some early explanations for ghosts.

Houran, James, and Rense Lange (eds), *Hauntings and Poltergeists: Multidisciplinary Perspectives*. Jefferson, NC: McFarland, 2001. Includes contributions from some of the foremost researchers in the field, such as Tony Lawrence, Michael Persinger and William Roll.

Price, Harry, *The Most Haunted House in England*. London: Longmans, Green and Co., 1940. This is one of the most famous cases to be investigated by a ghost hunter, detailing Price's protracted and carefully documented on-site investigation of Borley Rectory.

Smith, Matthew D., (ed.), *Anomalous Experiences: Essays from Parapsychological and Psychological Perspectives*. Jefferson, NC: McFarland, 2010. Covers a range of parapsychological subjects, including hauntings, apparitions and séances.

INDEX